30-Minute Meals

Meals

FOR

DUMMIES®

30-Minute Meals FOR DUMMIES®

by Bev Bennett

WILEY

Wiley Publishing, Inc.

30-Minute Meals For Dummies®

Published by
Wiley Publishing, Inc.
111 River St.
Hoboken, NJ 07030
www.wiley.com

Copyright © 2003 by Wiley Publishing, Inc., Indianapolis, Indiana

Published by Wiley Publishing, Inc., Indianapolis, Indiana

Published simultaneously in Canada

For general information on our other products and services or to obtain technical support, please contact our Customer Care Department within the U.S. at 800-762-2974, outside the U.S. at 317-572-3993, or fax 317-572-4002.

Wiley also publishes its books in a variety of electronic formats. Some content that appears in print may not be available in electronic books.

Library of Congress Cataloging-in-Publication Data:

Library of Congress Control Number: 2003101938

ISBN: 0-7645-2589-1

Manufactured in the United States of America

10 9 8 7 6 5 4 3 2 1

1B/RU/QX/QT/IN

WILEY is a trademark of Wiley Publishing, Inc.

About the Author

Bev Bennett, the former food editor of the *Chicago Sun-Times,* writes a weekly food column on cooking for two for the Los Angeles Times Syndicate International. She also writes a weekly weight-loss column for the Los Angeles Times Syndicate International and a monthly cooking column for the *Chicago Parent* publication.

With degrees in home economics and journalism and having taken cooking classes in France, England, and the United States, Bev uses practical, everyday cooking skills to prepare innovative dishes.

She is a frequent contributor to *The Boston Globe* food section; Tribune Media Services; Content That Works, a Chicago-based newspaper and Internet syndicate; and *Better Homes and Gardens* magazine.

Her book, *Two's Company,* won first place in the KitchenAid Book Awards competition for Single Subject cookbook. This is Bev's eighth food book.

Dedication

To my loving husband, Linn, daughter, Rebecca, and son, Benjamin, who are always ready for dinner and the sooner the better. Thanks for your ready appetites, good humor, and honed palates.

Author's Acknowledgments

Thank you to my agent, Grace Freedson, for her years of friendship, wisdom, and encouragement. To Mike Baker, my project editor: I'm in awe of your professionalism, vision, and great advice.

For Dummies books have a team of experts who make writers like me shine. I'd like to express my gratitude to Norm Crampton, acquisitions editor; Esmeralda St. Clair, copy editor; Emily Nolan, recipe tester; Patty Santelli, technical reviewer and nutrition analyst; and Melissa Bennett, editorial assistant and champion formatter.

I'd like to thank the folks at Kansas State University Department of Human Nutrition for all the information that they've provided, including substitution and storage charts. And I also want to thank the National Cattlemen's Beef Association and Cattlemen's Beef Board for their descriptive info.

To friends Kim Upton and Lisbeth Levine, who were sounding boards for so many ideas, thanks for listening.

Publisher's Acknowledgments

We're proud of this book; please send us your comments through our Dummies online registration form located at www.dummies.com/register/.

Some of the people who helped bring this book to market include the following:

Acquisitions, Editorial, and Media Development

Project Editor: Mike Baker

Acquisitions Editor: Norm Crampton

Copy Editor: Esmeralda St. Clair

Acquisitions Coordinator: Holly Gastineau Grimes

Technical Editor and Nutrition Analyst: Patty Santelli

Recipe Tester: Emily Nolan

Editorial Manager: Jennifer Ehrlich

Editorial Assistants: Melissa Bennett, Elizabeth Rea

Cover Photos: © Getty Images

Cartoons: Rich Tennant, www.the5thwave.com

Production

Project Coordinator: Nancee Reeves

Layout and Graphics: Stephanie D. Jumper, Jacque Schneider

Proofreaders: John Tyler Connoley, Andy Hollandbeck, Susan Moritz, TECHBOOKS Production Services

Indexer: TECHBOOKS Production Services

Publishing and Editorial for Consumer Dummies

Diane Graves Steele, Vice President and Publisher, Consumer Dummies

Joyce Pepple, Acquisitions Director, Consumer Dummies

Kristin A. Cocks, Product Development Director, Consumer Dummies

Michael Spring, Vice President and Publisher, Travel

Brice Gosnell, Publishing Director, Travel

Suzanne Jannetta, Editorial Director, Travel

Publishing for Technology Dummies

Andy Cummings, Vice President and Publisher, Dummies Technology/General User

Composition Services

Gerry Fahey, Vice President of Production Services

Debbie Stailey, Director of Composition Services

Contents at a Glance

Recipes at a Glance

Salads

Sandwiches

Meat and Poultry

Fish and Seafood

Pasta

Meatless Main Dishes

Vegetables and Side Dishes

Dressings

Sauces and Condiments

Desserts

Entertaining

Especially for Two

20-Minute Main Dishes

15-Minute-or-Less Main Dishes

Table of Contents

Part III: Quick Meals without the Hassle 139

Chapter 9: Satisfying Soups 141

Chapter 10: Salad Selections 163

Introduction

· ·

*W*alking into a kitchen that's filled with cooking aromas is a delightful and comforting experience. The delicious food and the intimacy you enjoy in your home kitchen can't be duplicated in a restaurant, carryout joint, or fast-food line. Yet, between work, chores, family obligations, and a badly needed opportunity to unwind, you may find it difficult to get dinner on the table within the time limits that life imposes on you.

If you forgot how enjoyable a home-cooked meal can be or didn't think home cooking was possible, *30-Minute Meals For Dummies* is for you. This book can help you prepare wholesome meals that you may have thought were out of reach, given your busy schedule.

Cooking a great tasting meal isn't nearly as time-consuming as it's made out to be, and you don't have to be a chef to pull it off. Thirty-minute meals are simply a matter of putting a few tips, tricks, and techniques to work. This book helps you master the secrets of making delicious and quick meals by introducing you to marvelous ingredients that make cooking faster, as well as mouthwatering recipes that fit your deadlines.

If you're used to making reservations instead of dinner, be reassured that you can prepare delicious meals in minutes — in the comfort of your kitchen.

About This Book

I wrote this book for busy people who want to enjoy the pleasures of the table without the frenzied preparation. The ultimate payoff is creating fabulous meals in less time.

You've probably scaled back your dinner menus in recent years to speed preparation. We're all doing that. Maybe you can't remember the last time you served a couple of sides with the main course — unless it was Thanksgiving. But a plain piece of meat or chicken isn't dinner, so *30-Minute Meals For Dummies* shows you how to make one-dish meals that include vegetables, starches, and the traditional "meat."

This book transforms soup and salad side dishes into hearty main courses and turns your skillet into a one-dish dinner utensil. You often get everything a meal has to offer in one dish — well, besides adding a scoop of ice cream to the top of your jambalaya for dessert. And when you want a side dish, I have plenty of suggestions that are so easy to do that you can fit them into your 30-minute meal plan.

This book is structured around the equipment, ingredients, and recipe choices that fit your time frame. Each page is packed with my kitchen-tested suggestions for streamlining cooking. Even if you're an experienced cook, you can pick up useful hints. You get great recipes for classic meals, new dishes, and so much more in these chapters. You'll be pleased to know that you can fix nourishing and memorable dinners within your time frame.

Use the tips, ideas, and recipes in this book to prepare an occasional speedy meal or to make every night's dinner easier and more enjoyable. You can skim the book for dinner inspirations or ways to incorporate odds and ends from the refrigerator into your meal planning. No matter what your time frame for a given meal, this book provides answers. From 15-minute entrees to 2-hour cooking sessions (that produce several 30-minute meals), I cover it.

Conventions Used in This Book

To know what to do when recipes call for certain ingredients, see my considerations in the list that follows:

- **Butter** is unsalted.
- **Broth** is canned broth, unless otherwise specified, because it usually contains less sodium than bouillon cubes or powder. Substitute bouillon if you prefer but taste before seasoning with salt.
- **Canola oil** is the oil that I prefer for cooking and for dressings unless I specify olive oil. Both are healthful choices.
- **Fresh herbs** are called for when the color and delicate flavor are important in a recipe. Substitute dry herbs if you prefer, using one third of the amount of fresh.
- **Fruits and vegetables** are washed under cold running water before using. Read labels on packaged salad greens to see if the manufacturer washed the greens; if so, skip that step.
- **Milk** is whole.
- **Pepper** is freshly ground black pepper. The job takes 20 seconds, and the taste difference is worth the time.
- **Salt and pepper** amounts are specified to my taste to save you time. Adjust seasonings to your preference.

And keep the following in mind as well as you peruse the recipes:

- Most of the book's recipes serve four. However, singles and twosomes can be just as pressed for time, and some of the book's recipes are designed to serve two. Most recipes for four can be halved or quartered for one or two servings. Or make the full amount and freeze the leftovers.

✔ When recipes list a range of servings, the recipe per serving info at the end of the recipe is based on the larger number — meaning the smaller portions.

✔ Food manufacturers change can and package sizes as often as I do hemlines. Don't worry if you can't find the exact size product that the recipe calls for. An ounce more or less of broth or frozen vegetables isn't going to change the flavor or texture of most recipes in this book. I specify cups or ounces for recipes that require exact amounts of ingredients.

✔ For vegetables, the recipes call for fresh, frozen, and canned products. Canned and frozen vegetables are more convenient. The food manufacturer does all the peeling, slicing, and dicing for you. Canned and frozen foods aren't nutritionally inferior. Don't feel guilty about using them. Fresh produce, however, is uniquely satisfying, especially when you buy it in season. You're getting vegetables at their peak of ripeness, so you don't have to do much to enhance their flavor. By all means, use fresh produce when it's in season and at its best quality. (Chapter 3 tells you how to substitute fresh for frozen or canned.)

✔ All recipe temperatures are in Fahrenheit. (Check out the appendix for information about converting temperatures to Celsius.)

✔ Whenever you're cooking from a recipe, read the entire recipe before you start to cook. Ten minutes before you serve dinner is no time to suddenly realize that you forgot to boil water for pasta.

Finally, this little guy ☺ alerts you to vegetarian dishes throughout the book. I define *vegetarian* as recipes that don't use eggs, meat, fish, seafood, or poultry.

Foolish Assumptions

Although I don't like to jump to conclusions, every author has to make a few assumptions about her audience, which includes you. So if you can identify with any of these descriptions, this book is for you:

✔ Between your frantic day and the demands of your personal life, you're looking for ways to free up a few minutes. Cooking is one of the activities that gets shortchanged (or cut out altogether), even though you'd like to make a nightly (or an occasional) meal . . . if only cooking didn't take so long.

✔ Tired of spending your evenings in your car, you long for some semblance of dining-at-home pleasure, instead of inching around a parking lot, waiting for your chance to order dinner from a metal box with a speaker.

✔ You buy every book with a black and yellow cover that you run across.

  ✔ You're not looking to prepare a five-course meal. You largely want self-contained meals (with side and serve-with suggestions) that please, satisfy, and basically get the job done with minimal hassle.

How This Book Is Organized

Starting with the introduction, the book is organized around the equipment, ingredients, and recipe choices that fit your time frame. This book is arranged in five major parts, and each part is divided into chapters that address specific subjects. Keep reading for the highlights of each part.

Part 1: Cooking Fast, Eating Well

This part tells you why you should cook even when you don't think you have the time. Driving up to a fast-food window with your kids in the back seat doesn't bring your family closer together, no matter what the advertisements suggest. I write about the foods that you can make in the same time that it takes to make the round trip to a burger joint.

I also take the opportunity to help you with some prep work. You could cover your kitchen wall to wall with appliances and gadgets, but only a handful of them are truly timesavers. Sort out the treasures that become your third hand in the kitchen. And every 30-minute cook needs staples — foods you store in the cupboard and use in a variety of cooked dishes. Supermarket shelves are crammed with ingredients that offer varying degrees of convenience. You can find out which ones are really handy and how some mouth-watering recipes can help you make use of staples. I also describe how to turn your kitchen into a model of efficiency that speeds you up instead of slowing you down.

Part 11: Mastering Skills for Speed

Thirty-minute skills start before you even step into the kitchen. I've always found fresh veggies to be a convenience food that can help you get to the table quickly, so I start this part off by providing my best tips for navigating the produce department. But when you get into the kitchen, you need cooking skills. Traditional techniques, such as sautéing, broiling, and steaming assure you of a dish in less than 30 minutes. Having the right ingredient for the technique helps. This part matches quick foods to preparations.

Having a flair for sauce can turn an ordinary steak into an extraordinary meal — quickly. I share my insight into sauce preparation in this part. You can also consider cooking as an investment. Bank a few hours on the weekend to make a large volume of food, and you have a pay-off in precooked ingredients throughout the week. Stock your freezer with leftovers, and you've saved time up for the future.

Part III: Quick Meals without the Hassle

You have all the right equipment and ingredients. You even have the right moves. This part describes all the meals that you can make in 30 minutes or less. Foods such as soups, skillet dinners, or two-fisted sandwiches aren't off limits to you, the 30-minute cook.

Don't ignore your sweet tooth or reach for a candy bar thinking that you don't have time for something truly scrumptious. Desserts aren't sacrificed in the quick cook's meal plan. This part also includes recipes and tips for desserts that satisfy anyone yet require minimal effort.

Part IV: Even Quicker Meals without the Hassle

Some days, I feel as if I'm the ball in a soccer game bouncing from one end of town to the other for errands and meetings. That's when I reach into my bag of desperation tricks. In this part, find out how you too can have almost instant dinner solutions. Serve traditional center-of-plate protein foods, such as chicken breast, beefsteak, or pork. Sauce up simple meats with pan glazes. You can also read about the revolution taking place in the meat department. Combine precooked meat, pork, chicken, and even bacon strips with a few personal touches and serve an almost instant meal.

Dinner may be waiting for you to notice it in the refrigerator. Doggy bags aren't even fit for a pooch if they linger too long. Put leftover entrees to good use in new dishes. Gather the bits and pieces in the refrigerator for an impromptu meal.

Manufacturers are paying attention to busy consumers, like you, offering a variety of foods that require minimal time and preparation. See how you can use (and improve) on these products to prepare meals at warp speed.

Part V: The Part of Tens

The Part of Tens, which appears in every *For Dummies* book, contains short practical tips for everything else I want to share. I provide you with a list of my favorite timesaving gadgets and some tips on how to take the stress factor out of the dinner hour (or half hour).

Icons Used in This Book

Those little eye-catchers in the left margins of this book call your attention to a variety of important information concerning 30-minute meals. Check these attention grabbers for the following:

Speed cooking can be distracting. This icon alerts you to potential dangers. The situations that this little piece of art accompanies can be hazardous to your health or the end product of your cooking endeavors.

Get two or three recipes from one by substituting ingredients. This icon suggests ways to vary your cooking without making it more time-consuming.

Cooking at warp speed takes skill. And although I hope that you remember every word that I've written, this icon reminds you of some of the more important pieces of info.

Sometimes you have to break the rules to get your meal together. This icon shows you the shortcuts for getting dinner to the table.

When a tidbit of information can bring greater ease or simplicity to your meal preparation, I let you know with this icon.

Where to Go from Here

Ladies and gentleman, start your ovens. One of the many great characteristics of all *For Dummies* books (including this one) is that they're written so that you don't have to read them cover to cover. Of course, you can read this book like any other, but you can also jump in anywhere you want and get tuned in. If you need a quick recipe, head over to the appropriate chapter. Or if you need to brush up on cooking techniques, check that chapter out first. It's all up to you. Just remember to have fun and relax. If you're white-knuckled with teeth clenched at the dinner table, you won't be able to enjoy the fruits of your labor.

Part I
Cooking Fast, Eating Well

The 5th Wave   By Rich Tennant

"I told her this was faster than the
food processor."

In this part . . .

Yes, you read the title of this book correctly. You can get a home-cooked meal to the table in 30 minutes or less. In this part, I start with the basics on how to assemble a meal within a limited time frame and why cooking at home can be preferable to eating out or ordering in. You don't sacrifice nutrition when you cook fast. To the contrary, in this part, I show you how easy it is to assemble a wholesome meal.

But you can't cook quickly if you don't have labor-saving ingredients and tools on hand, so I show you how to separate the essentials from the frills and streamline your meals. I also show you how to streamline your kitchen — a 30-minute cook is an organized cook. Find out ways to organize your kitchen and your cooking routine, so you're not slowed down. Clear the clutter from your countertop and start reading.

Chapter 1

Making Mealtime Matter

*W*hen your schedule is packed 24/7 or you experience occasional crunch periods, you still have to get dinner on the table as if you had all the time in the world. At times like that, you may nostalgically recall the calm, leisurely meals that you knew as a child. When you cook, you want to make the soups, stews, and hearty skillet recipes that nurture. You want to re-create your childhood dinner experiences.

Food gurus may give you the impression that a dish has to take hours of cooking to be worth eating. Maybe you read magazine recipes that tell you to simmer the dish for 3 hours, and you roll your eyes and wonder what world the food writer inhabits. Certainly not yours or mine!

It's simply not true that you can't make good food fast. In fact, cooking gets a bad rap as a time eater. I hate to see this happen, so I combat that myth in this chapter. I use these pages to outline all the benefits to cooking at home and offer some advice on how easy it is to pull off an at-home meal in a jiff. You can get nutritious and satisfying meals that meet your expectations and serve memorable meals that take 30 minutes or less to prepare.

Dinner Doesn't Have to Slow You Down

To put the task of preparing dinner into perspective, compare cooking with other tasks that you do regularly around the house. You can get a meal to the table faster than you can

✔ **Blow-dry your hair and do your make-up.** Or wait for a member of your family to do the same. If you fall into that category, preparing dinner will seem to be much, much quicker.

✔ **Get the children to set the table.** This comparative estimate is actually based on repeating the "I've asked you twice, now!" warning five times.

✔ **Run the dishwasher.** In case you're thinking about doing double duty, a poached-salmon-in-the-dishwasher recipe occasionally makes the circuits on various Internet message boards and spiral-bound, school-fundraiser recipe books. It's not a technique that I endorse. I tried it, and my dishes had a fishy smell for days.

✔ **Watch the evening news on television.** Preparing dinner is also less depressing most of the time.

Making the Case for Cooking

You have demands on your time, but let me share some arguments in favor of your cooking dinner, even though you're on a tight schedule. I'm sure that some cook-at-home benefits have crossed your mind. (After all, you're reading this book.) If not, see what you think. I believe that cooking dinner at home provides three major benefits:

✔ Actually saving time by cooking.

✔ Eating a more healthful variety of foods.

✔ Spending more time with other members of your household, roommates, or friends, or quiet time for yourself that doesn't involve breathing exhaust fumes on your way to the nearest fast-food joint and reading menu boards after you arrive.

Saving time by avoiding the drive-thru

Yes, you read that line right. The food service industry tries to send the message that it's faster to drive to a fast-food restaurant window than to prepare and sit down for dinner. Fast-food commercials ask, "Why cook when you can cruise to your nearby burger joint and pick up a family's worth of burgers or fried chicken?"

One answer to the "Why not fast food?" question is that you don't really save time with that option. Plus, cooking at home is more convenient and less stressful than fighting evening traffic to get to a fast-food place. And after you make it to your local Burger-In-A-Box, you still have to face the energy-sapping aggravation and wasted time of waiting in line and getting home.

Time it from the moment you leave your home until you return with dinner. I bet the whole process takes at least 20 minutes, unless you live under two big, yellow arches. Carryout meals offer no advantage either. Standing in line at 6 p.m. at a rotisserie chicken store isn't as speedy as making a quick pasta or soup in your kitchen.

I've packed this book full of great meals that you can have on the table in around 30 minutes or less. Part III is a good place to start if you want to stack up the time factor and the quality of the recipes in this book against fast food and carryout, although almost every chapter contains at least a recipe or two. And if you're looking for even quicker meals, check out Part IV.

If you don't feel like flipping to Parts III or IV, check out the listing that follows for a few dinners that you can make instead of fighting the lines in your supermarket or carryout store. You can get these dishes to the table in ten minutes, guaranteed:

- **Chicken soup:** Heat a couple of cans of chicken soup with leftover or precooked chicken breast meat and a package of frozen peas. Add a dash of hot red pepper sauce and a squirt of lime juice.

- **Open-face pizza sub:** For each sandwich, slather pizza sauce on half a sub or hero roll. Layer on slices of mozzarella cheese, pepperoni, bell peppers, and onion rings. Microwave on high for 30 seconds or warm in a preheated 350-degree oven for 5 minutes.

- **Tortellini au gratin:** This dish is navel-shaped, stuffed tortellini pasta topped with grated cheese or buttered breadcrumbs — or both. Here's how to do it: Cook a package of fresh tortellini and drain well. Spoon the pasta into a shallow baking dish and sprinkle with a little grated Parmesan cheese. If you have breadcrumbs, add a handful, and dot with butter. Run the dish under the broiler for 30 seconds or until the cheese melts and the breadcrumbs are toasted.

Home cooking for the health of it

This book doesn't claim to be a health cookbook, but that's the beauty of it. Compared to eating in many restaurants, cooking dinner at home is an easy way to eat healthier foods. It's no secret that fast food and carryout dinners are loaded with fat and calories. Just click on the nutrition link of your favorite fast-food restaurant and see what you're eating. A burger with cheese and a medium order of fries alone have almost 900 calories and 45 grams of fat, and that doesn't include a beverage.

I'm not going to talk you out of eating fast food occasionally, and I'm not blaming dining out for the fact that more than half the adults in the United States are overweight or obese. However, I can assure you that dining in means that you're getting the wholesome foods that you want.

Taking control of what you eat

When you cook at home, you're mindful of the ingredients and the quantities of the foods you eat, so you're bound to eat healthier meals. You can make your favorite foods at home quickly — even the items that you love to order in fast-food restaurants — with significantly fewer calories. Your homemade hamburgers made from lean ground beef have fewer calories and less fat than their fast-food counterparts. (If you're a burger lover like me, check out my recipe for the ultimate burger in Chapter 11.) And a serving of frozen, oven-heated fries has 150 to 200 calories, half of what you get in a restaurant order.

When you get behind the wheel in the mealtime driver seat, you benefit because you

✓ **Cook healthier food.** You serve more fresh fruits and vegetables than you can order in fast-food restaurants.

✓ **Eliminate "super size" from your vocabulary and from your hips.** You control the portions of the foods that you serve. At home, no one is pushing you to eat the Super-Giant size of fattening foods for just 15 cents more.

✓ **Serve what you want to eat.** The selection of dinnertime foods that you get to choose from becomes almost limitless. Plus, you can add additional low-calorie, low-fat salads and vegetable side dishes, both of which are in limited supply in many fast-food restaurants.

✓ **Get veto rights on foods that you don't want to serve.** Try the I'm-not-running-a-restaurant line on the family. (However, if you're cooking for one, don't take this as a recommendation to start talking to yourself.)

Knowing what's in the foods that you serve means that you can make adjustments, cutting back on sodium, fat, and calories. The beauty is that you get to choose. For example, as an alternative to adding more salt, squeeze a little lemon juice over a dish. It makes all the flavors livelier. You can't ask the folks behind the counter of the Chicken Machine to do that for you.

According to Hoyle

To balance your nutritional goals with your time constraints, let the Food Guide Pyramid help you. The Food Guide Pyramid (see Figure 1-1) is a visual food plan designed by the U.S. Government. The pyramid shape emphasizes the role that foods play in relationship to each other. The foods that you should have the most servings of each day are at the base of the pyramid. The foods that you should eat sparingly are at the top. (For more information on the Food Guide Pyramid and planning healthful meals, check out the *Dietary Guidelines for Americans* online at www.health.gov/dietaryguidelines.)

Using the pyramid, you can choose from a wealth of from-scratch or convenience foods in every category. Take grains for example. Couscous, dinner rolls, pizza crust, pita breads, and tortillas all count in the grain category. Include whole grains, such as whole wheat bread or quick-cooking barley, in your choices.

I don't follow the pyramid religiously, but I do think about it when I plan meals. I ask myself whether 2 to 4 fruit servings and 3 to 5 vegetable servings are accounted for each day. If I'm falling short, I add an extra vegetable to a stir-fry or serve fruit sauce over frozen yogurt for dinner. (Speaking of stir-fry, it's one of the five techniques at the heart of 30-minute cooking that I detail in Chapter 6. And Chapter 14 has a couple of tempting dessert fruit-sauce recipes.)

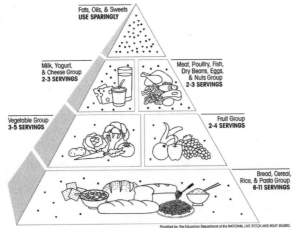

Figure 1-1:
The Food
Guide
Pyramid.

Cooking helps people connect

If you're cooking for more than one, and especially if you're cooking for children, the extra effort to prepare dinner at home pays off. Children who eat dinner at home with their parents eat more servings of fruits and vegetables and eat fewer fried foods and drink fewer soft drinks, say researchers. This one is just my opinion, so you're not going to get the expert citation, but when you cook, you're giving your family the message that cooking is an enjoyable experience. You get to spend time with and talk to other people. You're also raising a generation that can feed itself. Or as my daughter says, "At least I won't have to live on ramen noodles."

Creating a recipe that becomes your family's favorite is important. This is the dish that everyone asks for as a reward for hard work or good grades. This doesn't have to be a fancy dish as long as it's delicious.

Cooking is also a great excuse to spend time with friends. Having friends in for a home-cooked meal is a great way to connect without the noise of a restaurant interrupting your conversations. If your friends enjoy cooking as well as eating, have everyone help prepare the meal over a glass of wine.

Recalling the sweet-and-sour Chinese carryout dishes that nourished me through college when I didn't have a kitchen, I was inspired to make a version of this dish at home. It quickly became a mealtime favorite in my house. My Hot and Sweet Chicken recipe in this chapter eliminates the heavy breading and thick cornstarch sauce of the traditional takeout dish. With all the fruit and vegetables in the recipe, I can skip other courses, but I like a rice accompaniment, such as the Almond and Scallion Rice, also in this chapter.

If you add rice to a fast entree, start the rice first. As it simmers, cook the main course.

Making Good Meals Quickly is a Snap

At this point in the chapter, I paint quite a picture about all the reasons why cooking at home is superior to eating out. With all the benefits and considering all the hype about how time-consuming cooking is, you may think that getting a meal to the table in 30 minutes or less is difficult. Well it's not. And you don't have to have your own cooking show on TV or even be a veteran with many hours of cooking under your belt to pull it off.

All you need is a plan, and I just happen to have one:

- Forget about the way that your mom cooks (or the way that you think you should cook). You don't have to bake your bread from scratch, soak your beans overnight, or collect chicken bones to make your own stock. Take a look through that shoebox or computer file of recipes. Discard outdated recipes and menus to free you up for faster and fresher kinds of cooking. All you have to do is switch to a fun-and-easy style of cooking.

- Don't think of the dinner table as a Norman Rockwell illustration with platter upon platter of food being passed around. Big lavish meals are great at times, but this is the real world. Pare the number of dishes you fix. A one- or two-course dinner is perfectly acceptable, especially when your main dishes do double duty. Cooking a vegetable, starch, and protein together is faster than preparing each food separately.

That's the approach I take to my 30-minute meals. But don't worry: I provide plenty of suggestions and ideas for side dishes that you can make when you have the time, energy, and appetite. And I devote Chapter 14 to desserts.

✔ If you're not cooking for one, encourage helpers. I don't know of any law that says that you have to be the only one in the kitchen.

If you breathe a sigh of relief when you get to the front of the line at a fast-food restaurant, you're going to be even more relieved to find out how simple preparing quick meals is when you have a few cooking aids at home. If you can open boxes and have a can opener to handle the metal, you're ready for fast cooking. But you still may want to read Chapter 2 to get the scoop on blenders, food processors, microwave ovens, and other tools to speed you along. Using a few choice appliances and stocking your cupboards with a few key staples (see Chapter 3) can save time and an emergency call for pizza delivery.

Speaking of packages, the food industry offers so many products that have built-in convenience that you're never at a loss for shortcuts. Although I cover these products throughout the book, you may be especially interested in Chapter 5 on vegetables or see Chapter 15 about my love affair with prepared meat products.

But if it's been a while since you prepared a fast meal that you really liked, feel free to skip ahead to Chapter 4 for a bunch of quick tips on getting into a cooking groove. Or you may want to check out how simple the 30-minute cooking techniques are in Chapter 6.

Getting Dinner on in Even Less Time

I like to think that you're always going to have 30 minutes — the time that it takes to watch the evening news — to cook a meal, but I know it's not possible. Still, I value the dinner hour, even though it's shrinking. That's why you can use many of the recipes in this book to fashion delicious meals in 15 or 20 minutes tops.

In the Recipes at a Glance towards the front of this book, I outline recipes you can make in 20 minutes and recipes that take 15 minutes or less. Use this guide to quickly find inspiration for a meal when even 30 minutes is too long.

For recipes and meals that aren't salad or starch based, tear open a bag of mixed greens and top with the vinaigrette dressing in Chapter 5, one of the dressings in Chapter 10, or a packaged dressing. Add some whole-grain bread from your supermarket, and you have a satisfying menu.

Hot and Sweet Chicken

This tongue-tingling dish, inspired by the sweet-and-sour Chinese dishes of the '50s, takes a fraction of the time to prepare because it eliminates the lengthy deep-frying process. Your supermarket produce section features fresh pineapple cut into chunks, saving you a step.

Preparation Time: *5 minutes*

Cooking Time: *20 minutes*

Yield: *4 servings*

1 pound boneless, skinless chicken breast, cut into 1-inch cubes

2 tablespoons flour

½ teaspoon salt

2 tablespoons oil

1 sweet onion, peeled and cut into thin wedges

1 green bell pepper, cored, seeded and cut into thin strips

1 small jalapeno or serrano chile, seeded and minced

1 teaspoon grated fresh gingerroot

1 can (6 ounces) unsweetened pineapple juice

2 cups pineapple chunks in 1-inch pieces

½ cup shredded carrots (optional)

Pepper to taste

1 Place the chicken in a plastic bag. Add the flour and salt and shake to coat the chicken. Reserve the remaining flour.

2 Heat the oil over medium-high heat in a large, nonstick skillet. Add the chicken cubes to the hot oil and brown on all sides, about 5 minutes total. Remove the chicken and set aside.

3 Add the onion, bell pepper, chile, and gingerroot to the skillet and sauté 5 minutes. Sprinkle 1 tablespoon of the reserved seasoned flour into the skillet. Stir to brown the flour. Add the pineapple juice and scrape up any browned bits in the skillet. Add the pineapple chunks and chicken. Stir well. Cover and simmer 10 minutes or until the chicken is cooked through. If the mixture is too thick, add 1 to 2 tablespoons water. To serve, sprinkle on shredded carrots (if desired) and season with pepper.

Vary It! *Use a pound of pork tenderloin cut into 1-inch cubes in place of the chicken. Most pork tenderloins weigh between 8 to 12 ounces, so use two if necessary. Also, you can serve the dish over rice using ½ cup cooked rice per person.*

Per serving: *Calories 318(From Fat 89); Fat 10g (Saturated 1g); Cholesterol 63mg; Sodium 362mg; Carbohydrate 32g (Dietary Fiber 3g); Protein 24g.*

☞ *Almond and Scallion Rice*

Keep a bag of sliced almonds in the freezer (so the nuts don't turn rancid). Then sprinkle the almonds on rice dishes for a delicious crunch.

Preparation time: *2 minutes*

Cooking time: *18 minutes*

Yield: *4 servings*

1 cup long-grain rice	*2 tablespoons sliced almonds*
½ teaspoon salt	*2 tablespoons finely chopped scallions*

1 Combine the rice, salt, and 2 cups of water in a small pot. Bring the mixture to a boil. Reduce the heat to low, cover the pot, and simmer until the rice is tender and the liquid is absorbed, about 18 minutes.

2 Remove the cover, sprinkle the rice with the almonds and scallions and stir well. Set aside for 1 minute for the flavors to blend.

__Per serving:__ Calories 203 (From Fat 17); Fat 2g (Saturated 0g); Cholesterol 0mg; Sodium 293mg; Carbohydrate 41g (Dietary Fiber 1g); Protein 5g.

Chapter 2

Tools for Speed

As a professional food writer, I preview all the products that kitchenware manufacturers are ready to introduce each year before anything appears in stores. For a passionate cook like me, attending the International Housewares Show — which unfortunately isn't open to the public — is like a stroll through a gigantic toy store. Everything catches my eye. But I really look for products that are more than playthings.

Just like you, I want cookware and appliances that eliminate time-consuming preparation steps. I search for equipment that speeds up my cooking without sacrificing the good taste that I demand from food. When I find such products, they become permanent fixtures in my kitchen.

For a time-crunched cook, distinguishing the essentials from the frills and even the frivolous is important. My garage shelves are proof that I'm a fan of equipment. That's where I store my ice cream machine, bread baker, pressure cooker, slow cooker, and meat slicer. But the electric appliances that I'm partial to — the ones that truly save me time — are on my kitchen counter.

In this chapter, I share my suggestions on how to choose and use the appliances that will save you time. I review how to get the best results from your microwave oven. I help you to fight the urge to cover your counter with too many machines by listing the benefits and disadvantages of small electronics, so you can decide how many appliances you really need.

And because most of your cooking still requires conventional stovetop cookware, I cover the pots and pans that are the most versatile. And for your unplugged slicing, dicing, and chopping needs, you don't need knives that belong on the set of a television cooking show to produce your own prize-winning dishes. I provide you with a simple list of the knives you need.

The gadget addiction quiz

Take this tongue-in-cheek test to see if you could fall victim to every gadget pitch that manufacturers hawk.

1. How often do you blow a fuse in the kitchen?

A. Once a week.

B. Once a year.

C. I do everything manually, so I don't worry about electricity.

2. Can you see the surface of your counters?

A. Only if I remove the coffee maker, electric can opener, electric pepper mill, electric skillet, electric deep fryer, and the electric knife sharpener.

B. Yes, I see a bare patch, but that may be just the place to put the countertop grill.

C. My counters are bare, so I can spread out when I cook.

3. Which one of the following does your kitchen gadget drawer most closely resemble?

A. A department store display the day before Christmas.

B. A department store display the day after Christmas.

C. A Zen meditation center, stripped to its bare essentials.

4. How many of the following items do you own: cherry pitter, olive pitter, butter curler, escargot stuffer, and feather baster?

A. All of the above, but you forgot to mention the chicken feather plucker.

B. The cherry pitter but that doubles as an olive pitter and dried plum pitter, so it's multifunctional.

C. What's an escargot stuffer?

5. When you can't find a bottle opener, what do you usually do?

A. Go out and buy a new one.

B. Keep searching. I know I'll find it eventually.

C. Use my teeth.

If you answer **A** to three or more questions, you probably have more gadgets than you need. You may be a cook who is eagerly awaiting a better-designed eggplant polisher, but having too much equipment can slow you down just as much as having too few cooking helpers. Discover what items are really useful in this chapter.

If you answer **B** to three or more questions, congratulations! You're making practical choices based on your cooking style.

If you answer **C** to three or more questions, look through this chapter to find out how some utensils and small appliances can save you time.

Plug-in Speed: Small Appliances

Having the right appliances makes cooking faster and more pleasurable, whether it's a microwave oven that thaws meat you want to serve for dinner or an immersion blender for making frothy smoothies for breakfast.

Keep reading to find out the benefits and drawbacks of the most popular small appliances — microwave ovens, food processors, food blenders, immersion blenders, and countertop grills. You get some shopping tips, and I let you in on my preferences, but I also want to encourage you to choose the products that help with your specific cooking needs.

The Truth about Your Microwave, according to Bev

Nine out of ten kitchens include a microwave oven, and you probably have one of them. I can barely program my TV remote, so I'm not going to dive into the physics of how these work. The important concept for the 30-minute cook is that a microwave oven can shave minutes off of meal preparation.

Microwave oven devotees swear that the machine does a terrific job cooking food, but I'm not so sure. Microwave-cooked food doesn't have the fully developed aroma, color, and flavor of food cooked on a stovetop or in the oven. What's more, as a frequently harried cook, I don't like various stop-and-start steps. Cooking food for 2 minutes in a microwave oven, turning it, and then cooking it another 2 minutes isn't a convenient way to prepare food.

However, fans of microwave cooking and I do agree that microwaves are great in two instances — cooking veggies and in combination with other appliances and techniques.

Zapping your vegetables

Vegetables are excellent when cooked in a microwave oven. Broccoli and green beans remain a brilliant green. The vegetables can cook in a microwave with a minimal amount of water, so they don't lose as many vitamins and minerals when you wash that water down the drain.

Table 2-1 lists the microwave cooking times for vegetables that you're most likely to serve. Except for baking potatoes, you can cook vegetables, unsalted, in a covered dish with a small amount of water. Cook potatoes uncovered and without liquid on the microwave's tray. Spear potatoes in a few places with a knife tip before cooking them in a microwave. (Otherwise you have Exploding Potato Salad on the menu.) Allow 5 minutes resting time before serving the vegetables.

Table 2-1	Vegetable Cooking Times	
Food	*Quantity*	*Minutes (on High)*
Asparagus, in 2-inch pieces	16 spears	5 to 7 minutes
Broccoli	1 bunch, halved, trimmed	8 to 10 minutes
Brussels sprouts	1 pound, trimmed	5 to 7 minutes
Cabbage	1 small head, shredded	8 to 9 minutes
Carrots	4, trimmed and diced	7 to 9 minutes
Corn	Kernels from 4 ears	4 to 6 minutes
Green beans	1 pound, trimmed	10 to 12 minutes
Green beans	2 pounds, trimmed	16 to 18 minutes
Onion	2, coarsely chopped	5 to 6 minutes
Peas	2 cups, shelled	4 to 6 minutes
Potatoes (baking)	1 medium	4 to 6 minutes
Potatoes (baking)	4 medium	13 to 14 minutes
Spinach	1 pound, trimmed	6 to 7 minutes

Always pierce foods with a tight skin before cooking them in a microwave oven. This includes potatoes, squash, and sausages. This step prevents the food from bursting during cooking.

Combination cooking

Microwave cooking combined with conventional cooking offers the best of both techniques. Use this approach when you need to

- ✔ **Thaw:** If the meat that you're planning to serve for dinner isn't completely thawed, microwave the meat on the thaw cycle for a couple of minutes and then proceed with your recipe.

- ✔ **Get a head start:** Using a microwave to start long-cooking vegetables, such as hardshell squash and baked potatoes, cuts the total cooking time by half. Starting hardshell squash in a microwave oven also makes the vegetables easier to peel. If you've ever tried to peel a squash with the skin of an armadillo, you know how difficult it is.

Check out my Micro-Baked Butternut Squash recipe to find out how I get the rich, roasted flavor of oven-baked butternut squash — the long-necked tan-colored squash — in a fraction of the time by taking advantage of the strengths of a microwave.

⟳ *Micro-Baked Butternut Squash*

Maple sugar is a granulated version of maple syrup. Use this delightful sweetener as an alternative to brown sugar on squash and sweet potatoes. Maple sugar is sold in natural food stores and gourmet food shops. If you can't find it, substitute an equal amount of brown sugar.

Preparation time: *5 minutes*

Cooking time: *About 15 minutes*

Yield: *4 servings*

1 small butternut squash, about ½ to ¾ pound	*2 tablespoons maple sugar*
¼ cup apple juice, or water	*¼ teaspoon salt*
1 tablespoon butter	*¼ teaspoon pepper*

1 Preheat the oven to 400 degrees. Pierce the squash in several places with the tip of a knife. Place the squash in a microwave-safe, ovenproof dish and microwave on high for 3 minutes. Turn the squash over and microwave another 3 minutes.

2 As soon as you can handle the squash, peel it. Cut the squash into ½-inch thick rings. Scrape out the seeds and pulp. Return the squash to the dish. Pour in the apple juice. Dot the squash with butter and sprinkle with maple sugar, salt, and pepper. Bake the squash for 10 minutes or until fork tender. Spoon the butter and maple sugar glaze over the squash and serve.

Per serving: Calories 68 (From Fat 26); Fat 3g (Saturated 2g); Cholesterol 8mg; Sodium 150mg; Carbohydrate 11g (Dietary Fiber 1g); Protein 1g.

Logging on to dinner

Have you ever forgotten how to make Mom's prize-winning chicken casserole? Instead of calling her for the recipe, wouldn't it be great to send her an instant message using an Internet, refrigerator, and freezer combination. This is just one of the futuristic features that you can find (or will soon find) in your local appliance store to speed up dinner or make your meal preparation easier. Imagine having a refrigerator that keeps track of when you stored perishables and signals you when it's time to finish off the milk, eggs, or lunchmeats. Oh, did I forget to mention that I've seen refrigerator designs that also have built-in stereo speakers so you can listen to music while you cook? Of course, you can always save a few thousand dollars by sticking with that old portable radio you have on your counter.

Processing Food like a Professional

Makes it sound as if you're a chemist or the owner of a small food-manufacturing plant, doesn't it? But I'm talking about processing food with a food processor — a contraption that can help you make short work of your chopping, slicing, and shredding jobs. Place a food, such as a fruit or vegetable, into a container with a razor-sharp steel blade and turn the machine on; your food processor finishes the job in an instant.

Purchasing a food processor

If you regularly chop, mince, or shred vegetables for recipes, a food processor is a good investment, and the more vegetables that you need to process for a given meal, the more efficient using the machine can be.

If you're buying a food processor, look for a machine with a feed tube at least 4 inches in diameter so it can hold a whole, small onion or tomato. It should also include a steel blade, shredding blade, and slicing blade. Most food processors have an 11- to 14-cup bowl capacity. The more expensive models also come equipped with a mini bowl, so you can chop parsley or garlic and have a smaller bowl to clean.

Putting processing power to work

I don't mind preparing a recipe that calls for minced fruits and vegetables if I can toss everything into a food processor. But using a food processor demands that you pay close attention to what you're doing. In seconds, you can dice a whole onion. You can also turn an onion into a pile of mush in seconds, so a food processor isn't without its drawbacks.

Just because you have a food processor doesn't mean that using it is always the fastest option. Chopping a garlic clove is a good example. Mincing a clove of garlic in a food processor takes 20 to 30 seconds. Chopping one clove by hand takes as many seconds, and you have no machine to wash, so the overall chore is faster when you do it manually.

When washing a food processor, never leave the chopping blade in a sink full of suds. You can reach in and accidentally slice your finger. Wash the chopping blade separately, dry it immediately, and put it back in its holder.

Shopping for small appliances

Just as car prices come down as new models hit the showrooms each fall, department and discount stores slash the prices of small appliances as new versions hit the shelves by late spring or early summer. If you don't mind having last year's model blender, food processor, or other piece of equipment, look for sales starting in the spring.

And because small-appliance prices vary so much, check discount mass merchandisers and Web sites for good buys. Summer is also a fun time to peruse your neighbors' garage sales. Their counter clutter may be just the item that you need.

☞ Savory Corn Pancakes with Mango Relish

Pancakes flecked with corn, chives, and red pepper is a confetti-like dish to serve for Sunday brunch. Accompany this entree with a hot and sweet mango relish.

Preparation time: *10 minutes*

Cooking time: *4 minutes per side*

Yield: *About 12 pancakes*

⅓ cup chives

2 cups corn kernels, canned or frozen

1 small red bell pepper, cored, seeded and coarsely chopped

2 eggs, beaten

½ cup milk

1 cup flour

1½ teaspoons baking powder

¾ teaspoon salt

2 tablespoons butter

1 large mango, peeled and coarsely chopped

1 jalapeno chile, cored, seeded and coarsely chopped

1 teaspoon honey

1 Set the steel blade in a food processor. Add the chives, cover the machine, and process the chives with on/off bursts for 30 seconds or until the chives are minced. Remove 1 tablespoon of the chives and set aside.

2 Add the corn kernels and bell pepper to the remaining chives in the food processor. Cover the machine and process the vegetables with on/off bursts for 30 seconds or until the vegetables are minced. Scrape down the bowl. Add the eggs, milk, flour, baking powder, and ½ teaspoon of the salt. Cover the machine and process the batter with on/off turns for 30 seconds. Scrape down the bowl. Don't over process or the batter will be tough. Spoon the batter into another bowl. Wipe the bowl of the food processor clean with a damp paper towel.

3 Melt 1 tablespoon of the butter in a large nonstick sauté pan. Drop the batter by ¼-cup measures onto the skillet to form pancakes. Do not crowd, but cook the pancakes in batches. Cook the pancakes on medium high heat for 4 minutes on the first side and 3 to 4 minutes on the second side, or until the pancakes are firm and golden. Add the remaining butter when necessary and cook the rest of the batter.

4 Make the mango relish while the pancakes cook. Add the mango, the reserved 1 table-spoon of chives, and chile. Cover the machine and process with on/off turns for 30 seconds or until the mango is finely chopped. Remove the relish and spoon into a serving bowl. Stir in the honey and add the remaining ¼ teaspoon of salt.

Per serving: Calories 119 (From Fat 32); Fat 4g (Saturated 2g); Cholesterol 42mg; Sodium 329mg; Carbohydrate 19g (Dietary Fiber 2g); Protein 3g.

Blending with Ease

With its small blade and tall container, a blender is similar to a food processor, but produces different results. Food processors do an excellent job of chopping, slicing, and shredding food, but give poor results when it comes to purees. That's where blenders come in.

Buying a blender

Some machines come with a row of buttons for different degrees of chopping, blending, or pureeing. But two buttons — one for slow and one for high speed — are all that you need. By the time you decide whether you should choose the blending or pureeing speed, you could be done. Practically speaking — and this is from someone who hates to dust her computer keyboard — the more buttons you have, the more you have to clean.

A day in the life of your blender

The design of the blender's blade and container means the food comes into contact with more air than when you use a food processor. The result? Your creation is lighter and fluffier. If you haven't already experienced your blender's multitasking capabilities, try the following:

- **Making sauce and soup:** Blenders are wonderful when you want to make a satiny sauce or soup without chunks of the original ingredients ruining the texture.

- **Crushing ice:** Higher-priced and higher-quality models have powerful motors that grind ice for smoothies and mixed drinks. (They're perfect for making a frozen Margarita to enjoy while you prepare a 30-minute meal.) Blenders certainly surpass a hammer for making crushed ice.

- **Making baby food:** If you're only using a blender for baby food, choose an inexpensive model that purees ingredients.

- **Creating frothy, light smoothies:** Another great use for your blender.

Cheaper blender models vibrate as they puree foods. Watch the blender whenever it's operating to make sure that it doesn't march off the counter, taking your smoothie with it!

↻ Three-Berry Smoothie

Buy bags of frozen loose berries, so you can measure out what you need and keep the remainder frozen. Unsweetened berries are preferable, so you can adjust the sweetness to your preference.

Preparation time: *5 minutes*

Yield: *4 servings*

1 cup frozen raspberries	*2 cups buttermilk, plus more if desired*
1 cup frozen blueberries	*2 tablespoons honey*
1 cup frozen strawberries	*Dash of nutmeg (optional)*

1 Place the berries in a blender container. Add the 2 cups buttermilk, honey, and nutmeg (if desired).

2 Turn on the blender to low speed for 30 seconds, then increase the speed to high and blend for 1 minute or until the fruit is pureed and the mixture is light and frothy. If the smoothie is too thick for your taste, add more buttermilk by the quarter cup to reach the desired consistency.

3 Pour into cups and serve immediately.

Vary It! *Use 1 cup of vanilla yogurt and ½ cup of buttermilk.*

Per serving: *Calories 128 (From Fat 13); Fat 1g (Saturated 1g); Cholesterol 5mg; Sodium 131mg; Carbohydrate 26g (Dietary Fiber 3g); Protein 5g.*

Using frozen fruit instead of fresh fruit and ice cubes in a smoothie assures you of a frosty drink with undiluted fruit flavor. You don't have to wait for the fruit to thaw before you sip a luscious and nourishing blend of strawberries, blueberries, and raspberries. Keep a bag of your favorite berries or other fruits in the freezer, and you can have smoothies at a moment's notice. Read your blender information booklet to make sure the machine grinds ice before you start the smoothie recipe in this chapter.

Waving Your Magic Wand

The blender is one small appliance that I frequently use, but it has its limitations as well. When I want to make a hot cream soup, I have to pour the soup from the pot into the blender and then back into the pot to reheat before I serve it.

That's where the wonderful wand, better known as an *immersion blender* comes in handy. The blender is shaped like a long flashlight with a blade at one end (as you can see in Figure 2-1). Immersion blenders allow you to puree your food in the serving or cooking vessel that it's already in, instead of pouring the food into a blender container. To use it, simply place the blender in the mixture that you want to puree and turn on the switch. In seconds, you have a well-blended sauce, soup, or drink, without the mess of pouring liquids back and forth.

The more I use this gadget, the more indispensable it becomes. Ten years ago, I bought my first immersion blender to make cold Cucumber-Buttermilk Soup. (See the recipe in Chapter 9.) Now I use my immersion blender to make daiquiris in the pitcher, get the lumps out of mashed potatoes, and froth up a flattened smoothie.

Some hand blenders come with an ice crusher, and others are cordless and rechargeable. Instead of being tethered to the kitchen outlet, you can blend and serve cocktails and dinner on the deck. How's that for chilling out?

Figure 2-1:
The oh-so-handy immersion blender.

Grilling Food Indoors

I never saw George Foreman in a boxing match, but he's a knockout salesman for countertop grills. I certainly pay attention to his pitches. I've read what happens to boxers in the ring who ignore his delivery. But do you need a grill? The answer is a qualified yes.

First, there are two kinds of electric indoor grills:

✔ **The closed grill,** such as the George Foreman Grilling Machine, and many others from a wide range of manufacturers, features a cooking surface with metal plates that the food rests on (see Figure 2-2). Preheat the appliance, add the food, and shut the lid. The food, pressed in-between the top and bottom, cooks quickly and has grill marks on both sides.

✔ **The open grill** is a broad surface set over a drip pan. Turn the machine on to preheat it and add the food that you want to cook. Theoretically, it's like cooking on an outdoor grill. But no matter what manufacturers say, I can't reproduce the taste of outdoor grilled food indoors with a countertop grill.

If you frequently serve hamburgers, steak, fish, or boneless, skinless chicken breasts, a closed grill can be handy. It cooks quickly and cleans easily. Devotees like the fact that fat drips off, so you get a leaner, lower calorie food.

But unless you have more counter space than you know what to do with — and in that case, I'd like to sell you a couple of gadgets — I can't recommend an open grill. It's big and messy and never gets to a high enough temperature to cook food fast.

Figure 2-2:
A closed grill allows you to cook hamburgers without splattering your stovetop.

Almost scrub-free grilling

If your least-favorite outdoor chore is scrubbing the grill, an indoor closed grill gives you a break. It comes clean in a fraction of the time. After you finish cooking, turn off the grill and let it cool while you eat. Then turn the grill on again for one minute just to warm it up. Unplug the grill, put a wet paper towel on the surface, and shut the grill. After a minute, remove the paper towel while wearing an oven mitt — the paper towel is hot. The combination of the damp towel and the heat loosen any grime. You may have to do this two or three times depending on what you're cooking. Hamburger grease is easy to clean. Chicken may take three tries. After the third try, use a damp paper towel to wipe up any remaining residue.

Kitchenware Unplugged

Electric gizmos can only get you so far. You still need pots, pans, and good ol' fashioned knives to prepare a meal.

Department store cookware displays send out a seductive message: "Buy me and cook like the *bam* guy from TV." But choosing, maintaining, and storing a large collection of cookware is time-consuming. When you have a limited cooking schedule, you don't want to waste time pulling the butter warmer out of the cupboard, wondering whether you're better off using the copper or stainless-steel skillet, or choosing from among a block full of 30 different knives.

Being a passionate cook and one who loves cookware, I reluctantly realize that less is better when I'm in a hurry. Keep reading to find out how to lighten up kitchen clutter.

Boiling down your stock of pots and pans

Squatting down on the floor and rummaging through a cupboard in search of just the right pan or lid drives me to distraction. Having some family member pull out a different pot for every cooking chore and leaving everything in the sink for me to wash doesn't speed up dinner either.

My radical approach is to limit most of my cooking to four pots and pans, each with a lid. Why four? I cook on a standard four-burner stovetop, and I keep one pot on each burner. (The only drawback to my four-burner, four-pot scheme is that I have nowhere to put my teakettle!) The rest of my pots and pans stay in the cupboard until I absolutely need them.

This Spartan approach may not work for you, but before you indulge in cookware sets or extravagant pots and pans that have limited use, take an inventory of your cooking style.

Shopping with your inner chef

If your current cookware selection is limited or it's time to replace those sticking, formerly nonstick pans, keep the following in mind while you check out the shelves and then select cookware that meets your needs.

- **Pots or pans:** *Pans* have one long handle and come with or without lids. *Pots* have lids and handles on opposite sides. I recommend always buying cookware with a tight-fitting lid, which makes the cookware more versatile. I also prefer pans to pots. One handle means that I only need one potholder when I'm cooking. That's a personal quirk. You may feel more comfortable using pots.

✓ **Versatility:** My cooking instructors would slap my wrist, but I cook pasta in a Dutch oven, not a huge pasta pot that allows my spaghetti to float freely. A Dutch oven is large enough, so the pasta doesn't stick together, but small enough to fit comfortably on a stovetop burner. Cookware should be large enough to take care of several tasks but not so large that it doesn't do any well. Metal cookware handles are more versatile than wood or plastic ones, because you can put a metal-handled skillet in the oven without it melting.

✓ **Your cooking style:** Recipes in this book often tell you to sauté foods; to *sauté* means to cook them in a little fat over high heat. This speedy cooking technique requires a heavy-bottomed sauté pan that gets hot, retains heat, and doesn't buckle over high heat. Good materials include porcelain-coated cast-iron or sandwiches of metals including stainless steel and copper or aluminum. (For more information on sautéing, check out Chapter 6.)

✓ **Your physical comfort level:** If you want to lift weights, go to the gym. Cookware shouldn't be flimsy, but if your wrists buckle when you hold a skillet, go for something lighter.

✓ **Your budget:** You're only buying a few things, so buy the best quality you can afford. Cheaply made cookware has to be replaced more often, so it's no bargain in the long run. Look for better prices at discount general merchandise stores.

A pot or pan for every occasion

The items that I find essential for making most dinner recipes are in the following list. Select the cookware that allows you to make your family's favorite dishes quickly. If you're cooking for one or two, look for smaller sizes of the same kinds of pots and pans. As you can see from the list, versatility is key.

✓ **2-quart pan with a tight-fitting lid:** This is a great size for reheating canned soup, heating milk for hot chocolate, making one or two servings of rice, or preparing breakfast oatmeal for one or two.

✓ **3-quart pan with a tight-fitting lid:** Vegetables, sauces, and puddings are suited to this size.

✓ **12-inch sauté pan with nonstick surface and a tight-fitting lid:** Along with sautéing chicken, meat, and fish, I use this cookware to cook one-pot meals of rice, meat, and vegetables; risotto, the Italian dish of slowly simmered rice; and the occasional stir-fry. (I own a 12-inch skillet as well, but I don't use it nearly as often for my speed cooking.)

✓ **5-quart Dutch oven:** This is my all-purpose soup and chili pot and pasta cooker. A Dutch oven is a large pot with a tight-fitting lid that's often used for long-simmering soups and stews, but I find other uses for it.

For the recipes in this book, I call for cookware in relatively generic sizes, such as medium or large pots or pans. I don't want you to skip a recipe, because you don't have a specific size or shape cookware. In Table 2-2, I lay out approximate sizes that you can use to match my generic descriptions.

Table 2-2	Size Guide for Choosing Cookware
Description	*Size*
Small pot or pan	1 quart
Medium pot or pan	2 to 3 quarts
Large pot or pan	4 to 5 quarts
Dutch oven	5 quarts
Small skillet or sauté pan	6 to 8 inches in diameter
Medium skillet or sauté pan	10 inches in diameter
Large skillet or sauté pan	12 to 14 inches in diameter

Chopping, slicing, and dicing like grandma used to do

Preparing a small amount of food is faster using a knife and cutting board than a food processor or other gizmo that you have to set up and clean. But if your knives aren't sharp or aren't appropriate to the task, you're not saving time. A slip with a dull blade, and you may be spending dinner hour in the emergency room.

These knives should get you through most kitchen tasks.

- ✔ **Chef's:** Choose a knife with a 10- to 12-inch tapered blade for chopping and slicing.

- ✔ **Slicing:** Select a knife with an 8- to 10-inch thin, flexible blade for carving meat and poultry.

- ✔ **Paring:** Buy a well-made knife with a 3- to 4-inch blade for peeling, coring, and paring fruits and vegetables.

When shopping for knives, consider the following:

- **Balance:** Think like Goldilocks. You want a knife that's not too heavy and not too light.

- **Materials:** Excellent for home use, high-carbon stainless steel doesn't rust easily. (High-carbon steel does.) You can sharpen it at home with a *honing steel,* which looks like a toy sword.

- **Handles:** Most home cooks prefer knives with wood-riveted handles. Restaurant pros often choose heavy-duty molded plastic, because they're less likely to trap bacteria. With either choice, make sure that no gaps exist between the blade and the handle where bacteria can thrive.

Chapter 3

Staples for Speed

In This Chapter

▶ Stocking up on grains

▶ Cooking protein straight from your cupboard

▶ Putting canned and frozen veggies to work

▶ Seasonings make the difference

You can't whip up a quick dinner if your cupboard resembles Old Mother Hubbard's. Stock your kitchen with staples, and you'll have the fixings for a meal even when you don't have time to shop. This chapter covers the food products that form the basis for everyday entrees.

Having a well-stocked pantry doesn't mean predictable or boring meals. You're going to discover that many of the same ingredients that you enjoy in restaurants — herb-flavored pasta, fire-roasted tomatoes, and cannellini beans — are on supermarket shelves.

Boxes, cans, and jars are your shortcuts to dinner. In this chapter, I show you how to use staples as part of quick and innovative meals. Use a combination of fresh and convenient foods for the best color, aroma, and texture in your dishes.

I'm not going to describe every food that you can fit on your shelf. Instead, taking the building blocks of the Food Guide Pyramid (see Chapter 1) as inspiration, this chapter covers the various categories of staples (including grains, protein foods, and vegetables) that you're most likely to use every day — or when you have an emergency and can't get to a grocery store. And I can't ignore spices or fresh and dried herbs in a discussion of staples. They're the extra touch that assures you that your efforts are as flavorful as they are quick. Ladies and gentlemen, to your can openers!

Going with Grains

Grains provide the foundation for quick and hearty meals. A bowl of meat sauce looks meager but spoon it over spaghetti, and it's a rib-sticking entree. Grains come in many forms, but two types are primary — whole grains and refined grains:

- **Whole grains:** The manufacturer doesn't refine these grains, so they contain healthy fats and dietary fiber that you should be getting. Brown rice is a good example of a whole grain. Make whole grains, such as oats, whole wheat, barley, and rye, half of your daily servings, say diet experts. Whole grains have more nutrients than refined grains, but many also take much longer to cook, making them an occasional dish, not part of your 30-minute meal.

- **Refined grains:** These grains have been processed to remove the high-fiber bran and germ, leaving the starchy portion. White rice is a refined grain. Processed grains are usually white, easy to digest, and quicker cooking than their whole counterparts.

Keep the daily recommendations of the Food Guide Pyramid (see Chapter 1) in mind when you stock grains and other staples and plan your menus.

I love *serve-overs,* and not just because I play a lousy game of tennis. By serving a saucy meat, poultry, or seafood dish *over* one of the two most popular processed grains — spaghetti and rice — I turn a lightweight entree into a rib-sticking meal. That's why I always stock an assortment of pasta and rice products.

Using your noodle

Spaghetti is the little black dress of meal planning. Dress it up, or dress it down — either way, it's always in style. As soon as I use up one package, I buy another.

Health experts say a serving of spaghetti is one ounce, uncooked. But between you and me, 2 ounces of uncooked spaghetti — which turns into one cup of cooked spaghetti — is closer to what many people eat as a serving.

Make a circle slightly smaller than the size of a quarter with your thumb and forefinger. That's about the equivalent of 2 ounces of spaghetti, thin spaghetti, or linguine. (Check out Figure 3-1 for the exact two-ounce circle size.)

In addition to standard spaghetti, include chunky pasta, such as *farfalle* (butterfly shape), *conchiglie* (a frill-edged seashell shape), or *radiatore* (grooved curved shape), in your collection of staples for casseroles, stews, and skillet meals. *Orzo,* pasta shaped like a fat grain of rice, is excellent to use instead of rice for a little variety in soups, under stews, or in pasta salads.

Even though many pastas use the same basic ingredients of flour and water, different shapes trick you into thinking the flavor is different as well. That's something to remember if you're serving yet another pasta dish. Change the shape. (Of course, with all the quick and delicious recipes in this book, you're not going to suffer taste-bud fatigue.)

Cooking pasta is almost as easy as boiling water. Fill a large pot with 3 to 4 quarts of salted water. Cover the pot and bring the water to a rolling boil. Uncover, add 8 ounces of pasta, stir, and return to a boil. Cook 8 to 10 minutes for orzo or 10 to 12 minutes for spaghetti, farfalle, conchiglie, or radiatore. Drain and use in a recipe for four.

Salt raises the boiling point of water. If you don't salt water, it comes to a boil a few minutes sooner. When every minute counts, bring unsalted water to a boil, but don't forget to add the salt after the water is boiling.

Figure 3-1:
If your
handful of
spaghetti
is the same
size as
this circle,
you have
2 ounces of
spaghetti.

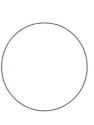

Following the grain trail

When archeologists search the sites of ancient villages, whole grains are often found among the ruins. According to *The Cambridge World History of Food* (Cambridge University Press), barley has been traced back to 7000 B.C., millet has its roots in biblical times, and the ancient Aztecs cultivated amaranth. The Aztecs toasted amaranth and even popped it like popcorn. Maybe this proves that snacking is in your genes. Even quinoa, the hot grain of the moment, traces its roots to Inca farmers in the Andes of Peru.

Pepperoni, Pesto, and Pepper Pasta Salad

Combine typical ingredients like olives and pepperoni in an antipasto plate and add farfalle pasta, and you have a meal. Serve this dish at room temperature for the best flavor.

Preparation time: 10 minutes

Yield: 2 servings

2 cups cooked farfalle pasta

6 ounces thinly sliced pepperoni

¼ cup pitted, chopped mixed Mediterranean olives

4 to 6 oil-packed sun-dried tomatoes, sliced

2 roasted red bell peppers, sliced

¼ cup tomato or basil pesto

1 to 2 tablespoon olive oil

1 tablespoon red wine vinegar

¼ teaspoon pepper

1 Place the farfalle in a salad bowl. Add the pepperoni, olives, tomatoes, and peppers. Toss gently but well.

2 Combine the pesto, 1 tablespoon of olive oil, vinegar, and pepper in a small bowl. Mix well. Spoon the pesto dressing over the salad. If the mixture looks dry, add the remaining tablespoon of olive oil.

Per serving: Calories 909 (From Fat 594); Fat 66g (Saturated 19g); Cholesterol 77mg; Sodium 2,385mg; Carbohydrate 48g (Dietary Fiber 3g); Protein 31g.

Sticking with rice

If spaghetti is the little black dress, rice is my favorite pair of jeans. The dinner plate always looks inviting with a side of rice. It goes with everything from soup to pudding. The types of rice that you're most likely to use include long-grain, parboiled, instant, and instant brown rice, each of which I describe in the following listing.

✔ **Long grain:** This long, slender rice goes with practically everything, from salads to skillet dinners, and it's the most popular kind of rice in American homes.

To cook long-grain rice, combine 2 cups of water and ½ teaspoon salt in a medium-size pot and bring to a boil. Stir in 1 cup rice. Cover pot, reduce heat to low, and simmer 18 to 20 minutes or until the rice is tender and the liquid is absorbed. Yields 3 cups.

✔ **Parboiled:** Sold as *converted* rice by a major food company, it's produced by a steam-treatment. That's a fancy way of saying that you get rice that doesn't clump together. It's not an advantage if you're eating with chop sticks and want rice that's easier to scoop up, but it's a plus in many skillet dinners.

To cook parboiled rice, combine 2¼ cups and ½ teaspoon salt in a medium-size pot and bring to a boil. Stir in 1 cup of rice. Cover pot, reduce heat to low, and simmer 20 to 25 minutes or until the rice is tender, and the liquid is absorbed. Yields 3 cups.

✔ **Instant:** Precooked and dehydrated rice. Despite what you may read in serious food publications, you won't be banned from the kitchen if you use it. Yes, instant rice has a pulpy texture. It's fine, however, when you need a quick base for a serve-over dish or you're preparing a skillet dinner that takes a little more time and you want to cut a few minutes of cooking.

Combine 1 cup of water and ¼ teaspoon of salt in a small pot and bring to a boil. Stir in 1 cup of instant rice and cover the pot. Remove the pot from the heat and let it stand for 1 minute. Fluff up the rice with a fork. This makes about 1½ cups.

✔ **Instant brown:** Another precooked and dehydrated rice, this time made from brown rice. Instant brown rice has a nutty taste and the nutrients of regular brown rice, but it's ready in a fraction of the time. Follow the same cooking instructions as you do for instant rice.

Of the rice varieties, I prefer parboiled rice, because it's indestructible. However, parboiled rice takes about 20 to 25 minutes to cook, and that means you have to be super-organized to make a skillet dinner using it. I wouldn't demand that level of organization from myself, and certainly not from you:

✔ If you're cooking without a minute to spare, substitute instant for parboiled rice in skillet dinners. (See Chapter 12 for a super fast and super tasty Spanish dish called *paella* that uses instant rice.)

✔ If you're just cooking rice to serve under a dish, prepare a large pot of parboiled rice when you have a chance, and refrigerate leftovers to use for a few dinners. Stir the cooked rice into a stew, soup, or skillet dinner to heat it.

Rice becomes hard at the center when it's refrigerated. To tenderize it, sprinkle a couple of teaspoons of water over the rice and reheat in a microwave oven.

Packing in Proteins

Most protein foods are perishables — meat, eggs, fish, seafood, and poultry. But you can stock plenty of cupboard choices as well, including canned tuna, salmon, and sardines. And beans are an often-overlooked source of protein, vitamins, minerals, and dietary fiber.

Fishing for some respect

What could be faster? Open a can of fish, and you're on your way to a main course. Different canned fish products offer different advantages. Check 'em out.

Tuning in to tuna

Unfortunately, you can't make mom's comforting tuna-noodle casserole in a time-crunched 30 minutes, but you can make plenty of other dishes with canned tuna. Choose the type that's appropriate for what you're cooking.

- **Albacore tuna** is a high-fat fish with a pleasing, firm, white flesh and a mild taste. It's usually the most expensive type of canned tuna. Use it in entree salads.

- **Fancy tuna** comes in large chunks. Spoon fancy tuna onto a platter with steamed vegetables and drizzle on the vinaigrette dressing (see Chapter 5) for a lunch entree.

- **Light meat tuna** doesn't specify the fish variety on the label. Base your selection on the grading. Use this type of tuna in salads — especially pasta salads.

- **Chunk tuna,** in smaller but distinct pieces, is great for tuna salad sandwiches and pasta salads.

- **Flaked tuna,** which comes in smaller shredded pieces, is appropriate for tuna croquettes.

Food companies also give you a choice of water-pack or oil-pack tuna. You'll probably drain tuna for most recipes, so save time and 100 calories per can with water-pack tuna.

Use albacore or chunk tuna in the Tuna, Pepper, and Rice Salad. If you only have oil-pack tuna, drain the oil and use it as part of the salad dressing in place of some of the olive oil.

Tuna, Pepper, and Rice Salad

Start with leftover cooked rice and add canned vegetables and tuna for a tasty dish. This recipe calls for canned, roasted tomatoes, which you can find in most natural food stores and some supermarkets. I like the smoky taste of the tomatoes. If you can't find this product, use your favorite canned, diced tomatoes. You can also make this rice salad a day in advance and chill. Adjust olive oil and lemon juice, adding more to taste if necessary.

Preparation time: *About 10 minutes*

Yield: *4 servings*

2 cups hot cooked rice

1 can (14 to 16 ounces) corn, drained

2 cans (6½ ounces each) white tuna, packed in water, drained

1 can (14½ ounces) roasted diced tomatoes, drained

1 can (4 ounces) diced chiles, drained

8 green onions, diced

1 small green bell pepper, seeded and diced

1 small red bell pepper, seeded and diced

2 teaspoons ground cumin

¼ cup chopped cilantro (optional)

2 garlic cloves, minced

3 tablespoons olive oil

2 tablespoons lemon juice

½ teaspoon salt

¼ teaspoon pepper

Place the rice in a large bowl. Add the corn, tuna, tomatoes, chiles, green onions, peppers, cumin, cilantro (if desired), and garlic. In a cup, stir together the oil, lemon juice, salt, and pepper. Add the dressing to the rice mixture. Toss gently but well.

Vary It! *Add a little variety by substituting 2 cups of cooked pasta or bulgur for the rice.*

Per serving: *Calories 385 (From Fat 120); Fat 13g (Saturated 2g); Cholesterol 30mg; Sodium 926mg; Carbohydrate 41g (Dietary Fiber 5g); Protein 23g.*

Plenty of other fish in the sea

Tuna isn't the only water-based, protein-providing, canned staple that you can use to whip up a quick meal. Canned salmon is a nutrition powerhouse. If you eat the soft bones, you get the equivalent calcium that you get in a glass of milk in each serving. Salmon also provides *omega-3 fatty acids,* the kind of fat that health experts say may reduce your risk of heart disease. All that with speed, convenience, and variety, too.

> ✔ **Sockeye or red salmon** has a deep orange-red color, firm texture, and meaty taste. Serve it with sliced tomatoes and mayonnaise or topped with sliced red onions on a slice of pumpernickel bread. Sockeye is also excellent in the chowder recipe in Chapter 9.
>
> ✔ **Pink salmon** has a light flesh and a soft texture. The flavor is mild. This is the salmon I'd serve to children who aren't crazy about fish. Use pink salmon for a salmon and macaroni salad.

Minced clams have the briny taste that seafood lovers expect but without the shells to fuss with. Find minced clams in 6- to 7-ounce cans in the same supermarket aisle as the tuna and salmon. Add minced clams to a canned clam chowder — to beef it up.

Check out my bare bones clams-to-the-rescue emergency dinner that follows:

1. Cook 8 ounces of spaghetti as I describe in the "Using your noodle" section earlier in this chapter.

2. Drain the spaghetti well and add a can of clams — or two if your family or friends are really hungry.

3. Open a jar of your favorite tomato-based spaghetti sauce and stir 2 cups (or more depending on your taste) in with spaghetti and clams.

4. Heat it all up until the dish is warmed through, and you're done.

Canned shrimp are convenient, but for my money, I'd rather use frozen shrimp. Canned shrimp usually taste salty and have a mushy texture.

That's a hill of beans

If I had space for only one protein food in the cupboard, I'd choose canned beans. Beans are filling, which is a great advantage when you're trying to feed a family fast. But more than that, beans are a good source of dietary fiber, which helps reduce your risk of heart disease, prevents you from overeating, and keeps you regular. Beans are loaded with *folate,* a B vitamin that reduces the risk of heart disease and helps prevent spinal defects in a fetus. Beans also contain some iron.

Enough of the nutrition lecture. You eat dinner, not nutrition, and beans are your ally when you're preparing a soup or stew in 30 minutes or less. What's more, beans come in so many varieties that you can serve beans every night of the week and not repeat yourself.

The five types of beans that I recommend that you stock along with suggestions for using them are as follows. (You can see what these little fellas look like in Figure 3-2.)

- **Black beans:** Also called *turtle beans,* these small beans have a rich black shell covering a white interior. Black beans taste sweet and not as starchy as some other bean varieties. Use them in soup, black bean, and white rice side dishes, or salads.

- **Chickpeas:** These beans also go by their alias, *garbanzo beans.* The round- to square-shaped, tan-colored beans have a firm texture and sweet, nutty taste. Chickpeas keep their shape well even after long cooking. They're good for soup, salads, and stews.

- **Cannellini beans:** Also called *white kidney beans,* this variety is sweet and mild with an almost buttery consistency. The bean falls apart after long cooking and helps thicken soups. Good for purees, soups, or as a side dish for meat. You can see how the starchy consistency of cannellini beans complements tender kale by preparing the Kale and Cannellini Beans recipe from this chapter.

- **Kidney beans:** These red beans with the pink-to-white interior have a full flavor that makes them a good match for meat. The lighter colored beans have a softer texture than those with a deep red skin. Choose them when you want a dish with a pulpy consistency. Use the firm beans for salads. They also work well in chili and soup.

- **Pinto beans:** This pink to tan-colored bean is meaty tasting, yet mild enough to blend with other ingredients. The bean holds up to cooking. Common uses include chili, soup, and refried beans.

For a healthful snack, drain chickpeas and dry with a paper towel. Dust with pepper and serve.

BEANS FOR EVERY DISH

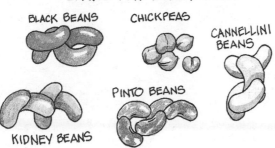

Figure 3-2:
Stockpile different types of beans. Size, shape, and color can vary.

☉ Kale and Cannellini Beans

Beans and greens make a hearty yet quick vegetarian entree. To boost the protein and calcium in the dish, sprinkle a tablespoon of grated Parmesan cheese over each serving. Serve this dish with whole-grain bread and a simple vegetable.

Preparation time: *10 minutes*

Cooking time: *17 minutes*

Yield: *4 servings*

1 tablespoon olive oil	*¼ teaspoon crushed red pepper flakes*
1 medium onion, chopped	*¼ teaspoon salt*
1 large garlic clove, minced	*¼ teaspoon pepper*
1 pound fresh kale, thick stems removed	*2 teaspoons fresh lemon juice*
1 cup vegetable broth	
1 can (15 ounces) cannellini beans, drained and rinsed	

1 Heat the oil in a 5-quart pot. Add the onion and garlic and cook over low-medium heat 2 minutes.

2 Coarsely chop the kale into 1- to 2-inch pieces. Place in a colander and run under cold water. Do not pat dry. Add the kale to the pot. You'll have about 12 cups, but it will quickly cook down. Cook over high heat 5 minutes, stirring frequently, until kale wilts.

3 Add the broth, beans, red pepper flakes, salt, and pepper. Cook at medium-high heat 10 minutes, or until the kale is tender, stirring occasionally. Sprinkle with lemon juice just before serving.

Per serving: *Calories 133 (From Fat 40); Fat 5g (Saturated 1g); Cholesterol 0mg; Sodium 511mg; Carbohydrate 20g (Dietary Fiber 6g); Protein 6g.*

Avoiding the consequences

Beans get a bad rap for causing flatulence. To reduce or eliminate that handicap, use a commercial product, such as Beano. You can buy this over-the-counter product in most drug stores and follow the package directions. If you start eating a small amount of beans, say ¼ cup at a meal, and eat them frequently, your body builds a tolerance to the beans, and you experience less flatulence.

Moving on to Greener Pastures

Shopping for fresh vegetables in season is one of my great pleasures. And a little fresh-veggie shopping know-how can save you plenty of time in the kitchen. That's why I devote a whole chapter, Chapter 5, to shopping for these green goodies. But I don't always have time to get to my farmers market or supermarket. And to be honest, I appreciate the fact that manufacturers prepare vegetables in ways that I don't have the time to do.

For example, it would take me 10 minutes to bring a pot of water to boiling, then scald, seed, and dice a couple of tomatoes. Opening a can of peeled and diced tomatoes takes one minute, tops. Do I have the time to scrape corn kernels from the cob? Not when I'm the designated driver for family activities. I'd just as soon use frozen or canned corn kernels. But what do you do if a recipe calls for a fresh vegetable and you only have the canned or frozen version? Don't worry. You can easily convert from fresh to canned or frozen using Table 3-1 in this chapter.

Table 3-1	Vegetable Conversion Chart	
Fresh	*Canned*	*Frozen*
2 large bell peppers	Not available	10-ounce package
1 pound broccoli	Not available	16-ounces frozen
1 pound brussels sprouts	Not available	2 (10-ounce) packages
4 to 6 carrots	16-ounce can	10-ounce bag
4 ears corn	16-ounce can	10-ounce bag
8 ounces green beans	14-ounce can	10-ounce bag
2 pounds shelled peas	16-ounce can	10-ounce bag
3 tomatoes	14.5-ounce can	Not available

But are you getting nutritionally inferior vegetables when you opt for the canned or frozen variety? Not for a minute. Studies from the University of Illinois show that canned vegetables are on a nutritional par with fresh ones.

Recommendations from health experts to eat 3 to 5 servings of vegetables a day don't specify fresh, canned, or frozen. Serve whatever form fits into your schedule.

Tomatoes to the rescue

Canned tomatoes are one of my favorite convenience foods. You can find diced, sliced, pureed, and whole tomatoes. Manufacturers offer tomatoes with garlic, onions, chiles, Italian seasonings, Mexican seasonings, and more. Just open a can, and you're halfway to dinner. And that's just for starters. You also have your choice of tomato paste, tomato sauce, or pureed tomatoes. With so many choices, what should you stock? Start with these tomato products:

- ✔ **Tomato paste** is a thick tomato concentrate. It's available in cans or tubes. I prefer tubes, because I can use what I want and refrigerate the remainder. It's less messy than half-opened cans. Add a tablespoon of tomato paste to pasta sauce, soup, or chili for an intense tomato taste.

- ✔ **Tomato puree** is a thick liquid made by cooking and straining tomatoes. Add tomato puree to soups and stews. Pasta sauce recipes often call for adding a can of tomato puree to a mixture of ground beef and seasonings.

- ✔ **Tomato sauce,** the thinnest and least intense of the three tomato products, has the consistency of a thick juice. Use it in soups, stews, pasta sauces, or as part of a sauce for meat or poultry.

Canned tomatoes are a boon during the off-season when you can't find good-tasting, fresh tomatoes, but I also choose diced tomatoes when I'm pressed for time. Your cupboard should include plain and flavored diced tomatoes. If you do much Tex-Mex cooking, stock diced tomatoes with chiles; if you prefer Italian cooking, buy tomatoes with garlic. You'll also find fire-roasted diced tomatoes, which give your dishes a delicious smoky taste.

Tomatoes are high in *lycopene,* a substance that may reduce your risk of certain cancers. Cooked tomatoes are higher in lycopene. Your body is better able to absorb lycopene when it's in a dish with some fat. So mix a little olive oil and a can of diced tomatoes with garlic and pour it over a package of spaghetti for a real quick, healthy dish.

If you want to get a bit more involved with your canned tomatoes, try my Chicken Stew with Winter Vegetables recipe or the Sweet Potato and Bean Soup.

Chicken Stew with Winter Vegetables

Use canned tomatoes and their liquid to make this saucy stew. Vary the tomatoes, substituting fire-roasted tomatoes or tomatoes with roasted garlic to change the flavor each time you make this recipe. Take a look at the chicken thighs when you're shopping. Choose brands that are trimmed of fat, saving you time and money. For an accompaniment, open a bag of mixed greens and add your favorite salad dressing.

Preparation time: *8 minutes*

Cooking time: *20 minutes*

Yield: *4 servings*

¾ cup long-grain rice

1 pound, boneless, skinless chicken thighs, trimmed of fat

1 tablespoon olive oil

¼ cup flour

½ teaspoon salt

¼ teaspoon pepper

¼ teaspoon curry powder

¼ teaspoon ground cumin

1 can (14½ ounces) diced tomatoes, undrained

2 canned sweet potatoes, cut into ½-inch pieces

1 Prepare the rice while the chicken is cooking. Combine 1½ cups of water and ¼ teaspoon salt in a medium-size pot and bring to a boil. Stir in the rice. Cover the pot, reduce the heat to low, and simmer 18 to 20 minutes, or until the rice is tender, and the liquid is absorbed.

2 While the rice is cooking, heat the olive oil over medium-high heat in a large nonstick skillet. Place the chicken in a plastic bag with the flour, salt, and pepper and shake to coat. Add the coated chicken to the skillet in a single layer and brown 3 minutes per side. Remove the chicken from the skillet and set aside.

3 Add the curry powder and cumin to the skillet. Add the tomatoes with their liquid. Using a wooden spoon, scrape up any browned bits from the bottom of the skillet.

4 Return the chicken to the skillet and add the sweet potatoes. Stir well. Cover and simmer the dish for 5 minutes or until the sweet potatoes are hot.

5 Serve by dividing the rice among 4 plates and topping each serving of rice with a portion of chicken and sauce.

Per serving: Calories 428 (From Fat 109); Fat 12g (Saturated 3g); Cholesterol 76mg; Sodium 512mg; Carbohydrate 52g (Dietary Fiber 3g); Protein 26g.

Sweet Potato and Bean Soup

This hearty soup is flavored with the sweet, nutty taste of roasted garlic. Just open a can of diced tomatoes with garlic. Round out the soup with salad from a bag.

Preparation time: *10 minutes*

Cooking time: *20 minutes*

Yield: *2 entrees; 4 first-course servings*

1 tablespoon olive oil	¼ teaspoon ground cumin
1 medium onion, chopped	¼ teaspoon pepper
1 can (15 ounces) chickpeas, drained and rinsed	Salt to taste
	2½ cups chicken broth
1 medium sweet potato, peeled and cut into ½-inch dice	1 tablespoon minced fresh basil (optional)
	¼ cup grated Parmesan cheese
1 can (14½ ounces) diced tomatoes with roasted garlic	

1 Heat oil over high heat in a medium pot. Add onion and sauté 3 minutes. Add chickpeas, sweet potato, tomatoes, cumin, pepper, salt, and chicken broth. Bring to a boil. Reduce heat to low and simmer for 15 minutes or until potato is tender.

2 Stir in the basil (if desired) and simmer for 1 minute more. To serve, spoon into 2 large soup bowls and garnish each serving with 2 tablespoons of grated Parmesan cheese.

Speed It Up! *Cut the total preparation and cooking time to 10 minutes by substituting 1 cup of canned, diced sweet potatoes.*

Vary It! *For a vegetarian dish, use vegetable broth in place of the chicken broth. For a heartier dish, add a cup of leftover cooked chicken or pork cubes.*

Per serving: *Calories 431 (From Fat 150); Fat 17g (Saturated 4g); Cholesterol 14mg; Sodium 2,932mg; Carbohydrate 55g (Dietary Fiber 10g); Protein 15g.*

Corn on the can

Although tomatoes are the heavy hitter in the canned veggie world, corn is also an important ingredient to have on hand. Corn is getting sweeter all the time. When farmers plant a variety called Candy Corn, they're not kidding. If you want to add a naturally sweet flavor to a dish, corn is a great and healthful way to do it. For example, add a can of corn to a hot chili recipe. You'll calm the flames. I'm not suggesting anything corny, but the following list shows how you can improve other quick recipes using canned corn:

- Buy a box of corn muffin mix. Add a cup of drained, canned corn with the liquid ingredients.

- Add a cup of canned or frozen corn kernels to 2 cups of fresh salsa or salsa in a jar.

- Stir a cup of canned or frozen corn into packaged corn chowder.

- Stretch your own homemade vegetable soup with corn. A cup of corn would be a great addition to the Harvest Vegetable Soup in Chapter 9.

When buying canned corn, choose *vacuum-pack corn,* because it's packed with minimal liquid, which you're probably draining off anyway. Why pay for something you're feeding to the plumbing? I prefer yellow corn to white, because I want more color in my cooking, but that's a matter of individual style.

Indulging yourself

Okay. You won't go hungry if you don't stock your favorite splurge items. But cooking fast doesn't mean that you can't have fun. If you love to try new foods, cruise your supermarket's gourmet counters for items like imported olives or sun-dried tomatoes. They're not really staples, but they go to show that you don't need to add much to transform the taste of an ordinary dish into something special. These are foods that I rely on to dress up meals:

- **Canned artichoke hearts:** Add artichoke hearts to salads, toss with cooked pasta just before serving, or sprinkle chopped artichoke hearts on a frozen pizza before baking. You'll turn a simple dish into a glamorous one.

- **Bottled olives:** You'll find dusky brown kalamata olives that have a tangy, herbal flavor and meaty-tasting niçoise olives along with the classic pimiento-stuffed green olives. Add olives to a skillet chicken or pork dish as a seasoning agent. The taste will be slightly piquant and richer. Olives are a fruit (I know they're listed in this vegetable section, but I figured you'd let me slide on this one) to serve as a savory ingredient or food.

- **French fried onion rings:** I'll admit I'm a sucker for fried onion rings. Instant texture and taste with the flip of a lid. Make a skillet dinner and sprinkle on fried onions, and you've transformed the dish.

Seasoning in a Snap

Even when I'm cooking as fast as I can I don't want to forego flavor. What's the point in making a quick dinner if it's inedible? That will never happen when you prepare the 30-minute dishes in this book. And that's because I cook with spices and herbs. Spices and herbs are important tools of the quick-cooking trade. You can impart a ton of flavor in just a few seconds. The following section shows you how to use spices and herbs.

Adding some spice to your life

Spices are aromatic seasonings that come from the bark, buds, seeds, or roots of various plants or trees. Spices are roughly divided into two main categories:

- ✔ **Savory:** Pepper, cumin, paprika, and cayenne pepper are the savory spices that you're most likely to use. Add savory spices to entrees and side dishes to develop full robust tastes. You don't have to cook savory-spiced foods for long to benefit from their flavors and aromas.

- ✔ **Sweet:** You don't have to relegate common sweet spices, such as cinnamon, nutmeg, clove, and ginger, to dessert recipes. A pinch of cinnamon rounds out the taste of beef stew. Add a dash of ginger to pork and make the taste more intense. Cinnamon and ginger can get you through most dessert recipes.

If you dine out in Mexican, Indian, Thai, or other Asian restaurants, you know about the wonderful foods that combine sweet and savory spices. Think about those marvelous Indian curries that use cinnamon, ginger, cumin, and cayenne. The combination of spices adds up to a well-rounded flavor in which no one spice predominates. You can experiment with these spices to add zest to your cooking as well. Start with small amounts and introduce one seasoning at a time. You don't want to overwhelm your palate or those of your family and friends.

Spices release their flavors when heated. Sprinkling cumin on a dish of cooked chili won't taste as good as when you add cumin and then simmer the chili. Fortunately, it doesn't take a long time for the flavor to blend into the dish. You can get plenty of satisfying taste from a spicy dish cooked for 10 or 30 minutes. Fat also releases the flavor and aroma of spices. Use spices in recipes that also call for a little oil or butter.

You can buy spices in two basic forms — whole and ground — and each brings something different to the table in terms of time and taste:

- ✓ **Convenience and storage:** Using pre-ground spices is faster than having to grind whole spices. Ground spices, however, lose their freshness and distinctive aromas more quickly than whole spices. Buy ground spices for the seasonings that you use most often, such as cinnamon, ginger, allspice, and cumin. Buy whole spices for seasonings that you use on an occasional basis, such as cloves or nutmeg.

- ✓ **Flavor:** Ground and whole spices also flavor foods in different ways. Cumin seed is subtler than ground cumin. Use cumin seed for long-simmering dishes, so the taste is released gradually; use ground cumin for rubs or for quick soups. Seed spices, such as caraway, fennel, and sesame seeds, are usually sold whole.

Pepper is my one exception to the ground rule. I always buy whole peppercorns for their sharp, distinctive taste. The children get the chore of filling the pepper mill.

Herbs to the rescue

Herbs are the aromatic leaves of plants. Some herbs, such as chives, are mostly leaves; others, such as rosemary or bay leaves, grow on woody stems. You may be familiar with parsley, sage, rosemary, and thyme from the lyrics to an old Simon and Garfunkel song. But even if you can't hum along, you can choose different herbs that make your dishes sing.

Some suggestions for herbs that match nicely with these foods are as follows:

- ✓ **Beef:** Oregano, basil, rosemary, thyme, and bay leaf. Always remove the indigestible bay leaf before you serve your food.
- ✓ **Chicken:** Oregano, basil, and thyme.
- ✓ **Eggs:** Thyme, chives, dill, and chervil.
- ✓ **Fish:** Tarragon, chives, mint, oregano, basil, dill, cilantro, and chervil.
- ✓ **Lamb:** Rosemary, thyme, and oregano.
- ✓ **Pasta:** Oregano, mint, thyme, chives, and basil.
- ✓ **Pork:** Rosemary and sage.
- ✓ **Potatoes:** Dill, thyme, oregano, and chives.
- ✓ **Tomatoes:** Basil, parsley, mint, and thyme.

Herbs come in two basic varieties — *dry* and *fresh.* Dry herbs have a more pungent aroma and flavor than their fresh counterpart. However, they require cooking to make their flavor mellow. Dried herbs taste harsh unless they're cooked first. See the following quick-cooking herb breakdown on when and how to use each type of herb:

- ✔ **Dry:** Use dry herbs in a dish that you'll be cooking for *at least* 5, preferably 10 minutes.

- ✔ **Fresh:** Add fresh herbs to food during the *last* 5 to 10 minutes of cooking. They lose their potency if overcooked.

If a recipe calls for fresh herbs and you only have the dry version, use one-third the amount called for. Instead of 1 tablespoon of fresh basil, substitute 1 teaspoon of dry basil. Don't forget to add the dried basil during cooking, not at the end. And always crush dried herbs with your fingers to release the flavoring oils before adding the ingredient to a food.

As much as I rely on dry herbs, I treasure having a few herb pots in the kitchen. During the winter, when I can't remember what a green lawn looks like, I reach for the thyme plant and smell the scent of spring. (Check out Figure 3-3 to see what thyme and some other fresh herbs look like.) It adds a quick burst of flavor to my meal and a hint of sun to my disposition. Rosemary, chives, and parsley round out my indoor garden. To harvest and store fresh herbs:

1. Hold the plant under a spray of cold water to rinse the leaves

2. Take a small pair of scissors and snip the leaves directly into the food that you're cooking. Don't go overboard in trimming herbs, or you'll kill the plant.

3. Wrap stem ends of fresh herbs with a damp paper towel. Place the herbs in a plastic bag with a resealable top. Close the bag, squeezing out excess air.

4. Refrigerate the herbs up to a week, changing the paper towel every other day.

Coming out of the closet with spices

Light and heat destroy the color and flavor of spices. The expert advice is to keep spices in tightly covered jars in your cupboard. But I disagree. As someone who can be easily distracted when cooking, I want my spice arsenal at arm's reach, not tucked away on some dark shelf. My spices sit under the kitchen windowsill in a shaded area. Look around and see if you can find an area near the stove but away from direct heat and light.

Figure 3-3: These are the herbs that you'll rely on for quick, delicious, and fragrant dishes.

Chapter 4

Focusing on Efficiency

In This Chapter

▶ Clearing the clutter and the cobwebs

▶ Multitasking in the kitchen

▶ Approaching meal preparation with a plan

All the best and sure-fire 30-minute meals can turn into 60-minute meals if you're disorganized. A nothing-is-where-you-can-find-it kitchen can throw a monkey wrench into the best-laid plans of mice and chefs.

Getting organized not only makes you a faster, more efficient cook but a less frantic one as well. Knowing where the butter is without ripping the refrigerator apart can have a calming effect. Putting a pot of water on to boil as soon as you go into the kitchen saves you time when you're going to cook spaghetti or boil vegetables.

Kitchen organization isn't something that comes naturally, but you'll discover that you can keep your kitchen organized if you make it a habit. I know that you didn't buy this book to have someone lecture you on cleaning up your cupboards, and I won't do that. However, I will share the tips that can help you find the ingredients that you need in record time.

I also provide some tips and techniques that you can use when you're actually ready to cook as well. Doubling up on some cooking chores also shaves time. I show you how to multitask without getting frazzled. This chapter shows you how to put rhythm into food preparation and provides all the coaching that you need to become more efficient in the kitchen.

Organizing, Schmorganizing

Dismissing kitchen organization is easy. Most likely your life, like mine, is pretty structured. Having one area in which you can let loose is a relief. Besides, you may think that putting things away in a specific place is one more chore that eats into your schedule. Getting organized the first time isn't much fun, but after you're set up, your going to gain plenty from your new-found organization:

- ✔ **Money:** I'm embarrassed to admit all the times that I've discarded slimy lettuce, because I forgot that it was in the refrigerator until the greens were well past their prime.

- ✔ **Space:** If you never have enough room for the groceries, check to see what you're stocking. Maybe you're buying duplicates of foods that you already have instead of eating down your inventory. Being organized can prevent this duplication. And consciously arranging all those boxes, cans, and jars may free up even more space.

- ✔ **Time:** During the five minutes that it takes to find the lid for the sauté pan, you could put your feet up and take a look at the newspaper.

Developing Storage Options

The displays at your local storage or linens store can provide you with plenty of storage ideas. You can also look for functional and well-built storage pieces in restaurant supply houses. Wire bins on metal frames allow you to see what's in each compartment without pulling out drawers. Look for storage units on wheels that you can roll out of the way when you want more space.

Buy a waist-high set of drawers on wheels and add a butcher-block top to the unit. You not only get storage options, but you gain another work surface as well. (Check out one version in Figure 4-1.)

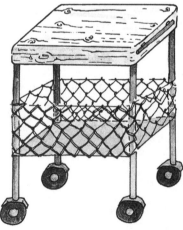

YOU CAN MAKE YOUR OWN STORAGE UNIT/COUNTERTOP COMBINATION USING WIRE BASKETS ON WHEELS TOPPED WITH A WOODEN CUTTING BOARD.

Figure 4-1:
Rolling
down
Organization
Avenue.

Dangerous storage spaces

Household accidents can result from carelessly storing everyday items. Here are a few scenarios you may want to think twice about:

✔ **Using a microwave as a storage space.** Avoid storing papers or packaged foods here. You don't even have to turn on the microwave to spark a fire, say the experts from Underwriters Laboratories, an independent, not-for-profit product-safety testing and certification organization. A power surge can trigger a fire in the microwave oven. Keep an oven empty unless you're using it. (Visit Underwriters Laboratories on the Internet at www.ul.com/consumers for all kinds of household and general safety advice.)

✔ **Storing items in a toaster oven.** Turning a toaster oven on requires only light pressure to the switch. If you inadvertently flip the switch, any contents could go up in flames.

✔ **Repackaging nonfood items in food containers.** Poisoning can occur when people eat what they think is food because it's in familiar food packaging. Various poison-control centers often receive reports of people drinking weed killer or other dangerous household chemicals that are stored in food containers such as old juice jars.

✔ **Repackaging food in different food containers.** You don't want someone with food allergies accidentally eating a food that he or she is allergic too because that person thought it was something else. Keep food in its original containers with the original labels. Occasionally this isn't practical. For example, you may want to transfer opened canned food to a plastic container with a lid so the food is less likely to spill if the package is knocked over. In that case, take the original label and paste it on the container just to be safe.

See the following listing for more storage ideas:

✔ For compact storage, buy bottles of herbs and spices and place them in a heavy-duty clear plastic box. If you have spices, say cinnamon, that you always measure (instead of simply shaking), remove the perforated top, so you can get a measuring spoon into the jar faster. Mark the lid of each jar with the name of the seasoning, so you see what you need at a glance. Then store the box in a cupboard or on a kitchen counter away from heat and light.

✔ Attach a measuring spoon on a colorful piece of yarn to your coffee canister, so you don't have to hunt for a spoon every morning. You can also tie a tablespoon measure to your bottle of olive oil and keep the bottle near the stove. You'll be ready whenever a recipe calls for olive oil.

✔ If you use much flour in your cooking (to flour chicken or thicken sauces, for example), place the flour in a canister and keep it on the counter. I also bury a graduated measuring cup in the container.

✔ Transfer your brown sugar to a container with an airtight lid to keep it from getting hard. If it's too late, soften hard brown sugar in your microwave. Spoon, or chop, the amount you want, place it in a microwave-safe bowl, and heat it at medium or medium-high for 1 minute. Repeat if necessary.

You can also soften a rock-hard sugar lump by adding a few apple slices, sealing the container, and setting it aside for a day. Supermarkets also sell granulated brown sugar. The granulated variety isn't appropriate for cakes and cookies, but it's fine in most other recipes.

✔ Pour sticky honey into a small bottle with a squirt cap, so it's less messy to use.

✔ Buy squeeze bottles or tubes of your favorite condiments. Just add a squirt of mustard to a vinaigrette dressing instead of spooning it out of a jar.

✔ Buy a plastic spray bottle for cooking oils and spray your pots and pans with oil. You'll save time measuring the oil and probably use less of the highly caloric fat. If you cook with both olive oil and a vegetable oil, buy two bottles in different colors.

✔ Keep coarse salt in a small open bowl as chefs do. Reach for a pinch to season foods as you cook.

✔ Use a magic marker to date everything that you put in the cupboard and fridge. It only takes a minute and then you don't have to worry about how long you've kept a food.

Discard canned foods that bulge or leak. Don't open and taste any food to see whether it's okay. The most deadly toxins don't have an off-taste. Also, don't toss the damaged cans or opened cans of spoiled food in a shallow garbage can or box where children or pets can get to them.

Getting organized can make cooking more enjoyable. If this idea really appeals to you, pick up *Organizing For Dummies* by Eileen Roth and Elizabeth Miles (Wiley) for more in-depth organizing guidance.

Ready, Set, Cook!

If you're like me, doing two things at once is probably the bane of your day. But handling more than one chore at a time in the kitchen is actually a time-saver, not a headache. If you've ever opened your mail while chatting with a friend or read the newspaper while drinking coffee, you can multitask in the kitchen without feeling frenzied.

Making mealtime easier

I probably do some food preparations simply because that's what I was taught, and now they've become a habit. I guess you do likewise. But, when you're in a time bind, decide whether all the prep that you do is really necessary. I try to eliminate the following:

✔ **Potato peeling:** If you cook and serve potatoes with the skins on, you not only skip the peeling part, you also increase the amount of dietary fiber that you get.

✔ **Thawing frozen vegetables:** For soups or skillet dinners, simply add your vegetables while they're still frozen, breaking up any solid blocks with a wooden spoon.

Chefs have years of experience cooking 50 to 100 meals a night to guide them. But they still start each day making a schedule for themselves and their staffs. Writing out your plan gets you in the habit of moving efficiently. Keep a list on the refrigerator of what you should be doing to get dinner ready. After the moves become second nature, scrap the list and keep mental notes.

Some cooking steps don't need your constant attention — thank goodness — so you're free to take care of other kitchen chores. For example, in the 10 to 15 minutes it takes a pot of water to boil, you can do one of the following cooking-related activities:

✔ Sauté boneless, skinless chicken breasts, chicken thighs, shrimp, or fish fillets.

✔ Make a quick sauce to serve over pasta. Sautéing chopped onions, garlic, and tomatoes takes about 10 minutes.

✔ Make a salad and dressing. (Chapter 10 has excellent salad suggestions.)

✔ Set the table — or better yet, call someone else to set the table.

✔ Heat up bread in the oven. (For garlic bread, start by slicing a *baguette* — a loaf of French bread — lengthwise. Then mix garlic salt with butter that's softened from being left outside the fridge. Spoon and spread the mixture in between the slices, wrap the loaf in foil, and bake for 10 to 15 minutes.)

✔ Uncork a bottle of wine. Take a taste.

✔ Put your feet up for 5 minutes.

Cooking vegetables and pasta together

Fresh pasta cooks in one-third to one-half the time of dried pasta. As a marvelous coincidence, pasta cooks as fast as many vegetables. Taking advantage of that means that you can add fresh pasta and vegetables to one pot of boiling water. You won't have extra cookware to wash or additional steps to take. Just don't tell my Italian cooking instructor what I'm suggesting, or she's going to call on me with her rolling pin in hand.

Tortellini and Sugar Snap Peas with Alfredo Sauce

Tortellini are stuffed pasta squares (filled with meat, cheese, vegetables, or a combination of these ingredients) folded and formed into rings. I recommend using fresh tortellini, because it's plumper and more filling, and it cooks faster. Find fresh pasta in the supermarket refrigerator cases near the cheese products. Add a salad of mixed greens and a vinaigrette dressing to round out this meal.

Preparation time: *10 to 15 minutes*

Cooking time: *10 minutes*

Yield: *4 servings*

1 tablespoon salt

2 packages (9 ounces each) cheese-filled tortellini

4 cups sugar snap peas, 8 to 9 ounces, well rinsed

1 cup half-and-half

¼ cup butter

¼ cup grated Parmesan cheese

2 tablespoons minced fresh chives

¼ teaspoon pepper

1 Bring a large pot of water to a boil. Add the salt. Add the tortellini and sugar snap peas. Cook 5 minutes or until the tortellini are tender and float. Drain the tortellini and sugar snap peas well and return them to the pot.

2 Add the cream, butter, cheese, chives, and pepper. Cook over medium heat for 3 to 5 minutes or until the cream thickens slightly and coats the tortellini.

Speed It Up! *Substitute 1½ cups of Alfredo sauce for the cream, butter, and cheese. You can find refrigerated Alfredo sauce near the fresh pasta. You can also use a jar of Alfredo sauce. Include the fresh chives for color and flavor.*

Per serving: *Calories 541 (From Fat 236); Fat 26g (Saturated 15g); Cholesterol 77mg; Sodium 716mg; Carbohydrate 58g (Dietary Fiber 9g); Protein 22g.*

Cooking shrimp and pasta together

Cooking shrimp in water while it's coming to a boil has two advantages: The shrimp aren't exposed to the high heat that makes them tough, and you finish half the cooking while the water heats up. Unfortunately, this method has one downside. Shrimp and other protein foods produce an unpleasant-looking brown foam as they simmer. Use a slotted spoon to skim off the foam before you start cooking the pasta.

Linguine with Shrimp and Broccoli

This all-in-one meal takes almost no effort on your part, yet it yields an elegant dish. It doesn't hold up well, so make the dish just before you're about to sit down to dinner. You can put a kitchen helper to work browning a small, chopped onion in a little butter. Add the onion to the finished dish just before serving.

Preparation time: *5 minutes*

Cooking time: *25 minutes*

Yield: *4 servings*

1 tablespoon salt	*¾ cup half-and-half*
1 pound raw, large peeled shrimp	*⅛ teaspoon crushed red pepper flakes*
8 ounces dry linguine	*⅛ teaspoon pepper*
4 cups broccoli florets, cut into 1-inch pieces	

1 Fill a large pot with water and add the salt. Add the shrimp. Partially cover and cook over high heat for 10 minutes or until the shrimp are pink and firm and the water just comes to a boil. Scoop out the shrimp with a slotted spoon and set aside. Skim off any foam from the water. Keep the water over high heat.

2 Add the linguine and cook 8 minutes. Add the broccoli and cook another 2 to 3 minutes or until the linguine and broccoli are both tender. Drain the pasta and broccoli well and return to the pot. Add the shrimp, half-and-half, crushed red pepper flakes, and pepper. Cook over medium heat 1 minute or until the half-and-half thickens slightly and coats a spoon.

Vary It! *Substitute asparagus cut into 1-inch lengths for the broccoli.*

Speed It Up! *Substitute 1 pound frozen, cooked shrimp for raw. To change the recipe, bring the water to boiling. Add the linguine and broccoli as directed. If the shrimp are still frozen, add them with the broccoli. Otherwise, add thawed shrimp with the half-and-half.*

Per serving: *Calories 359 (From Fat 66); Fat 7g (Saturated 4g); Cholesterol 185mg; Sodium 369mg; Carbohydrate 45g (Dietary Fiber 5g); Protein 28g.*

Breakfast in a pan

You know how you can cook more than one food in a large pot. But keep reading to discover how you can also get double or triple duty from a sauté pan. Preparing a hearty brunch, including toast, eggs, and bacon in one pan requires that you have all your ingredients in place. The inspiration for the Hole-in-One Farmer Breakfast recipe in this section is a favorite camp recipe from my childhood, called Moon Over Miami. (See Figure 4-2 for the particulars. And for other, non-breakfast, one-pan meals, see Chapter 12.) You can make this recipe in your kitchen or over a campfire.

THE HOLE-IN-ONE EGG BREAKFAST

1. MAKE A HOLE IN THE CENTER OF A SLICE OF BREAD. THE HOLE SHOULD BE ABOUT 2" IN DIAMETER—THE SIZE OF A RAW EGG.

2. PLACE THE BREAD IN A SAUTÉ PAN WITH MELTED BUTTER.

3. DROP THE RAW EGG INTO THE HOLE AND FRY THE EGG UNTIL FIRM.

FORE!

Figure 4-2: A complete breakfast in a pan or skillet.

Music is the speed demon's muse

Okay. Call me perverse, but I can't listen to soothing music when I'm in a hurry. Ordinarily, I'd love to sit back and listen to a little Bach, but when time is of the essence, give me James Brown. When I blast that voice through the kitchen, I move to a quicker beat. Do you have a favorite radio station that supplies upbeat, high-energy music? Turn it on. While you're turning the dial, check out my fave five when it comes to cooking:

- ✔ "Good Golly Miss Molly" by Little Richard
- ✔ "Papa's Got a Brand New Bag" by James Brown
- ✔ "I Got You (I Feel Good)" also by James Brown
- ✔ "I Heard it Through the Grapevine" by Marvin Gaye
- ✔ "Great Balls of Fire" by Jerry Lee Lewis

Farmer Breakfast

Bacon, eggs, and toast — all the fixings of an old-style farm meal — come together in minutes. Serve this for Sunday brunch for two with a fruit salad on the side.

Preparation time: *5 minutes*

Cooking time: *13 minutes*

Yield: *2 servings*

4 strips bacon	*¼ teaspoon salt*
2 slices sourdough bread, sliced ½-inch thick	*¼ teaspoon pepper*
2 eggs	*2 slices cheddar or provolone cheese*

1 Arrange the strips of bacon in a large nonstick sauté pan. Fry the bacon over high heat 2 minutes per side or until crisp. Remove the bacon to a plate lined with paper towels. Cover and keep warm while making the rest of the dish.

2 Pour off all but 1 tablespoon bacon fat in the skillet. Using a cookie cutter, cut a 2-inch hole in the center of each bread slice. Add the bread to the skillet and sauté 1 minute.

3 One at a time, break each egg into a cup and then pour them into the holes in the center of the bread slices. Season each egg with ⅛ teaspoon salt and a dash of pepper. Fry 3 minutes to slightly set the eggs. Using a spatula, gently turn the eggs over. Arrange the cheese slices over each egg. Cover the sauté pan and cook 2 to 3 minutes or until the eggs are set and the cheese is slightly melted. If the bacon is cold, return it to the pan for 1 minute to heat through. Serve immediately.

Vary It! *Slice a couple of tomatoes and sauté them with the bread slices.*

Speed It Up! *Use precooked bacon slices instead of raw. To start the recipe, melt 2 tablespoons of butter or margarine in the sauté pan. Add the bread, eggs, and cheese as directed. Either add the bacon strips during the last minute to heat through or heat separately in a microwave oven, following the package directions.*

Per serving: *Calories 489 (From Fat 252); Fat 28g (Saturated 12g); Cholesterol 259mg; Sodium 922mg; Carbohydrate 35g (Dietary Fiber 2g); Protein 25g.*

Getting a Head Start

Cooking more food than you serve for one meal gives you a head start on the week's dinners. Accept it as a bonus in your menu planning. I know I do. In fact, I cook extra portions of ingredients that I know I'm going to use in two consecutive dinners. You'll find that you save time and energy by doubling up on some cooking steps.

The pinch hitters

All cooks, even the most organized of them, have reached onto the shelf for an ingredient only to find that they've run out. It happens to me, and I bet it happens to you too. When the cupboard is bare, don't panic and don't rush to the store to waste your cooking time in a grocery line. Instead be flexible and think about substitutions you can make. The Cheat Sheet at the front of this book suggests things that you can use in place of the ingredient you're missing. You may want to rip that page out of the book and put it on your refrigerator door.

But I do have one additional bit of advice to keep in mind when you're tinkering with substitutes: Taste as you cook. You may want to add or eliminate other ingredients to compensate for the changes. For example, if you're using a bouillon cube instead of broth, taste your dish before you add salt because bouillon cubes are salty. And your homemade ketchup may not be as thick as the store-bought version, so you may want to cook it over high heat for a couple of minutes to thicken it.

In this section, I describe foods you can prepare in bulk for maybe a little more time than it takes to cook smaller amounts. Your reward is having cooked ingredients on hand for other recipes. (If this concept appeals to you, check out Chapter 8 for information on big batch cooking in the truest sense.)

I often double up on the six ingredients that follow to jumpstart subsequent meals:

- **Eggs:** Hard-cook 5 or 6 eggs at a time. Store the extras in a bowl in the refrigerator to add to a pasta or rice salad (or for the egg salad sandwich in Chapter 11).

- **Rice:** Cook double the amount of rice you need for a recipe. Two cups of rice cooks in the same amount of time as one cup of rice. Store the leftovers in the refrigerator to use for rice salad. Or for a quick light meal or snack, stir rice into chicken broth for soup.

    Rice becomes hard at the center when it's refrigerated. Sprinkle a couple of teaspoons of water over the rice and reheat it in a microwave oven or add it to a dish that you're cooking. As the cold rice heats up, it becomes as tender as just-cooked rice.

- **Couscous:** My family loves toasted couscous, a large pearl couscous that's also called *Israeli couscous*. Although toasted couscous sticks together when cooked and chilled, it separates into individual pearls when you add it to a soup or stew for an additional meal.

✔ **Ground beef:** Browning twice the ground beef that you need for a given meal only takes a few more minutes, and you only have to clean up once. Refrigerate cooked, browned beef for up to two days or freeze it for up to one month. (You can use the cooked ground beef in my 8-Minute Chile in Chapter 17.)

✔ **Onions:** Chopping extra vegetables takes only a little more time, and you save yourself from washing that skillet again. Store cooked onions in the refrigerator and pull out your convenience food every time a recipe begins with "brown the onions."

✔ **Vinaigrette:** Pouring oil and vinegar into measuring spoons isn't a big deal, but if you can do it less often, why not? Fill a fancy bottle with vinaigrette dressing and keep it around. I prefer to refrigerate vinaigrette dressings, though not everyone agrees with me. Remove refrigerated vinaigrette and bring it to room temperature about 15 to 30 minutes before dinner.

Part II
Mastering Skills for Speed

The 5th Wave   By Rich Tennant

CONDUCTOR IRA MENDELBAUM REHEARSES HIS QUICK COOKING TECHNIQUES.

Ravel—3rd movement, Mendelbaum—2nd course.

In this part . . .

In this part, you can find out about some of the techniques, skills, tricks, and tips for getting food to the table in minutes. And it all starts at the supermarket — before you even enter the kitchen on a given evening. When you go to the supermarket, keep speed in mind when you peruse the produce if you want to shave minutes off your prep time.

When you get back from the store, you can master quick-cooking techniques, such as sautéing, broiling, and stove-top grilling. I also share what I consider a quick-cooking secret weapon — great sauces. And then I wrap up this part with cooking in large quantities. It's a technique that may not seem conducive to 30-minute meals at first glance, but after reading how you can turn a bit of extra effort into numerous 30-minute meals, you'll be hooked.

Chapter 5

Vegging Out: Fresh and Fast Produce

In This Chapter

▶ Buying vegetables with built-in convenience

▶ Discovering the vast array of available greens

▶ Salad bars to the rescue

▶ Preparing precooked and partially cooked vegetables

Fresh vegetables add color, texture, and flavor, as well as valuable nutrients, to your meals. Imagine how much better a meatloaf looks on a plate when you add a side of peas or carrots. Plus, knowing that you're adding wholesome and delicious foods to the family's menu always makes you feel good.

Thanks to recent advances from farmers and packing companies (like preservatives to prevent spoilage and packaging that keeps vegetables fresh longer) you can enjoy the benefits of fresh vegetables without much time-consuming labor. Pared, peeled, and partially or fully cooked vegetables now fill supermarket produce aisles. The food industry calls these convenience-added vegetables. And you can understand why. You're getting all the nutrition, flavor, and satisfaction in less time and with less work.

In this chapter, I provide some fresh ideas for using the quickest veggies and vegetable products. Perusing the produce aisles of your favorite grocery store, you can find a wide variety of greens and put together a salad in a jiffy. I show you how to take advantage of the chopped, sliced, and cleaned vegetables available at gourmet supermarket salad bars and produce shelves. See how you can speed meal preparations by using partially prepared produce items to save time.

You don't have to forego healthful vegetables in your dinner planning — even if you don't have the time it takes to peel, chop, and cut.

Shopping for Timesaving Produce

You can find what's called convenience-added fresh vegetables in super-markets' refrigerated produce sections and in supermarket salad bars. *Convenience-added* fresh vegetables are ready-to-eat veggies that have been cleaned, rinsed, and cut. A quick glance at the fresh produce section also offers *partially prepared produce* — partially or completely cooked vegeta-bles. Manufacturers not only peel the potatoes — they cook them for you. Read package directions to see what's left for you to do.

Be prepared for sticker shock at first. You're paying anywhere from 20 to 200 percent more for not having to peel carrots or dice potatoes, for example. The good news: Prepared vegetables are 100 percent edible, and you'll save money when you don't have woody broccoli stalks or tough outer lettuce leaves to discard. If you value saving time, you may have scraped your last carrot.

Tossing Variety into Your Salads

Chefs seek out wild, or at least uncommon, leafy vegetables to replace typical garden-variety lettuces. They use a variety of these greens for the vegetables' sharp, spicy, herbal, or buttery tastes. When chefs use greens with distinctive flavors, they don't have to include many other salad ingredients. Sounds like a real timesaving idea to me.

The best part? Savvy marketers are making greens with multi-syllable names available to supermarkets. Some stores, especially natural-food markets, sell exotic greens in bulk. (See the "Bagging, washing, and storing bulk salad greens" section, later in this chapter.) Other stores carry bagged gourmet greens. (For more information, check out the "Taking the wrap: Packaged salad greens" section, later in this chapter.) "The exotic greens guide" section, coming up next in this chapter, can help you choose the best of the greens (or the reds, and even the yellows).

Knowing the flavors of various greens, you can put a deluxe salad together in a jiffy. These greens are so delicious that you don't even need to spend time adding other vegetables to the salad bowl if you're in a real hurry.

Arranging a handful of exotic greens on a dinner plate gives you an instant and impressive side dish.

The exotic greens guide

If you need to, photocopy this guide to fancy greens and take it to the super-market with you. Or you could just bring the whole book along. Check out Figure 5-1 to see what the greens in this guide look like.

Arugula (uh-roo-gu-lah), also known as rocket

Looks: A long oval or scallop-shaped light green leaf. The mature plant has edible small white and brown flowers.

Taste and use: Spicy. The older the plant is, the sharper the flavor. Serve raw and mixed with milder-tasting greens. Mature leaves can be cooked in a little olive oil.

Baby romaine (row-maine)

Looks: Small, green, oval leaves. Baby red romaine has a green and red leaf.

Taste and use: Sweet with a hint of sharpness. Baby romaine has a more delicate taste than it's full-grown relative. Use as the only ingredient in a salad or mixed with other greens.

Chervil (chur-vuhl)

Looks: Small lacy green leaves.

Taste and use: A hint of anise. Mix with mild-tasting greens in a salad; also use as a garnish.

Dandelion

Looks: Long, narrow, dark green leaves.

Taste and use: Mild to slightly bitter when young; very bitter and tough-textured as the plant matures. Add baby dandelion leaves to mixed salads; mature leaves should be sautéed or steamed.

Frisée (free-zay), also known as curly endive

Looks: Pale green to yellow with frizzy long-toothed leaves.

Taste and use: Mild to slightly bitter. Add raw in a mixed salad or cook with a little bacon.

Japanese red mustard

Looks: Large, oval-shaped leaf that's deep green with dark red to rust-colored veins.

Taste and use: Slightly pungent to very sharp tasting. Similar to horse-radish. Use in small amounts raw in salads; add to a roast beef sandwich for a kick.

Mâche (mahsh), also known as lamb's lettuce, field salad, or lamb's tongue

Looks: Its dark green leaves have a delicate texture.

Taste and use: Slightly sweet, nutty and similar to Bibb lettuce. Serve plain or mixed with other greens in a salad.

Mizuna (ma-zoon-ah)

Looks: Light green, long jagged leaves.

Taste and use: Spicy-sharp. Mix with other greens in a salad.

Purslane (purse-lane)

Looks: Little plump, succulent deep green leaves.

Taste and use: Slightly sour with a hint of cucumber. Use as a salad ingredient mixed with robust-tasting greens or as a garnish.

Radicchio (rah-dee-key-oh), also known as red leafed Italian chicory

Looks: Shaped like a loose-leafed cabbage. Color is ruby red with white veins. Some varieties of radicchio are red-tinged and bear a resemblance to romaine lettuce.

Taste and use: Pleasantly bitter. Small amounts can be mixed with delicate greens in a salad. Grill or sauté and serve hot, with bacon and/or nuts.

Tat Soi (tat soy)

Looks: Deep green leaves, which are oval to round in shape.

Taste and use: Mild and with a slight mustard flavor. Serve raw in salad or add at the last minute to a stir-fry dish.

Watercress

Looks: Small dark green round leaves on a long stem.

Taste and use: Pleasantly pungent and peppery. Its strong flavors have the most appeal in small amounts. Mix with greens in a salad; use as a garnish for entrees or as an ingredient in cold vegetable soups.

I devote a whole chapter of this book to salads, Chapter 10 to be specific, but many of the exotic greens you run across at the supermarket are mild tasting and fine-textured, such as mâche. A thick cream dressing or a vinaigrette with a high proportion of lemon juice or vinegar (like many of the dressings I cover in Chapter 10) would overpower these types of greens. So I've come up with a good one for delicate greens. Use the balance of oil and vinegar that the Vinaigrette for Mâche recipe in this chapter features. Throw this dressing over some gourmet greens, and you have a nice side salad.

Pulling a fast one on your appetite

Studies conducted at Penn State University show that people are used to eating a certain volume of food every day. You can use this piece of information to your advantage. "Trick" your appetite into accepting less fat and fewer calories by presenting a large volume of food that's lower in fat and has less calories than the food you're used to eating. Big servings of salads and vegetables are a good choice if you want to take this route.

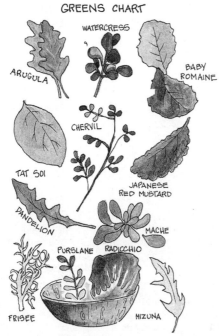

GREENS CHART

WATERCRESS

ARUGULA

BABY ROMAINE

CHERVIL

TAT SOI

JAPANESE RED MUSTARD

DANDELION

MACHE

PURSLANE   RADICCHIO

FRISEE

MIZUNA

Figure 5-1: Bagged salad greens often contain these common yet exotic-looking greens.

Bagging, washing, and storing bulk salad greens

Produce departments in natural or upscale supermarkets often feature bins of loose exotic salad greens that you can help yourself to. Mixtures usually include radicchio, frisée, arugula, and baby leaf lettuces. (Check out "The exotic greens guide" section, earlier in this chapter, for descriptions.) Most stores sell bulk exotic salad greens by the ounce. This can be a real bargain. You're getting the same combination of salad ingredients that your local bistro serves, but for a fraction of the cost. Bulk salad greens are cheaper than comparable packaged mixtures.

☙ Vinaigrette for Mâche

This dressing is a snap to make and keeps well. Double the recipe and store the remainder in a covered container in the refrigerator. Bring the dressing to room temperature before serving. Use 2 cups of mâche not packed into the cup, for each salad.

Gourmet greens are very delicate. Dress them lightly just before serving so the leaves don't become soggy.

Preparation time: *1 minute*

Yield: *4 servings*

1½ tablespoons red wine vinegar	*5 tablespoons extra-virgin olive oil*
¼ teaspoon salt	*Pepper to taste*

Place the vinegar and salt in a bowl and stir to dissolve the salt. Add the olive oil and whisk to blend. Season with pepper.

Per serving: *Calories 150 (From Fat 150); Fat 17g (Saturated 2g); Cholesterol 0mg; Sodium 146mg; Carbohydrate 0g (Dietary Fiber 0g); Protein 0g.*

Take a good look before you dive in. The salad vegetables should be true to their original colors with no yellowing or dark spots. The leaves should look fresh and firm, not limp, slimy, or slick, which means the greens are too old to eat. You should see a good variety of colors and shapes.

After you're satisfied that the bulk salad meets your standards, make your selection. Don't buy more than you'll use in a couple of days because these salad ingredients are highly perishable. Measure four scoops of greens or two ounces for a generous side salad for four.

If you can't find tongs or a scoop at the produce section, use a plastic bag as a glove. Put your hand in the bag then take fistfuls of greens, which is about one serving, while protecting other shoppers from your germs. And never nibble on bulk greens before you wash them. Other people's germs may have contaminated them.

Washing greens as soon as you get them home means that you won't have an extra step to do at dinnertime. If you're buying farmers market vegetables, wash them promptly in case the produce hosts insects. Use a salad spinner to wash and dry the greens (an easy method, which in my opinion is a lot of fun), or wash them by hand. To wash by hand, place the greens in a fine-mesh colander and hold under a gentle cold-water spray. Then place the greens in a single layer on a cookie sheet lined with paper towels. Air dry at room temperature.

After you've washed the greens, place them in a perforated plastic bag and keep in the refrigerator vegetable crisper. Inspect greens every day. Discard any leaves that are turning dark or slimy or browned around the edges, and use the remainder that night.

Taking the wrap: Packaged salad greens

You may not know arugula from artichokes, but salad growers do. Why not let food companies create a delicious blend of greens for you? You'll find various combinations starting with familiar hunks of iceberg lettuce and shredded cabbage to exotic Asian mixtures of spicy, peppery mizuna and red mustard in plastic bags in the refrigerated sections of produce departments.

At first, the package labeling might be confusing. What's a *spring salad mix* and how is that different from *field greens?* Here's the scoop on what's in the bag. (Check out the "The exotic greens guide," earlier in this chapter, for more info.)

- ✔ Spring salad mix, also called mesclun (*mess*-klun), usually includes arugula, mizuna, tat soi, frisee, oak leaf, red chard, radicchio, and mustard greens.
- ✔ Field greens often feature mâche, a wild green.
- ✔ The Asian greens assortment usually includes mizuna, tat soi, and red mustard.
- ✔ Gourmet greens may feature a mix of radicchio, arugula, and even nasturtium blossoms.
- ✔ Herb salads are a mix of delicate greens flavored with chervil, and occasionally watercress and basil. You'll also see packages of baby romaine lettuce, baby arugula or baby spinach.

Some brands claim to be *premium.* This designation doesn't mean anything to you as a shopper. A product labeled *organic* has to meet certain standards of growing, harvesting, and packaging. However, you can't be assured that an organic salad mix doesn't contain bacteria. You have to assume that nothing that grows in the ground will be sterile. Unless the package label indicates that the contents have been thoroughly cleaned, wash your salad greens before serving.

Bagged salads that contain croutons are very expensive and unnecessary when you can make your own. Toast a slice of French bread then rub it with a cut garlic clove. Tear or slice the garlic toast into bite-size croutons.

Some manufacturers wash their greens before they package them. You may question whether these are really safe to eat right from the bag. Independent laboratory tests concluded that pre-washed greens are safe to eat.

◌ *Asian Greens and Radish Salad*

Pair sharp-tasting Asian greens with radishes for a pungent salad. Buy bagged, trimmed radishes without the tops.

Preparation time: *10 minutes*

Yield: *4 servings*

6-ounce bag Asian greens	*1 tablespoon lemon juice*
1 cup sliced radishes	*1 teaspoon Dijon-style prepared mustard*
¼ cup olive oil	*Salt and pepper to taste*

1 In a salad bowl, toss together the Asian greens and radishes.

2 In a cup, stir together the oil, lemon juice, mustard, salt, and pepper. Pour over the salad and toss gently but well. Serve immediately.

Per serving: *Calories 135 (From Fat 125); Fat 14g (Saturated 2g); Cholesterol 0mg; Sodium 195mg; Carbohydrate 3g (Dietary Fiber 2g); Protein 1g.*

If you're buying greens from a reputable packer and the label says pre-washed, relax. You can save a step. However, washing greens only takes a couple of minutes, so for peace of mind, go ahead and wash pre-washed greens if you prefer. If the package contains no mention of washing, treat the greens as if they haven't been touched and do a thorough job of cleaning.

Elegance made simple with grape tomatoes

Grape tomatoes are a wonderfully convenient and a great way to jazz up salads and sides. These tomatoes are consistently sweet any time of the year, so I'm always assured of having a flavorful ingredient on hand. The grape tomato's counter life — tomatoes should be kept at room temperature — is about a week . . . if you can resist.

Put a bowl of grape tomatoes on the kitchen table, so the family can help themselves to a healthful instant snack. Although you can cook grape tomatoes, you'll lose some of the sweet taste. Use Roma or beefsteak tomatoes for cooking. (In just a bit, I eat my words and suggest one truly delicious cooked grape tomato recipe that you can serve as a side dish.)

Topping a baked potato

With quick-cooking baking potatoes, you can have a side dish or an entree in minutes. Split open a baked potato and add one of the following:

✔ Goat cheese mashed with a little milk and chopped green onions.

✔ Grated Southwestern-flavored cheddar cheese and a dollop of salsa.

✔ Heated, canned or leftover chili.

✔ Plain yogurt mixed with a dash of white prepared horseradish.

✔ A spoonful of heated, condensed cream of celery or broccoli soup and a few bacon crumbles.

Fancier food stores stock yellow and red teardrop shaped tomatoes as well. These expensive teardrops are salad (not cooking) tomatoes. Whenever I want to play chef at Chez Bennett, I serve a salad that's an arrangement of halved yellow and red teardrop tomatoes on a bed of mixed greens. In five minutes flat, I'm a culinary genius!

Shopping the Salad Bar

Salad bars offer more than a convenient carryout lunch. Salad bars allow you to stock up on ingredients for quick dinner salads and for cooked dishes. Find out how to judge a salad bar's quality by asking yourself the following:

✔ Are the ingredients kept in bowls over ice so the perishables remain cold? Vegetables shouldn't be directly on ice, or they'll freeze.

✔ Is the area clean? Are the items neatly arranged in their own bowls, or do you frequently find one ingredient dribbled into another? This is a problem if you have specific food requirements. For example, if you're a vegetarian, you don't want bacon bits in your chopped green peppers.

✔ Does the food turnover or are the same ingredients left out all day? The produce manager should be able to tell you how often the salad bar is replenished.

✔ Are the foods protected from consumers' germs by a plastic shield? Many municipalities require it.

✔ Does the salad bar have the variety you want?

You're probably paying more per pound for vegetables at a salad bar than in the produce counter. Make your purchases count by choosing vegetables that are otherwise expensive, such as artichoke hearts, olives, or snow peas.

⏲ *Sautéed Grape Tomatoes*

Grape tomatoes were first cultivated in China. The seeds were brought to the United States less than a decade ago. Now U.S. farmers grow more grape than cherry tomatoes.

Lightly sautéing grape tomatoes brings out their natural sugars. I add a splash of balsamic vinegar to balance the sweetness. You can serve this dish hot or at room temperature.

Preparation time: *5 minutes*

Cooking time: *6 minutes*

Yield: *4 servings*

1 tablespoon olive oil

1 shallot, peeled and minced

2 cups grape tomatoes, halved lengthwise

1 teaspoon white balsamic vinegar, or 1 teaspoon white wine vinegar and a pinch of sugar

¼ teaspoon salt

¼ teaspoon pepper

1 Heat the oil in a medium non-stick skillet. Add the shallot and sauté 1 minute over medium heat or until tender. Add the tomatoes and cook over low-medium heat about 3 minutes or until the tomatoes are slightly pulpy and hot.

2 Add the vinegar and stir to blend. Season with salt and pepper and remove from heat. Serve the tomatoes hot or at room temperature.

Per serving: *Calories 50 (From Fat 33); Fat 4g (Saturated 1g); Cholesterol 0mg; Sodium 153mg; Carbohydrate 5g (Dietary Fiber 1g); Protein 1g.*

If you think salad bar vegetables are just for the salad bowl, you're missing out on a great resource. You can also get chopped, pared vegetables to use in other recipes — like recipes for soups in Chapter 9 or the skillet dinners in Chapter 12. Check out the following ideas:

✔ Take advantage of the salad bar to avoid mundane tasks, such as chopping onions — the kind of tasks you'd gladly pay a dollar or two to get out of doing. Buy a pound of chopped onions, and you can sauté onions for soups and skillet dinners without shedding a tear. (Another onion-chopping solution is to buy bags of fresh, chopped onions. You can find them in the supermarket produce section.)

✔ If you don't have time to trim, pare, and chop broccoli for a steamed vegetable side dish, buy a couple of cups of broccoli from the salad bar instead. Save all the preparation time and toss the broccoli in your steamer.

↙ Suppose you're using packaged soup for a quick dinner for one or two, and you know the product doesn't provide enough food to satisfy you. Simmer the soup with a handful of salad bar vegetables and you have a more nourishing meal.

When you visit the salad bar with a recipe in mind, you may want to know how to substitute cut vegetables for whole. Check out Table 5-1, which contains equivalent measures for common salad bar veggies.

Table 5-1	Measuring Salad Bar Veggies
Whole (average size)	*Cups*
Broccoli	4 cups
Carrot	½ cup
Cauliflower	5 cups
Corn	½ cup
Lettuce, head of iceberg	6 cups
Onion	1 ½ cups
Bell pepper	1 cup
Tomato	½ cup
Zucchini	½ cup

Be sure to pack vegetables in separate cartons to use for cooking. Write the purchase date on each carton. Refrigerate any cut vegetables, including tomatoes. (Store whole tomatoes at room temperature but away from direct sunlight.) Use soft, cut-up vegetables, such as tomatoes within one to two days. Chopped onions and bell peppers will keep three to five days, and broccoli, cauliflower, carrots, and radishes should stay fresh up to a week.

Handling Partially-Prepared Produce

Partially prepared fresh produce is either half cooked or completely cooked. But even if you buy fully cooked produce, you're going to have to heat it to restore the "fresh" taste. Using these products may make the difference between your family having a balanced meal and one that's veggie-lite. You may not use these convenience foods all the time, but have them on hand for emergencies.

Unfortunately, you have to treat partially prepared produce, such as par-cooked potatoes or mashed potatoes, differently from their whole counter-parts. After the processor peels, pares, and precooks your vegetables, the freshness clock starts ticking, and the foods have to be used soon.

Note the use-by date on food packaging and serve unopened food before the freshness date passes. After you've opened a product, you reduce its storage time. Serve the vegetable in the next day or two even though the use-by date may still be in the future.

Also examine processed vegetables, such as partially cooked potatoes, which have a short shelf life. Check for discoloration, slimy texture or sour odor. These are all signs of spoilage. Discard the vegetables.

Cutting Down on Trimming and Paring Time

If you hate to trim and pare, you can now relegate the vegetable scraper and paring knife to the attic. You can buy fresh vegetables with the inedible parts removed.

Babying your carrots

Count baby carrots as the first and biggest hit of the produce counter, and no wonder. Just think of the time you save by not searching your drawers for the swivel peeler. Serve baby carrots and you don't have to peel, pare, or cut the carrots into appealing shapes. You don't even have to clean the parings out of the sink. What a convenience.

The original baby carrots were harvested before the plants grew large and woody. No bigger than your thumb and as sweet as a sugar beet, the carrots were a hit in restaurants, and they still remain on many a menu.

The baby carrots that you buy in supermarkets, however, are similar to the restaurant version in name only. Bagged baby carrots begin as a variety of long thin carrot. Vegetable processors cut the carrots into pieces they send through a lathe to shape into uniform widths.

So consumers won't mistake the pared carrots for the true babies, the gov-ernment will soon require that full-sized, trimmed carrots carry an explana-tion on the label.

Unfortunately, peeled carrots have a shorter shelf life than unprocessed ones. Examine the carrots. They should be a vivid orange color and moist, without liquid accumulating in the package. If the pieces are dull with a white caste, they have lost moisture and won't be sweet. Don't buy them. But, if you have a bag of dried-looking carrots in the refrigerator, simmer them with a little chicken broth and a pinch of sugar, and they taste as delicious as fresh. Avoid carrots that look slimy. Toss out any spoiled carrots — don't taste them first.

Keep one bag of baby carrots handy for snacking and tuck another away in the refrigerator for a delicious cooked side dish. Simmering baby carrots until they're fork-tender brings out their sweetness.

○ Baby Carrots with Dill

Lemon and dill add a citrusy and herbal taste to carrots. Serve the carrots as a side dish for chicken, fish, or steak.

Preparation time: *2 minutes*

Cooking time: *15 to 20 minutes*

Yield: *4 servings*

1 (1-pound) bag baby carrots	*1 teaspoon fresh minced dill weed*
1 cup reduced-sodium chicken broth	*¼ teaspoon pepper*
Grated zest of 1 lemon	

Place carrots in a small pot with chicken broth. Bring to a boil. Partially cover pot and cook 15 minutes or until carrots are tender and most of the liquid has evaporated. Stir in lemon zest, dill, and pepper while you hold the lid of the pot away from you to avoid steam.

Speed It Up! *Instead of chopping dill weed on a cutting board, hold a dill sprig over the carrots and snip a little dill into the carrots. You won't have to wash the cutting board.*

Per serving: *Calories 47 (From Fat 6); Fat 1g (Saturated 0g); Cholesterol 0mg; Sodium 195mg; Carbohydrate 10g (Dietary Fiber 2g); Protein 2g.*

Carrot processors, who haven't had such a hit since Bugs Bunny became unofficial spokesman, are attempting to make their crop more convenient in other ways as well: Look for wave-cut carrot slices and coarsely shredded carrots in bags in your produce department. Serve the wave-cut carrots when you want to dress up Sunday pot roast with a fancy-looking vegetable. The shredded carrots make a great salad tossed with raisins, sunflower seeds, and a little mayonnaise.

Focusing on broccoli and cauliflower florets

Give a heads-up to broccoli and cauliflower florets, too. While well past their infancy, the packaged vegetable heads, minus the tough stalks, cook faster and are sweeter tasting, so the family is more likely to eat them.

Don't worry about wasted stalks, however. Shredded broccoli stalks, sold as *broccoli slaw,* are available packaged in most supermarkets. You can mix half broccoli and half cabbage for a nutritious side salad.

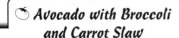

⌘ Avocado with Broccoli and Carrot Slaw

Look for bags of already combined shredded carrots and broccoli, also called *broccoli slaw,* in your supermarket's chilled produce section. The crisp, shredded vegetables are a great match for buttery avocado. If this salad is going to sit for more than 10 minutes, toss the avocado with the dressing and then add the carrots. The lemon juice in the dressing will prevent the avocado from browning.

Preparation time: *About 10 minutes*

Yield: *2 servings*

1 small avocado, peeled and cut into thin wedges	*1 tablespoon lemon juice*
½ cup shredded carrots	*2 teaspoons soy sauce*
½ cup shredded broccoli	*1 teaspoon sugar*
1 tablespoon vegetable oil	*1 teaspoon sesame seeds*

1 Arrange the avocado slices, carrots, and broccoli on a serving plate.

2 For the dressing, stir together the oil, lemon juice, soy sauce, sugar, and sesame seeds in a cup. Pour over the avocado and shredded carrots.

Vary It! *If you prefer, skip the shredded broccoli and double the carrots.*

Per serving: Calories 263 (From Fat 210); Fat 23g (Saturated 3g); Cholesterol 0mg; Sodium 332mg; Carbohydrate 14g (Dietary Fiber 6g); Protein 4g.

A Bunch of Other Veggie Products to Speed Dinner

Take a look in your supermarket produce area and see how quick and easy side dishes are to prepare. From precooked potatoes that you heat and eat to special veggie packaging that you can use in a microwave, you have plenty of choices for healthful and fast vegetables.

Preparing precooked spuds

In the time that it takes to bake, boil, or roast a potato, you could have an entire meal on the table. It's enough to frustrate all but the most devoted spud lovers. Fortunately, the potato wait is over.

Refrigerated, diced, cooked potatoes are available in the produce department. They make potatoes a viable side dish for time-strapped cooks. Buy herbed or spiced varieties of potatoes if you're short on time. If you prefer to flavor potatoes to your own liking, choose plain diced, cooked potatoes.

Be aware that even though the potatoes are fully cooked, you still have to heat them according to the package directions for optimal flavor and texture. Heat potatoes following the label and then cool the potatoes for such dishes as potato salad.

Discover what a convenience shredded, raw potatoes are for hash browns or potato pancakes. The newest take on timesaving spuds is refrigerated, prepared mashed potatoes. Just heat and serve. Talk about a quick side dish. These potatoes, which use dairy products, are highly perishable. Treat them as you would milk or meat products and store them in the refrigerator. You may not want to use fully cooked potatoes all the time, but it's good to know they're available for emergencies.

Zapping veggies in their wrappers

Sometimes, it's not the cooking that slows you down, but the prep work or the clean up. Maybe it takes you five minutes to steam vegetables, and another five minutes to wash the pot after dinner and put it away. Short of having a kitchen robot, you could do very little, until now.

Your scrub-free life begins with fresh vegetables sold in packaging designed for microwave cooking. The U.S. Food and Drug Administration approved certain materials for both storage and cooking. The label indicates whether you can cook in the bag. Puncture the bag of vegetables with a fork, place it on a microwave-safe dish and follow the label directions. No water to boil, no pots to wash.

Baking potatoes wrapped in microwave-safe film are another innovation. One brand, Potatoh! is a pre-washed, 8-ounce potato. Puncture the wrapping and microwave according to package directions. The wrapping creates a crisp-skinned microwave-cooked potato.

Don't reuse the bags for other foods and don't attempt to microwave foods in bags that aren't designated for that use.

Chapter 6

Fast Cooking Techniques

*H*aving a few core cooking techniques in your bag of culinary tricks makes all the difference when you want to get a great-tasting dish on the table in less than 30 minutes. Don't worry; I'm not suggesting that you enroll in a chef's training program to acquire skills to rival those of the best French chefs. I know that you don't have time in your busy schedule for that. In fact, I avoid the fancy stuff of glossy magazines. Instead, I focus on the skills that you need every day, whether you're cooking the recipes in this book, or improvising in the kitchen. This chapter can change your mealtime for the better — and speedier.

Concentrating on the kinds of cooking that you already do, I show you how to polish those skills to make food preparation go faster. I pass along tips that professional chefs have shared with me. Using this practical advice helps me, and I'm confident that it's going to turn you into a faster cook as well.

But if you don't know stovetop grilling from sautéing, don't worry. These cooking methods are easy to follow, even if you're on a deadline. In this chapter, I cover five *speed* styles — sautéing, broiling, pan broiling (and it's cousin stovetop grilling), steaming, and stir-frying — and the tools you need.

Each type of cooking method is appropriate for one or more kinds of foods, and I tell you which is the best technique for a particular food. For example, steaming beef turns its color to gray and changes its flavor to bland and boring, but sautéing or stir-frying beef strips gives you much tastier results.

I'm guessing that you've already incorporated some quick and easy ways to cook food, even if you don't attach names to your techniques. But you can cut your cooking time and your kitchen aggravation in half by taking full advantage of the methods that I share with you in this chapter.

Choosing the Right Cookware for the Job

I'm not a cookware snob. I believe that a few pots and pans will take care of most of your cooking needs, especially for those quick, everyday dinners. In Chapter 2, I discuss cookware essentials. However, having the right cookware, and the right size cookware for the job will make cooking faster.

For example, you wouldn't bring a 6-quart pot of water to the boil to cook a handful of asparagus, when you can do it in half the time with a pot half the size. I have a few tips to help you match the cookware to the task, or the technique.

- ✔ Make sure your cookware is large enough to hold food without crowding. Food that's packed into a skillet steams but doesn't brown properly.

- ✔ If you're sautéing food, which means you're cooking food at a high temperature in a little fat, choose cookware with a thick layer of metal at the bottom. The cookware should spread the heat evenly without burning your food. Cast-iron or thick, stainless steel cookware is a good bet.

- ✔ Choose cookware that's easy to clean. I used to be the last one out of the kitchen until I invested in high-quality nonstick cookware. Now I even have volunteers to wash nonstick pots and pans. Department and discount stores carry many fine brands of nonstick cookware. As a general rule, you get what you pay for in cookware quality. Buy a brand that claims a long-lasting finish.

A skillet for all seasons

Using a cast-iron skillet or sauté pan for quick cooking is a great advantage. You can use cast-iron cookware at high temperatures without damaging the metals. Before you use cast-iron cookware for the first time, season it — not with salt and pepper — with a coating of vegetable oil. Use cottonseed or soybean oil and generously coat the interior of the pan or skillet, so you have a thick layer of oil. Then place it over low heat and let it sit until you see a little smoke rising. Do not leave the cookware untended. Immediately take the pan off the heat and let it cool at room temperature. Wipe out the oil with a paper towel and repeat the steps once more. After you season a piece of cookware, you should wash it in warm water and dry it with paper towels. If the pan is particularly messy, clean it with a mild detergent. Don't use strong detergents and don't put the cookware in a dishwasher or it has to be seasoned again.

Sautéing for Fun and Profit

Sautéing (which is also known as *pan frying*) is cooking food in a hot, open sauté pan or skillet with a little oil or butter to prevent sticking. Although sautéing may seem intimidating, because it's a restaurant-menu term (and it's French), I think that this is the easiest and fastest quick-cooking technique. If you can heat oil and butter, you're going to be a sauté champ. In this section, I walk you through each step of the technique. So get ready, get set, sauté!

Using the right cookware

Choose a piece of cookware that's heavy or at least has an evenly thick bottom. You don't want to burn some parts of the food while other parts remain raw. Heavy-bottomed stainless steel and cast-iron are both good for sautéing.

Although cooks — including this one — sometimes use the terms interchangeably, skillets and sauté pans have different shapes and different uses. A *skillet,* also called a *frying pan,* has sloped sides, sometimes with pouring indentations for getting rid of grease. Think of grandma's cast-iron skillet and you get the image. A *sauté pan,* on the other hand, has straight or slightly curved sides that are slightly higher than those of skillets, and it comes with a lid. You can sauté in either piece of cookware, but when you need to start hot and then cover and simmer, a sauté pan with a lid is the answer.

Sautéing 101

Starting with a heavy-bottomed pan (see Figure 6-1), work through the following steps to sauté.

1. **Read the recipe and understand all the cooking steps before you start.**

    When you're cooking fast over high heat, you can't leave the stove to consult your directions.

2. **Select a fat — either oil or butter — that you want to use and add it to the pan.**

    I like canola oil, because it doesn't burn even when I use it to cook at a high heat, and it's considered one of the healthier oils that you can use. But, at the end of the day, nothing can beat the taste of butter. When you want the butter taste, use it. Or use half butter and half oil.

3. **Place the pan containing oil or butter on the stove and heat for about 30 seconds (or as long as the recipe directions indicate).**

   The first few times that you sauté food, be sure to have all your ingredients ready before you start. After you feel comfortable preheating cookware, put the waiting time to good use and take care of some last-minute recipe preparations.

4. **Add your food to the pan and brown it on one side.**

   As soon as the steak, pork chop, lamb chop, or whatever you're cooking hits the heat, the food firms up and forms a golden crust. Wait a minute and then give the sauté pan a little shake so the food doesn't stick.

5. **When you notice that the sides and edges of the food are no longer red or raw-looking, turn the food over with a spatula or large fork and brown the other side.**

   Steps 4 and 5 are just for giving food a gorgeous tan. You're not completely cooking the food at a high heat.

6. **After you brown your food on both sides, reduce the heat, and continue cooking until the food is cooked to your preference.**

While you're sautéing food, resist the temptation to poke, prod, or pierce food. Doing so just lets the juices escape. Have a little patience. Food doesn't cook faster just because you're doing something to it. Piercing food while it cooks just dries it out.

Figure 6-1:
Sauté
foods in a
nonstick
pan with
just a
little fat.

SAUTE' PAN

Selecting foods that work

Sautéing is an excellent technique for the following:

- ✔ **Boneless, skinless chicken breasts:** Pounding chicken breasts to an even thinness helps the chicken cook quickly and evenly. (For more info on pounding chicken breasts, see Chapter 13.)

- ✔ **Boneless, skinless chicken thighs:** Succulent chicken thighs don't dry out as easily as chicken breasts and are delicious when you sauté them. Again, pounding makes for even cooking.

- ✔ **Bay or sea scallops:** Dust scallops lightly with flour mixed with a dash of salt and pepper. If the sea scallops are more than a half-inch thick, cut them in half horizontally before cooking. That way, the centers can cook before the outsides burn.

- ✔ **Meat:** Lamb chops and pork chops are great. Pan-fried strip steak is another winner. Meat cuts should be about an inch thick so that the outsides get nicely browned while the insides stay rare to medium doneness.

- ✔ **Fish fillets:** Cooking thin fillets, such as sole is tricky. The fish is delicate and can fall apart, so watch carefully as you cook. If you're nervous about your first sauté experience, start with perch fillets that aren't as dainty.

- ✔ **Vegetables:** In our household, a hamburger isn't complete without a topping of sautéed onions and mushrooms. Melt a little butter in a skillet and add a small thinly sliced onion and as many mushrooms as the skillet will hold. Cook for 2 minutes or until the onions are tender and your kitchen is aromatic. I think it's time for hamburgers tonight.

Broiling Like You Mean It

Broiling is cooking food under a direct heat source in your oven, one side at a time. Broiling means that your edibles get a blast of intense heat, which is similar to what happens during grilling. However, it just never touches the heat source. Like grilling, broiling doesn't call for adding liquid to food. You're dry cooking, and the result is that broiled foods have a crusty, brown exterior that locks in the juices, so the interior is succulent and tender.

The mouthwatering contrast of the crisp exterior and tender interior of a steak in the broiler sells you on this cooking method if nothing else does. When I pull a steak from the broiler, no one quibbles that it's a quick meal. What a marvel to get such flavor without spending much time at it.

Getting the gear

When I bought my first oven, it came equipped with a *broiler pan* (see Figure 6-2), a two-piece utensil consisting of a rack or slotted metal tray and a pan underneath that fit into the broiler under my oven. Some expensive stovetops have broiler units as well. These are usually narrow so you have to choose your pan accordingly. Most broiler pans come in one of two approximate sizes: 9-x-13-inches or 13-x-17-inches. I prefer the larger size in case I want to broil larger amounts of food for parties.

Before shopping, measure your broiler space to make sure it accommodates the size broiler pan that you choose.

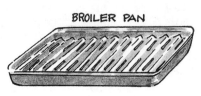

Figure 6-2:
Slap on a
steak for a
super-easy
and
delicious
meal.

BROILER PAN

Broiling basics

Of the cooking techniques that I discuss in this chapter, broiling is the easiest. Oops! I already said that about sautéing, didn't I? Well, broiling is also the easiest. You didn't think I was going to suggest anything challenging when you're in a rush to get dinner, did you?

But don't let the ease of preparation lull you into thinking that the food takes care of itself. It doesn't. Broiling is deceptively simple but precise at the same time. Choosing the wrong food or looking away for a minute can turn your dinner into shoe leather.

Broiling cooks food at a steady, high temperature. You can't turn the broiler down to say, 325 degrees or up to 400 degrees. Instead, you regulate the heat by how far away you place the food from the heat source. Broiler rack adjustments vary with each brand of oven, but in general, you can set broiler racks from 3 to 6 inches away from the heat. Place foods that you want to cook quickly close to the heat; place foods that take more time further away from the heat. That way, the outside of the longer-cooking food doesn't burn while the insides are still raw.

You can broil many of the same foods that you sauté (such as scallops, steaks, hamburgers, and boneless skinless chicken breasts or thighs). Make sure the foods are an even thickness, so they don't cook faster in one part. (See Chapter 13 for directions on pounding chicken breasts to a uniform thickness.)

For broiling:

1. **Adjust the broiler rack of the oven to the desired position.**

   For hamburgers, chicken breasts or thighs, and steaks, place the rack about 3 to 4 inches from the heat source. To broil vegetables that burn easily, keep the rack about 5 to 6 inches away from the heat.

2. **Turn on the broiler.**

3. **Place your food on the rack of the broiler pan.**

   Don't brush foods with oily or sugary sauces that can burn.

4. **Place the food in the broiler and cook foods on one side, following the time in the recipe instructions.**

   Each piece of food cooks at its own schedule. Check the food for doneness about 30 seconds to 1 minute before the recipe indicates it should be done.

5. **Remove the broiler pan and the food. Flip the food over and cook the second side.**

   It's unlikely that you're going to broil food as long on the second side as you do on the first, so pay attention and check the food for doneness about 1 minute before the recipe indicates that it should be done.

If the food happens to ignite, douse the flames with baking soda. (Then turn to Chapter 17 where I tell you how to cook a substitute meal at warp speed.)

Cleaning broiler pans is a hassle, and you may be tempted to cover the broiler-pan rack with foil to make cleaning easier. Don't do it. Covering the grates prevents the fat from dripping down, thus gathering in a pool on the foil and causing potential flair-ups. Some cooks use a sheet of heavy-duty foil in place of a broiler pan. This can be dangerous for the same reason: You're creating a pool of highly flammable fat.

For easier clean-ups, tackle the broiler as soon as you start washing dishes:

1. Discard any accumulated fat from the broiler pan.

2. Fill the pan with hot water and set it over a stove burner on low heat about 5 minutes.

3. Using a wooden spoon, dislodge any stuck particles of fat.

4. Pour the greasy water into the sink and wash the pan and the rack with warm, soapy water.

Letting a broiler pan sit around while you're entertaining friends or helping with family activities means that the grease is harder to remove in a couple of hours. Better cookware stores sell broiler pans that are coated with nonstick finishes to make washing easier.

Reviewing the contestants

You may notice that many of the foods that I suggest you sauté also top my list of broiler-friendly grub. Tender meats, seafood, and poultry are all excellent when cooked with dry heat, which includes broiling and sautéing. Cooking a steak in a lot of liquid (stewing or braising) wouldn't taste as good. Broiling is an excellent technique for the following:

- ✔ Boneless, skinless chicken breasts, cut or pounded to an even ½-inch thickness.
- ✔ Boneless, skinless chicken thighs, pounded to an even ½-inch thickness.
- ✔ Bread. For toast or an open-face grilled cheese sandwich.
- ✔ Sea scallops.
- ✔ Steak.
- ✔ Thin fish fillets, such as sole or filleted trout.
- ✔ Thin hamburgers.
- ✔ Pale foods. Your broiler is a tanning salon for casseroles. Place a pallid casserole under a broiler for 30 seconds to one minute to give it a golden finish.

To spice up your meal with some fancy bread, try a broiler delight that Italians call *bruschetta* (*brew*-sheh-tah):

1. Cut coarse bread, such as sourdough, into 1-inch thick slices.

2. Rub with a peeled garlic clove and drizzle lightly with olive oil.

3. Place the bread on the rack of a broiler pan and run the bread under the broiler about 30 seconds per side or until browned.

Grilling and Broiling in a Whole New Light

Ladies and gentlemen, step right up, and let me introduce you to a modern marvel — your stovetop. Yes, you read that sentence correctly. That appliance you so often take for granted can do some pretty cool things:

- ✔ Your stovetop can transform itself into an indoor grilling machine, letting you grill foods without heating an outdoor grill.
- ✔ Your stovetop can also broil foods just like an oven broiler.

Because stovetop grilling and pan broiling are so similar, most cookbooks don't make a distinction between these two techniques and refer to both as *pan broiling*. But I want to take a minute to distinguish between them. The difference is in the cookware:

✔ For *stovetop* grilling, you use a stovetop grill pan, which looks like a skillet with ridges on the bottom. The food sits on the ridges and gets those neat stripes that replicate an outdoor grill.

✔ For *pan broiling,* you use a cast-iron skillet or heavy-bottomed skillet.

Both techniques start cooking food on a very hot utensil, usually without added oil or butter, on high heat, and on top of the stove. So, if you can pan broil you can grill. These techniques are basically the same thing — with a different stripe. They give food the same crusty finish that it gets from oven broiling or outdoor grilling with some advantages:

✔ Stovetop grilling gives food snazzy grill marks without heating the outdoor grill — a big plus during a rainstorm or when it's 20 below zero.

✔ Pan broiling lets you see the food as it cooks and control the timing with more accuracy than an oven broiler.

✔ Both techniques fill the kitchen with the scent of beef crackling in the pan. You don't waste a minute getting anyone to come to dinner once that aroma circulates through the house.

These techniques generate plenty of smoke, especially when you cook foods, such as steak, that contain a moderate amount of fat. Neighbors may respond to the loud beeping of your smoke alarms, asking, "What on earth is the matter?" To avoid this intrusion, open all your windows and start the fan over the stove before you begin cooking.

Getting in the groove and pumping iron

Heavy cast-iron or enamel on cast-iron skillets or sauté pans with ridges is ideal for stovetop grilling (see Figure 6-3). The ridges raise the food above the pan's surface while the fat drips down into the grooves. Then, when you finish cooking, you can pour off the accumulated fat. Stovetop grilling not only gets dinner to the table quickly, it also helps you trim excess fat and excess calories from your food. As an added bonus, if your pan is hot enough, the ridges create the same attractive stripes that you get when you grill food.

Figure 6-3:
Ridges are
perfect for
stovetop
grilling.

GRILLING PAN

For stovetop broiling, use a heavy cast-ion or enamel on cast-iron skillet without the ridges. If Grandma is ready to hand over her skillet to you, you're all set. (For more info on cast-iron, see the sidebar, "A skillet for all seasons," in this chapter.)

Cookware with ridges is usually heavy, expensive, and designed to last a lifetime. Make sure that you want to do this kind of cooking often enough to justify spending as much as $100 to $150 for a pan. In Chapter 2, I discuss electric countertop grills that are similar to stovetop grilling pans. The electric units are easy to use, but harder to clean and take up valuable real estate space on the counter.

Stepping up to the stove

Setting up your food and equipment before you begin stovetop grilling or pan broiling means that your dish will cook faster and that the cooking process will be smoother.

1. **Bring your food, whether it's steak, chicken, or fish, to room temperature for about 30 minutes beforehand.**

2. **Wipe the food and the cookware dry, or your dinner will sputter rather than sizzle.**

3. **Preheat the utensil.**

4. **When a drop of water sizzles and evaporates in 30 seconds or less, place the food in the pan.**

5. **The most important advice that I can offer about this technique: Leave the food alone.**

   Don't move, poke, or prod the food.

6. **Let the food hit the heat for at least a minute or two.**

   Then take a peak and see whether the underside is cooking to your satisfaction.

7. **When the underside is cooked, and you see that the sides of the food are browning as well, flip the food over.**

   Stovetop grilling or pan broiling a 1-thick steak for 2 to 3 minutes per side should result in medium-rare steak. If the top and bottom of the food are well-browned but the sides look raw, the food isn't cooked enough. Turn the heat down to medium-high and cook each side another minute or two.

As with broiling, check your food on the second side about a minute before the recipe indicates that it's done.

Stovetop grilling and pan broiling buddies

Use these high-heat techniques for the following:

- ✔ Boneless, skinless chicken thighs, pounded to an even ½-inch thickness
- ✔ Salmon steaks, but brush with oil first
- ✔ Steak

Steaming Along

Steaming is a cooking technique in which you cook food over, not in, the hot vapors from a boiling liquid like water or broth. Steaming may seem like a plain, ordinary cooking technique, but it can also be elegant if you steam foods like seafood, preserving their delicate flavor and texture.

Steaming is one of the most soothing techniques for food. Think of how relaxed you feel after a steam bath. Steaming is just as gentle on food. Unlike boiling, steaming doesn't cause foods to fall apart or toughen.

Because the food stays above the cooking liquid, the nutrients stay in the food and aren't washed away in the liquid.

Even though steaming doesn't subject food to the intense heat of say, broiling, it's a quick cooking method for vegetables and seafood. Broccoli steams in about 10 minutes; a large lobster in less than 20 minutes.

Steam heat can burn. When you check the doneness of food, lift the steamer lid away from you so you don't get the full brunt of the steam on your face or hands, and be sure to use a potholder.

Steamers, steamers, everywhere

Stovetop steamers come in many styles and sizes. All steamers have three parts:

- ✔ **Bottom:** Holds the liquid
- ✔ **Lid:** Prevents the steam from escaping
- ✔ **Perforated basket:** Holds the food

You can buy or put together many versions of a steamer, but my choice for steaming is a shallow perforated insert that fits in my pasta pot (see Figure 6-4). I recommend it for two reasons. First, I get both a steamer and a pasta cooker in one pot. Second, the insert is big enough to hold a head each of broccoli and cauliflower, so I can steam extra vegetables to serve in salads later in the week. (In the "Steaming veggies, fish, and seafood" section later in this chapter, I suggest other ways to use leftover steamed vegetables.)

If you're short on space or you steam small amounts of food at a time, you can pick up a collapsible metal basket in many supermarkets or discount stores. Set the basket in a pot or pan that contains a small amount of steaming water — not enough to touch the food — and cover with a lid. Cookware stores also carry multi-tiered aluminum steamers. The layers stack and sit on top of a pot or pan with a little water. (Again, the water shouldn't touch the food.) Placing a different food in each tier means that you can steam an entire meal in one utensil on one burner.

Figure 6-4:
A food
steamer has
several
parts.

Step-by-step steaming

Anytime you steam food, you cook it in vapors from a simmering or boiling liquid. But the liquid is up to you. The most common choices are water and broth, but other liquids, including beer or wine, work, too.

Keep a kettle of water on to simmering, so you can refill the bottom of the steamer if necessary. Don't add cold water, because it slows the cooking process.

Using leftover broccoli stalks

Many recipes tell you to use sweet and fast-cooking broccoli florets, including my Broccoli and Cauliflower with Lemon-Butter Sauce recipe in this chapter. But unless you cook the stalks as well, you're paying full price for broccoli while you use half the vegetable. That's plenty of waste. You can use the woody but very nutritious stalks in several quick and easy ways.

First, peel the tough skin off the stalks and discard. Then you have some choices:

✔ Cut the stalks into ¼-inch thick slices and add raw to a salad.

✔ Cut the stalks into ¼-inch thick slices and steam them as you would broccoli florets. Serve the broccoli "coins" with lemon butter or make skewers for Christmas parties by alternating broccoli slices with cherry tomatoes.

✔ Cook the broccoli stalks in enough water to cover until they're tender. Puree and add broccoli to sour cream dip. Or puree and add the mixture to mashed potatoes for St. Patrick's Day — or anytime that you want to brighten the vegetable course.

Following these steps, set up your steamer with your food.

1. **Fill the bottom of the steamer with your cooking liquid.**

   The top level of the liquid should be an inch or more below the bottom of the steamer basket. If possible, allow space between the sides of the steamer and the food that you're steaming as well.

   For quick-cooking foods, such as spinach, broccoli, or peas, use boiling water. For delicate foods, such as fish fillets, use simmering water. Also simmer longer-cooking foods, such as potatoes, so that the water is less likely to evaporate before the food is cooked.

2. **Add a few marbles — yes, marbles — to the liquid.**

   As the liquid simmers, the marbles knock together. If you don't hear a noise, then the liquid has evaporated, and you need to add more liquid.

3. **Arrange the food in the steamer basket in the steamer.**

   You can put cauliflower or broccoli florets, Brussels sprouts, carrots, and small potatoes directly in the steamer basket. You can also steam delicate scallops or fish.

   To get a bonus sauce for the same time you spend steaming fish or seafood, place these foods in a stainless steel bowl in the steamer basket. As scallops and fish cook, they give off flavorful juices that gather in the bowl. Add a little melted butter and lemon juice, and you have an instant sauce with no extra effort.

4. **Cover the steamer and cook for the amount of time that your recipe recommends.**

   Broccoli, cauliflower, thin asparagus, small Brussels sprouts, and green beans cook in about 10 minutes; add another 10 for small new potatoes.

5. **Test the food for doneness.**

   For vegetables, insert the tip of a knife into the vegetable. If the knife gives easily, remove the steamer lid, take the pot off the heat, and serve the food.

   Test fish for doneness by gently prodding in the center of the fish piece to see the interior. The fish should be opaque and firm, not translucent.

Steaming veggies, fish, and seafood

Steaming is an excellent technique for cooking up the following:

- ✔ Small vegetables, such as peas or sugar snap peas

- ✔ Fresh vegetables cut in small pieces, such as broccoli or cauliflower

- ✔ Small, firm vegetables that you want to maintain their shape, such as new potatoes or baby carrots

- ✔ Delicate fish

- ✔ Delicate seafood, such as sea or bay scallops

Steaming retains or even brightens the natural colors of veggies. Steam broccoli, for example, and you get a vegetable the color of a forest in May. My family is more likely to eat green vegetables that are a vibrant shade than those that are cooked to a faded, drab color. I'll bet that you'll see the same results at your table, if you haven't already. Avoid steaming foods, however, that you want to turn to golden brown, such as meat or poultry.

Overcooking vegetables turns their colors drab and their textures mushy. Overcooking also destroys some nutrients, such as vitamin C. Being a quick cook means that you're never tempted to leave the vegetables to steam too long.

The recipe I provide in this chapter for steamed broccoli and cauliflower yields about 6 cups of cooked vegetables. If you are cooking for a small household, or one that isn't as crazy about vegetables as I am, you'll have leftovers. No problem. Steamed vegetables such as the broccoli and cauliflower — or carrots, Brussels sprouts, and asparagus — can be put to delicious and quick use in one of the following ways:

✔ Add leftover vegetables to a pasta or rice salad.

✔ Puree the vegetables and add to a can of cream of broccoli soup.

✔ Puree the vegetables and add to a yogurt or sour cream dip for vegetables.

✔ Toss the cold vegetable leftovers with a little bottled Italian dressing and serve as a salad.

⭮ *Cauliflower and Broccoli with Lemon-Butter Sauce*

White cauliflower and green broccoli make a lovely color combination as a side dish on your dinner table. These vegetables, which are cousins by nature, have similar sweet rich tastes. Unfortunately, this family tastes and smells a bit like sulfur — imagine rotten eggs — when mishandled. Choose broccoli and cauliflower heads that are firm, with tight buds and no discoloration. Most importantly, avoid overcooking your vegetables. It brings out the sulfur odor.

Preparation time: *10 minutes*

Cooking time: *10 minutes*

Yield: *6 servings*

3 cups cauliflower florets	*1 tablespoon lemon juice*
3 cups broccoli florets	*3 tablespoons melted butter*
1½ teaspoons salt	*¼ teaspoon pepper*

1 Wash the cauliflower and broccoli florets, which are the buds and the inch or so of tender stems.

2 Place the cauliflower, then the broccoli in a steamer basket over a steamer pot or large pot that has a lid. Add water to about an inch below the bottom of the basket and 1 teaspoon of the salt to the pot.

3 Bring the water to a boil over high heat. Cover the pot and reduce the heat to medium. Cook at medium heat for 7 minutes for tender-crisp or 10 minutes for tender, or until the cauliflower is tender when you pierce it with a fork.

4 Remove the broccoli and cauliflower and place it in a serving bowl. Add the lemon juice, melted butter, the remaining ½ teaspoon salt, and the ¼ teaspoon of pepper. Toss well.

Per serving: *Calories 72 (From Fat 54); Fat 6g (Saturated 4g); Cholesterol 15mg; Sodium 599mg; Carbohydrate 4g (Dietary Fiber 2g); Protein 2g.*

Stir-Fry and Serve

The food flies, and the wok swirls. A dramatic cooking style, stir-frying makes me feel as if I'm a chef at the top of my game, and my family is always impressed. What I don't tell my family watching my stove-side performance is that I chose this technique because it's fast and easy. They're thrilled with the results — crisp-tender vegetables, succulent meat, poultry, or seafood, and intense seasonings. In fact, whenever my children say, "We haven't had stir-fry in a while," it's a gentle reminder to get out the wok. I certainly don't mind hearing this phrase, and I know that you won't either, after you master some basic techniques.

As the name suggests, *stir-frying* means that you stir food while cooking it in oil at a high heat. Stirring keeps the food from burning while subjected to high temperatures.

Picking out the hardware

Woks, which are cooking utensils that have tall sides, are designed for stir-frying. (Check out the wok in Figure 6-5.) You can find woks with one handle or two. I prefer the single handle for tossing foods, but then I'm a showman — or showmom. I like to bring fun to food preparation. But whether you entertain your dinner guests with a little wok show or not, you'll want to read through the following list to get an idea of what your wok choices are:

- ✔ Traditional woks have a round bottom designed to concentrate heat on the food in the utensil. The round bottom makes the wok tipsy, so I suggest buying a metal ring within which you can set the wok for support. Round woks are excellent if you cook with gas.

- ✔ You can also use flat-bottomed woks for gas stoves. However, if you have an electric stove, be sure to select a flat-bottomed wok.

- ✔ Electric woks don't reach a high enough temperature for stir-frying, and I don't recommend them.

A large and heavy-bottomed skillet is an excellent substitute for a wok, and I frequently use a 14-inch cast-iron skillet for stir-frying.

Woks are available in carbon steel, iron, stainless steel, and with nonstick surfaces. If you're selecting carbon steel or iron, season your wok before you first use it. (Follow the seasoning advice that I provide in the "A skillet for all seasons" sidebar in this chapter, of course.) Seasoning a wok makes it easier to clean and prevents food from sticking as it cooks.

You also need a wire strainer for scooping foods out of a wok and a utensil for pushing the food around. Use a wooden spoon or a heat-resistant silicone spatula for woks made with nonstick materials; use stainless steel, wood, or silicone with iron or carbon-steel woks.

Figure 6-5: Work it and wok it!

Whipping out your wok

Being prepared makes all the difference between having a perfectly cooked dinner and having your meal go up in smoke. In fact, you're going to spend more time chopping and cutting food than you will cooking it. Never stop to chop an ingredient or measure out a seasoning when you're in the middle of stir-frying.

You may find the steps dizzying the first time that you try it, so I suggest experimenting with a single food, such as broccoli, before you move on to an entree. Because preparation is so essential to stir-frying, I'm going to go over the key elements. If you're doing stir-fry cooking for the first time, follow the directions carefully. If you're a stir-fry pro, take a look as a brush-up.

✔ Read your recipe thoroughly before you start to cook.

✔ Wash and dry vegetables. Wet vegetables steam; so make sure to pat vegetables dry with paper towels.

✔ Chop, dice, or slice all the ingredients into uniform sizes, so they cook at the same rate.

✔ Measure all the ingredients and keep them within reach as you start to cook.

✔ Measure and blend seasonings in advance.

After you have all your ingredients sliced, diced, and measured, you're ready to wok and roll.

1. **Start the stir-fry process by preheating a wok on medium-high heat for a minute.**

2. **Add 2 to 3 tablespoons of oil.**

   Some cooks prefer peanut oil, which can cook at high temperatures without disintegrating; others choose healthy canola oil, which also cooks at high temperatures. As you pour in the oil, trickle it around the sides of the wok. You're coating the sides with oil, making them stick-free.

3. **Add a crushed garlic clove or slice of crushed gingerroot and cook for a minute to flavor the oil if you like.**

   Don't let the garlic burn. Remove it as soon as it colors slightly.

4. **If your recipe uses meat, cook it first, and then scoop it out with a wire strainer.**

   Stir-frying is the motion of moving a spatula through a wok, tossing the ingredients. Let meat set for a few seconds before tossing, so it gets a chance to brown.

5. **After you've removed the meat, stir-fry your vegetables, adding the densest vegetable first.**

   Some common stir-fry vegetables, such as broccoli and carrots, take longer to cook than others, such as onions and cabbage that have higher water content.

   Keep the vegetables jumping, using a tossing motion, from the second that they hit the wok.

Stirring up some ingredients

Stir-frying is an excellent technique for the following:

- ✔ Tender cuts of pork (such as pork tenderloin), beef, or chicken, cut into small pieces
- ✔ Vegetables cut into small, even pieces

Hot Shrimp and Vegetable Stir-Fry

Stir-fry cooking usually takes more preparation than cooking time, and this recipe is no exception. Take care of the vegetable slicing and you're ready to cook.

Preparation time: *10 minutes*

Cooking time: *6 minutes*

Yield: *4 servings*

2 tablespoons oil

3 slices (¼-inch thick) gingerroot, unpeeled

1 pound small raw, peeled shrimp

2 cups sliced shiitake mushrooms

2 baby bok choy, thinly sliced (about 2 cups)

1 teaspoon minced fresh chile

¾ cup chicken broth

2 tablespoons finely chopped scallions

1 tablespoon lime or lemon juice mixed with 2 teaspoons cornstarch

2 cups cooked rice

1 Add the oil to the wok and heat 30 seconds over high heat. Add the gingerroot and heat 1 minute. Scoop out and discard the ginger.

2 Add the shrimp and stir-fry for 1 minute over high heat or until the shrimp turn pink. Scoop out and set aside. Add the mushrooms, bok choy, and chile, and stir-fry 1 minute or until the vegetables are limp.

3 Stir the chicken broth, scallions, and the lime juice and cornstarch together. Add to the wok and stir 30 seconds or until the liquid thickens slightly. Return the shrimp to the wok. Reduce heat to medium-high and cook 1 minute or until shrimp are cooked through and hot.

4 Immediately dish out the shrimp and vegetables and serve over rice.

Per serving: *Calories 313 (From Fat 83); Fat 9g (Saturated 1g); Cholesterol 169mg; Sodium 397mg; Carbohydrate 36g (Dietary Fiber 3g); Protein 22g.*

Chapter 7

Sauces in Seconds

Sauce makes the difference between a plain, boring entree and a lick-the-plate-clean dinner. Ladling a sauce on steak or over noodles makes your quick meal taste like a dish that you devoted plenty of time to making. Long-simmering, complex traditional sauces, however, can't be part of a cookbook about 30-minute meals. So relax and put away the whisk. In this chapter, I offer a saucy and spicy approach. Mexican, Greek, and Thai cuisines inspire some raw sauces that are fresh, vibrant, and quick.

With a handful of ingredients and the flick of a blender button, this chapter helps you jazz up flavorful toppings for meat, fish, and chicken. A few all-purpose international sauces can really pep up your dishes. Plus you don't have to do it all on your own. You've probably seen supermarket shelves full of international sauces. You can use these sauces straight from the bottle and/or customize them for your cooking. I also provide a new twist on that old standby — salad dressing.

Making Magic with International Sauces

I'll bet sauces aren't first on your agenda when you're trying to get dinner to the table quickly. But a quick sauce can come to your aid, adding flavor and interest to a plain-looking piece of fish or pile of vegetables.

Check out how you can use sauces, particularly uncooked sauces like the ones I cover in this chapter:

✔ **Create a quick side dish.** Top off a baked potato with tomato-based salsa to add color and low-fat, low-cal zest. Add a dollop of Tzatziki Sauce to steamed broccoli or carrots to perk up the flavor.

✔ **Disguise foods that diners dislike.** Sauces (such as *pesto,* a basil and garlic sauce that you can buy in a jar) are wonderful paired with mild-tasting, pale-colored fish, such as halibut, sole, and swordfish. You can also hide dreaded vegetables, such as Brussels sprouts, under a seductive blanket of sauce.

✔ **Revive food.** Cooking pork chops or fish steaks for a couple of minutes too long spells *dry entrees.* When you accidentally overcook dinner, add a dash of sauce — salsa or bottled teriyaki sauce for moisture.

✔ **Stave off hunger pangs.** Scrambling to get dinner ready is less stressful when you're not doing it on an empty stomach, so nibble while you cook. Make a salsa or another uncooked sauce — Tzatziki Sauce, for example — add some chips or hunks of crusty bread for dipping.

✔ **Turn an ordinary dish into an extraordinary one.** A plain, bland chicken breast becomes a mouthwatering beauty of an entree when you top it with salsa.

The sauces that I outline in this chapter work particularly well with many of the dishes that you can turn out using the fast-cooking techniques covered in Chapter 6, and I often match them up with the beef, poultry, pork, and seafood dishes covered in Chapter 12. (Chapter 13 also has a recipe for *chimichurri,* an uncooked sauce of herbs, garlic, oil, and vinegar that people in Argentina slather on grilled meat. Check it out, too.)

Homemade sauces that busy cooks all over the world prepare are often mixtures of cold vegetables and herbs. Originally, this approach was a way to stretch and flavor cheap cuts of meat or chicken, but these rough-hewn sauces are also appreciated for their distinctive advantages:

✔ **Vegetable-based:** You're serving healthy vegetables.

✔ **Made with a minimal amount of fat:** They're usually low-cal, too.

✔ **Almost instant:** In the time it takes to peel and puree, you have a sauce.

Saluting Salsa

Salsa, which means *sauce* in Spanish, is as popular as ketchup in the United States. Keep reading to find out what makes salsa such a valuable ingredient for 30-minute meals, in addition to being an aphrodisiac. Just kidding with the aphrodisiac thing.

Choosing prepared salsas

Salsa is a combination of chopped tomatoes, chiles, cilantro, onions, and garlic. Your supermarket probably sells as many versions of bottled salsa as it does ketchup. Bottled salsas have to be cooked to prevent spoilage. Unfortunately, cooking makes a salsa taste more like tomato or pasta sauce. I don't recommend bottled salsa unless you have no other choice. Commercially prepared fresh salsas have a livelier taste.

Adding freshly chopped cilantro to commercially prepared salsa gives it a lively flavor. Cilantro (sih-*lan*-troh), also called Chinese parsley or coriander, is a leafy herb that tastes like mild licorice. The flavor fades after you chop it, so don't prepare cilantro in advance for tomorrow night's dinner. Take a good look when you're shopping. Cilantro, which is in the herb section of your produce counter, looks like Italian parsley.

Add one or more of the following to bottled salsa to perk up the taste:

- ✔ Dash of fresh lemon or lime juice
- ✔ Teaspoon of minced, fresh chiles

Because commercially prepared fresh salsas usually don't use preservatives, these salsas are highly perishable. Check for a use-by date on the package and observe it. As salsa spoils, it starts to ferment. You can tell by the tingly, slightly fizzy taste. Discard the salsa immediately.

Salsa from scratch

When you make your own salsa, you avoid the waste of old salsa or the disappointment of salsa that tastes like bottled tomato soup.

You can also customize your salsa to your taste preference. Varying the ingredients or the intensity of the chiles changes the character of the dish. Mild to medium hot *jalapeño chiles* yield a salsa that's excellent with fish or chicken. Substituting a *habanero chile* (a small, yellow, square-shaped chile) makes for a smokin' hot salsa. Save this version for Saturday night or a Super Bowl party. (Check out the "Some like it hotter" sidebar in this chapter for more chile info.)

And who says salsa has to be red? Check your supermarket for *tomatillos* (tom-ah-*tee*-ohs) — a green husk-covered fruit that's similar to tomatoes. Tomatillos are firmer and tarter though less juicy than red tomatoes. Use tomatillos in place of tomatoes and make a great salsa verde.

☞ *Blender Salsa*

Use a variable-speed blender or food processor fitted with a steel blade to chop vegetables for this medium-heat salsa. When done, the vegetables should be finely chopped but not slushy. You can also chop the vegetables by hand, which is the traditional way to make salsa.

Before adding the chile to this recipe, however, take a tiny taste of it. If you're using a fiery hot habanero, you may want to add only a teaspoon of minced chile. If you're using a milder tasting jalapeño chile, use the whole pod, minus the seeds. (See the sidebar "Some like it hotter" in this chapter for more on chiles.)

Preparation time: *8 minutes*

Yield: *4 servings*

1 small garlic clove	*1 tablespoon coarsely chopped fresh cilantro*
Juice of ½ lime	*2 medium-large tomatoes, cored and coarsely chopped*
2 tablespoons coarsely chopped scallion	
1 small chile, cored, seeded, and coarsely chopped	*¼ teaspoon salt*
	¼ teaspoon pepper

Place the garlic, lime juice, scallion, chile, and cilantro in a food processor fitted with a steel blade. Process with on/off pulses until the mixture is finely chopped. Add the tomatoes, salt, and pepper and turn the machine on and off a couple of times just to mince the tomatoes.

Vary It! *If you accidentally puree the mixture, don't worry. Add a dash of olive oil, and you have gazpacho, the famous chilled soup from Spain.*

Per serving: *Calories 20 (From Fat 3); Fat 0g (Saturated 0g); Cholesterol 0mg; Sodium 153mg; Carbohydrate 5g (Dietary Fiber 1g); Protein 1g.*

Chives and scallions are sometimes too pungent. Tame the taste by dipping the fresh greens into a pot of boiling water for 10 seconds and then draining. This step, called *blanching,* strips the bitter taste.

Some like it hotter

Chiles give salsa its zip and come in different varieties. But what about the variety of spellings? *Chili* and *chile* can't be blamed on my lack of spelling skills. Generally, *chile* refers to the plant or pod, which means the individual fruit. *Chili* is what you call a dish that contains meat and chiles. But you also use *chili* to refer to the powdered mixture of *chiles* and other seasonings that you use in cooking. No wonder it's confusing.

Handling chiles is easy by comparison. Use gloves when you seed and chop fresh chiles and make sure that you remove all the chile seeds, because the seeds carry much of the heat. Above all, don't rub your eyes after handling chiles. The chiles' volatile oils can burn your eyes. The fresh chiles that you're most likely to find are

- **Anaheim:** Also known as the *California chile,* the Anaheim (anna-*hime*) is green-skinned, thin, and about 6 inches long. It has a mild taste and adds more color than fire to a dish. You can also buy the sweeter red Anaheim chile.

- **Habanero:** A small, wrinkled, square-shaped chile, the habanero (ha-bah-*nay*-roh) is the hottest chile that you're likely to experience — if you can stand it. It can blister your mouth.

- **Hungarian cherry pepper:** This fire-engine red chile is the size of a large cherry tomato. It's sweet and mild, although you're apt to taste hot versions of this fruit as well.

- **Jalapeño:** This chile, about 2 inches long and tapering at the end, is probably the most popular hot chile in the United States. The jalapeño (hal-uh-*peen*-yoh) is sold green or red, but the red is slightly sweeter. I've noticed that jalapeño chiles aren't as hot as they used to be, so I advise you to taste a chile before using it in a salsa.

- **Poblano:** The dark green poblano (poh-blan-o) is 4 to 5 inches long and about 3 inches wide. Poblano chiles are usually baked or cooked, not chopped raw for salsa.

- **Serrano:** About an inch long and thin, the serrano chile is hot and slightly tart. Cooks pickle serrano chiles or chop them raw for salsas.

A Taste of the Mediterranean

If salsa is the ketchup of Mexico and Central America, then yogurt is the condiment that Greek cooks rely on. The fabulous Greek gyro (*yee*-rowh), spiced, minced lamb packed into a loaf and cooked on a vertical spit, is a natural partner with yogurt. Ask for a *gyro sandwich,* a pita bread pocket packed with thin slivers of gyros and a dollop of Tzatziki Sauce — yogurt flavored with garlic and onions. It's part salad and part condiment.

Health experts, touting the Greek diet to prevent heart disease, often mention the benefits of Tzatziki Sauce. In Greece, Tzatziki Sauce is often made with goat's milk yogurt. To satisfy your curiosity, look for goat's milk yogurt in natural food stores. The product has a tangy and clean taste, and good news — it does *not* smell like goats!

☺ Tzatziki Sauce

This sauce should have a thick consistency, so I avoid fat-free varieties, which get watery after standing a few minutes. I have to warn you, this sauce is intensely garlicky. Serving a store-bought lemon sorbet after a dinner with tzatziki eliminates some of the effects that garlic has on your breath.

Preparation time: *5 minutes*

Yield: *4 servings*

1 cup plain yogurt	*1 tablespoon coarsely chopped fresh dill weed*
1 small cucumber, peeled and coarsely chopped	*1 tablespoon coarsely chopped fresh mint*
¼ teaspoon salt	*1 tablespoon olive oil*
1 small garlic clove	*1 teaspoon white wine vinegar*
	⅛ teaspoon pepper

1 Place the yogurt in a blender container. Add the cucumber, salt, and garlic. Blend the mixture to a puree.

2 If you want emerald green-colored sauce, add the dill and mint to the blender and blend again until the herbs are finely minced and tint the sauce. If you want your sauce to remain white with flecks of green, remove the sauce from the blender to a serving bowl. Finely mince the dill and mint and stir them into the sauce.

3 Add the olive oil, vinegar, and pepper. Stir well.

Vary It! *Substitute ½ cup sour cream for half the yogurt for a thicker and richer sauce. You can also try stirring 1 cup of ricotta or cottage cheese into the tzatziki sauce; then add a handful of diced radishes and serve the dish as a refreshing brunch entree.*

Per serving: *Calories 75 (From Fat 40); Fat 4g (Saturated 1g); Cholesterol 4mg; Sodium 190mg; Carbohydrate 6g (Dietary Fiber 0g); Protein 4g.*

Stirring in Sauces from the Shelf

If you want to include Asian dishes, sauces, or flavorings to your menu, you don't have to head to the nearest carryout. Zesty and pungent Asian seasonings and sauces are available in supermarkets, so you can prepare intensely flavored food in minutes. Just as you use salsa as more than a dip, you can use various Asian sauces, even if you don't have a wok.

The array of products in supermarkets is so tempting that you may not know what to choose. To start, I recommend limiting yourself to one all-purpose stir-fry sauce, so you're not crowding your refrigerator with bottles. This condiment usually contains soy sauce, ginger, *hoisin sauce* (which is soy beans, garlic, chiles, and a sweetener), and seasonings. Some stir-fry sauces also contain cornstarch, which thickens a sauce. Stir-fry sauce is a versatile Asian condiment that you can use in so many ways:

- ✔ **Dressing:** Top cooked rice noodles in a salad or put over stir-fry vegetables, such as broccoli or cauliflower.

- ✔ **Basting sauce:** Baste grilled ribs about 10 minutes before the ribs are done, so the sauce doesn't burn.

- ✔ **Marinade:** Steep chicken, pork, or shrimp in it before cooking.

After you're hooked on stir-fry sauce, I suggest that you make your own. Start with my Asian Stir-Fry and Seasoning Sauce, and customize it as you become more comfortable working with the ingredients.

Prepare a big batch of sauce for future meals. Pour your stir-fry sauce into a thoroughly clean bottle. Keep it refrigerated and use it within 10 days.

Asian Stir-Fry and Seasoning Sauce

Spoon this pungent and sweet sauce over cooked Asian buckwheat or rice noodles and shrimp for a quick dinner or side. To use this sauce for stir-fry cooking, which I describe in Chapter 6, stir a teaspoon of cornstarch into the chicken broth and then add the remaining ingredients as the recipe directs.

Preparation time: *7 minutes*

Yield: *about ½ cup; 4 servings*

2 tablespoons chicken broth

1 teaspoon grated fresh gingerroot

1 teaspoon dark sesame oil

¼ cup hoisin sauce

2 tablespoons dry sherry, or additional 2 tablespoons chicken broth

1 teaspoon sugar

In a bowl, stir together the chicken broth, gingerroot, sesame oil, hoisin sauce, sherry, and sugar.

Per serving: *Calories 56 (From Fat 16); Fat 2g (Saturated 0g); Cholesterol 1mg; Sodium 290mg; Carbohydrate 8g (Dietary Fiber 1g); Protein 1g.*

Making Sauces from Dressings

Lettuce not forget (you know I've been waiting to work that line into this book) that salad dressing is more than a vegetable topping. Salad dressings double as marinades, sauces, and condiments. How does salad dressing benefit the quick cook's repertoire in so many ways? A *salad dressing formula* is a combination of oil, vinegar, and seasonings — a trio of ingredients that's the base for a variety of other sauces you use every day.

Marinating meats

Marinades are mixtures of oil, acid (usually vinegar), herbs, and sometimes spices. Soaking seafood or chicken in a marinade, what's known as *marinating* the food, flavors it. You can measure out all the ingredients that you need for a marinade, or you can pour some Italian dressing into a bowl, add your seafood or poultry and refrigerate. Pretty easy, isn't it?

To marinate foods, select a dressing with the word *vinaigrette* — your clue that the product contains oil, vinegar, and seasonings. Italian dressings are basically vinaigrettes, so choose an Italian dressing, if you prefer.

Then place the meat, poultry, or seafood in a glass or stainless steel bowl or in a resealable plastic storage bag and pour on enough dressing to coat. Refrigerate beef, lamb, or pork in a marinade in the morning and you have flavor-infused meat to cook for dinner. Marinate more delicate foods like seafood or chicken in the refrigerator for one hour, turning after 30 minutes.

Soaking raw food in dressing contaminates the dressing with bacteria. Discard leftover salad dressing that has been used as a marinade.

Basting for moisture and flavor

Basting sauce is marvelous for painting a chicken golden brown as it roasts or for flavoring ribs as they grill. Again, you can prepare a basting sauce recipe or open a bottle of dressing. Vinaigrette dressings or sweet and sour dressings are your best bets for basting foods. Read the ingredient label. If sugar, corn syrup, or fructose is high in the ingredient list, the dressing contains many sweeteners. Foods with a high sugar or sweetener content burn easily, so baste with these dressings during the last 10 minutes of cooking. Baste with unsweetened dressings, according to your preference.

Seasoning your salad dressing

Starting with your favorite condiments, such as mustard, ketchup, or mayonnaise, mix in a tablespoon or two of salad dressing, and you're making a new and delicious sauce. My favorites include

- ✔ Equal amounts of sour cream and blue cheese dressing to slather on a steak
- ✔ Two parts Dijon-style mustard with one part Italian dressing for a basting sauce for roast chicken or broiled shrimp
- ✔ Equal amounts of mayonnaise and Thousand Island dressing for a sandwich spread

And see how you can use salad dressings to whip up side dishes in seconds:

- ✔ Poppy seed dressing with an equal amount of pineapple juice poured over precut fruit salad
- ✔ Ranch dressing with an equal amount of sour cream for steamed vegetables such as broccoli, carrots, or asparagus
- ✔ Vinaigrette dressing mixed with half the amount of chicken stock, in a two-to-one ratio, for a low-fat sauce for pasta salad

Chapter 8

Big-Batch Cooking

In This Chapter

▶ Cooking up a storm that'll pay off later

▶ Storing beef and poultry in the fridge and freezer

▶ Putting a big chicken on the fire

▶ Cooking brisket

▶ Ground beef: It's not just for burgers

*E*ven though I typically cook for my family of four, I sometimes make enough for a small army — like the high school football team is coming to chow down. Fortunately, the football team has yet to show up all at once. Although this book promises meals in 30 minutes or less, I reserve this chapter to talk about the advantages of cooking in quantity — admittedly a time-consuming job. But I'm sold on its future benefits — not the least of which is having ready-made dinners on hand that take less than 30 minutes to go from your refrigerator to the dining table.

Yes, the big-batch recipes in this chapter take longer than 30 minutes to cook. But, if you look closely, you'll notice that the prep time is consistently less than 30 minutes. But wait, it gets better. I like to think of these big-batch recipes as starting points for other dishes. The pay-off for some extra up-front time in the kitchen is wonderfully varied. Tonight's aromatic meat sauce can be Monday's tongue-tingling chili or the Latin-inspired picadillo that you serve when friends come for dinner. Now, check out the meals that you can produce from the first big batch recipe. Yep, that's right: 30 minutes or less. So you could say that this chapter obeys the spirit of the law — helping you prepare wholesome, satisfying meals quickly — even if it breaks the letter of the law.

In this chapter, you'll see how easy big-batch cooking is. Your work doesn't double or triple just because the amount of food that you produce does. Even with the promise of a food bonus, you don't want to be tied to a stove. I don't either. That's why I design the recipes in this big-batch chapter to be pretty effortless. Chicken roasts and beef braises while you put your feet up for a well-deserved rest.

Starting Big

In this chapter, I feature three basic starter recipes using ingredients that everyone loves — chicken, a beef roast, and ground beef. These starter recipes provide so many options that your family won't know that you're reworking a previous meal, unless you tell them.

With each starter recipe, I also provide tips on how to buy and store the raw ingredients and how to keep the cooked leftovers safe, because meats and poultry are highly perishable.

Of course, you want to get cooking, so let me explain the game plan:

1. Make the starter recipe in each category. These launching pad recipes, though well seasoned, delicious, and appealing, allow for variations.

2. Try the two spin-offs that each starter recipe has. If you want to prepare both subsequent recipes, be sure to follow the recommendations on serving the starter recipes, so you have enough food left for other meals.

Check out the following tips for successful big-batch cooking:

✔ **Make sure that the key ingredients are readily available.** Call ahead to your supermarket and order a roasting chicken or brisket. In some areas, brisket is only available during limited times of the year.

✔ **Plan ahead, so your entree is ready to cook.** A frozen 8-pound chicken takes up to two days to thaw before you can roast it.

✔ **Read each recipe first.** Make sure that you have enough time to prepare the recipe from start to finish without interruption. Time your dish to serve dinner when the food is ready.

✔ **Larger quantities of food require larger pots and pans.** Brisket, for example, roasts in an 11-x-17-inch pan. Crowding food can ruin the results, so make sure that your cookware and your oven can accommodate the necessary pans.

✔ **Serve one-third of the dish immediately and then pack away the remaining two-thirds for two more meals.** That means midnight snacks sabotage the plan. You can put a lock on the fridge or tell yourself and everyone else not to nibble on leftovers.

Of course you can tailor the plan to your needs. For example, serve the starter recipe for a dinner party and use the leftovers for one follow-up meal.

✔ **Wrap and appropriately store the remaining food after each meal.** This step is important for preventing bacterial contamination, and I provide you with some guidelines throughout the chapter.

✔ **Find a book or magazine to read.** You have to be available while your big-batch recipe cooks, but you can keep one eye on the food and another on your favorite reading material.

Big-Batch Basics: Roasted Chicken

A big, plump bird on the dinner table is such a rare treat. Most people only enjoy it for special occasions. Roast chicken is so easy to prepare, you may wonder why you don't make it more often.

You're roasting a whole chicken for its convenience but don't ignore the ceremony. Arrange roast chicken on your best serving platter, bring it to the table triumphantly, and take a bow for reviving the roast chicken dinner. Keep reading to find out what kinds of roasting chickens are available and how to handle your purchase for the sake of food safety.

Shopping for chicken

Chicken sizes vary according to the type of chicken. Large birds are a different variety from the small ones, not just better fed. Here are the two types of chickens you're most likely to see in supermarkets:

✔ **Broilers:** Also known as *broiler-fryers* or *fryers,* these young birds (from 6 to 8 weeks old) have a *dressed weight* — the bird's weight when stripped of everything but the skin — of about 3 pounds. A 3-pound bird yields 4 servings, enough for one meal. The broiler's tender meat makes it the best choice for frying. Broilers are sold whole or cut into serving pieces.

✔ **Roaster:** Similar to broilers, these chickens are 8 to 12 weeks older and have a dressed weight of about 5 to 8 pounds. An 8-pound roaster is about the same weight as a small turkey and serves 12. A roaster, as the name suggests, should be roasted, not fried.

Use a roaster for the Roast Chicken starter recipe in this chapter to ensure that you have enough chicken left over for the subsequent recipes. If you can't find a roaster, buy three broiler chickens and cook them together. Cooking times won't increase if you have three birds sharing the oven roost.

Two other types of chicken, hens and roosters, aren't practical for roasting because they're too tough.

Storing uncooked chicken

Supermarket sales offer a wonderful opportunity to stock up on chicken. That way, you have the makings of several meals in the freezer. My local supermarket sometimes has two-for-one sales on roasters. When the freezer is so full that my husband can't find the carton of his favorite ice cream, he knows roasters are on the menu. Use Table 8-1 for refrigerating or freezing raw chicken.

Table 8-1	Raw Chicken Storage Chart	
Chicken Part	*Refrigerate at 40 Degrees*	*Freezer at Zero Degrees*
Whole raw chicken	1 to 2 days	Up to 12 months
Raw chicken parts	1 to 2 days	Up to 12 months

Roasting chicken

Roasting a chicken is easier than roasting a turkey because you're often handling a smaller bird. Chicken roasts in as little as half the time of a turkey, depending on the size of the birds that you're dealing with. What's more, less pressure is on you when you make chicken versus the annual turkey feast.

Follow these quick and easy steps to prepare a chicken:

1. **Remove the bird from its wrapper.**

2. **Remove the sac that contains the neck and giblets from the cavity.**

   Giblets is a collective term that includes the chicken's liver, gizzard, and sometimes, the heart. You can freeze the neck up to one year to use in a chicken soup. Cook the chicken liver immediately or freeze it up to three or four months, until you have enough to serve as an entree. Serve the gizzard and heart to your cat. And if you prefer to serve liver to your cat, that's fine with me.

3. **Check the chicken for pinfeathers.**

   Pinfeathers are those little prickly feathers around the bird's tail. Pull them out with your fingers or with a pair of tweezers.

4. Season the chicken and oil it up.

Seasoning with a light dusting of salt, pepper, and herbs brings out the bird's natural succulent taste. Brushing chicken with olive oil burnishes the skin to a golden color that you'd think is only possible in the photos of food magazines.

Don't wash the chicken. Yes, you read that right. Older recipes tell you to rinse a chicken inside and out with cold running water. But washing chicken can spread poultry bacteria around the sink area, so food safety experts no longer recommend this messy step, which is a relief to me!

For roasting times, use Table 8-2 in this chapter. But remember that these times are approximate for an unstuffed bird and that a meat thermometer tells you when the bird is fully cooked. Insert the thermometer into the chicken's thigh, not touching a bone. When it registers 180 degrees, the chicken is done.

As a general rule, stuffed birds take about 30 minutes longer to cook than unstuffed birds. The larger the bird and the more stuffing, the more time it will take. If you're stuffing the bird, take the stuffing's temperature, so you don't get sick. Warm, moist stuffing can harbor bacteria that cause food-borne illnesses. Cooking stuffing to 165 degrees means that the stuffing is safe to eat.

Some poultry companies package large chickens with pop-up timers. Don't rely on these gadgets to tell you when your bird is ready. At times, these devices don't register as done until your bird is overcooked. A meat thermometer is the most reliable indicator.

Table 8-2	Roasting Times
Chicken Weight, Unstuffed	*Time in a Preheated 350-degree Oven*
3 to 5 pounds	1¼ to 1½ hours
6 to 8 pounds	1½ to 2¼ hours

Allow 15 minutes resting time after you pull the chicken from the oven. Chicken, like most roasted meats, firms up and reabsorbs its juice during this time, making it succulent and easy to carve.

Roast Chicken

Feast on delicious chicken with gravy and roast vegetables. If you're cooking potatoes, you probably want to skip a stuffing.

Preparation time: *10 minutes, including gravy making*

Cooking time: *2 to 2¼ hours*

Yield: *12 servings*

1 roasting chicken (8 to 8½ pounds)	*8 small red potatoes (optional)*
¼ to ½ teaspoon salt	*2 cups baby carrots (optional)*
¼ teaspoon pepper	*½ cup water, or dry white wine*
¼ teaspoon crushed, dried oregano	*1 cup chicken broth*
1 tablespoon fresh lemon juice	*1 tablespoon cornstarch*
2 tablespoons olive oil	

1 Preheat the oven to 350 degrees. Remove the package in the chicken cavity containing the liver, neck, and any other parts. Discard these or use for another meal. Place the chicken on a rack set inside of a large, shallow roasting pan. Sprinkle the chicken with ¼ teaspoon salt, pepper, and oregano. Drizzle the lemon juice over the chicken. Spoon the olive oil over the chicken. Place the red potatoes (if desired) in the roasting pan around the chicken. Add the carrots (if desired). Sprinkle the potatoes and carrots with the remaining ¼ teaspoon salt.

2 Place the chicken in the oven for 2 hours. Remove the chicken and insert an instant read thermometer in the thickest part of the thigh, not touching a bone. The temperature should register 180 degrees. If not, return the chicken to the oven another 15 minutes and check again.

3 When the chicken tests done, remove it from the oven onto a platter. Cover loosely with foil and set aside for 15 minutes. This resting period makes chicken juicier and easier to slice. Spoon the vegetables into a covered bowl to keep them warm. Carve the chicken in the kitchen. Arrange one-third of the bird and the vegetables on the serving platter (saving the remainder for subsequent recipes).

4 Place the roasting pan on your stovetop. Using a large spoon, skim off any pools of fat. Add the water to the pan and turn the heat under the pan to low. Deglaze the pan by scraping up any browned bits using a wooden spoon. Because the roasting pan is probably twice the size of your burner, deglaze one side of the pan and then turn the pan around to deglaze the other side over the burner. Be sure to use an oven mitt.

5 Place the cornstarch in a cup. Stir the chicken broth into the cornstarch until it's smooth. Stir the cornstarch mixture into the roasting pan. Simmer, stirring constantly, about 2 minutes or until the pan gravy is slightly thickened.

Per serving: Calories 384 (From Fat 216); Fat 24g (Saturated 6g); Cholesterol 119mg; Sodium 411mg; Carbohydrate 2g (Dietary Fiber 0g); Protein 37g.

Chicken Strategy

You've read the safety warnings and shopping tips, and you know a roaster from a rooster. You've roasted the chicken perfectly. Now it's time to serve. Get out the platter that you save for company dinners and display the roast chicken, vegetables, and gravy. Use the directions in Figure 8-1 to carve the chicken, but don't put the entire bird on the table.

In order to get all three meals that I review in this chapter from your one roasted chicken, you can't serve the whole bird when you sit down for the starter meal. Instead, arrange one-third of the chicken with the vegetables and gravy.

Although these are my suggestions for getting three dinners from one roaster, you don't have to follow the plan. You can serve the whole roast chicken for a dinner party, or use leftovers for different meals. The chicken makes a great salad topper or sandwich filling.

Pack the remainder to use in the Chicken and Egg Enchiladas and Hot and Spicy Chicken and Rice recipes in this chapter. An 8-pound bird yields about 4 to 5 packed cups of leftovers, enough for two recipes.

Packaging leftover chicken

Chicken is highly susceptible to bacterial contamination. Removing the chicken meat from the bone as soon as you finish your meal will reduce the risk of bacterial spoilage. Wrap the boneless chicken in packages and refrigerate or freeze.

Chicken that you're using in a day or two needs an airtight wrapping, so it doesn't dry out. Put the chicken on a plate and cover with two layers of heavy plastic wrap or place the chicken in a refrigerator-freezer bag, press the air out of the bag, and seal. Store leftover cooked chicken in the fridge (at 40 degrees) for three to four days. If the chicken is covered with sauce, cut the storage time back to one to two days.

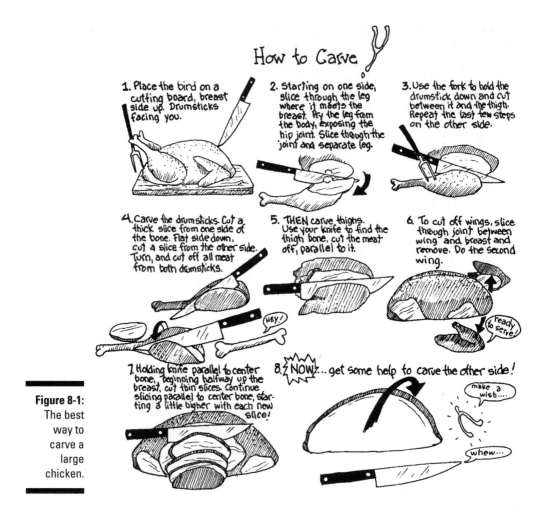

Figure 8-1:
The best way to carve a large chicken.

If you're freezing the leftover chicken, divide the chicken into one-recipe bundles, about 2 cups of cooked chicken per bundle. Place the chicken in freezer storage bags and press the air out of the bag. Cover each bag with a layer of heavy-duty aluminum foil. Label the package with the name of the item, the date that you freeze it, and the date that you should defrost and use the chicken. Store cooked chicken in the freezer (at 0 degrees) for four to six months.

The chicken and the egg

Don't wait long to make enchiladas with chicken — this recipe is that good. The chicken and egg filled tortillas answer the age-old question of which comes first. It's neither. The chicken and egg are on equal footing in this rich and satisfying dish.

Chicken and Egg Enchiladas

Cheese should melt into a velvety blanket for this luscious enchilada dish. Choose a traditional Mexican-style cheese, such as mild-tasting and quick-melting *asadero* (ah-sah-*deh*-row) available in supermarkets in areas that have a Hispanic clientele. Otherwise, use Monterey Jack cheese, which melts evenly. To bring up the heat level, select Monterey Jack cheese with crushed red pepper flakes.

Preparation time: *15 to 20 minutes*

Cooking time: *10 minutes*

Yield: *4 servings*

2 tablespoons butter	*¼ teaspoon pepper*
1 small onion, chopped	*2 hard-cooked eggs, chopped*
1 large celery stalk, trimmed and chopped	*2 cups diced cooked chicken*
1 tablespoon flour	*4 flour tortillas, each 9 inches in diameter*
½ cup milk, or half-and-half	*1 cup grated asadero, or Monterey Jack cheese*
1 can (7 ounces) diced mild chiles, undrained	
¼ teaspoon ground cumin	*1 tablespoon minced fresh cilantro*
¼ teaspoon salt	

1 Preheat oven to 425 degrees.

2 Melt the butter in a large skillet. Add the onion and celery and sauté over high heat 2 minutes. Stir in the flour and cook 1 minute to form a paste. Stir in the milk and cook 1 minute or until the mixture is thick. Stir in the chiles, ground cumin, salt, and pepper. Cook 30 seconds for the flavors to blend. Stir in the eggs and the chicken and heat through, about 1 minute.

3 Butter a glass 9-inch square baking dish. Working with one flour tortilla at a time, spoon ¼ of the chicken mixture down the center of the tortilla. Fold the sides of the tortilla tightly to the center to enclose the chicken filling. These tortillas are stuffed to capacity, so be careful placing each seam-side down in the baking dish. Repeat with the remaining chicken filling and tortillas.

4 Mix the cheese and cilantro together with your fingers. Sprinkle the cheese mixture over the tortillas.

5 Bake the enchiladas for 10 minutes or until the cheese melts. Remove the dish from the oven and let stand 1 minute.

Vary It! *Freeze leftover enchiladas so you can have a quick and filling lunch up to six months from now. Place individual enchiladas in small freezer containers and seal. Reheat at medium high in a microwave oven.*

Per serving: *Calories 534 (From Fat 263); Fat 29g (Saturated 13g); Cholesterol 189mg; Sodium 764mg; Carbohydrate 38g (Dietary Fiber 4g); Protein 30g.*

Chicken skillet dinners

Adding cooked chicken to a rice dish turns it into a substantial meal. As long as you have a box of rice in the cupboard and a package of cooked chicken in the freezer, you can have dinner on the table in less than 30 minutes.

Hot and Spicy Chicken with Rice

Fresh ginger has an alluring sweet and spicy scent that can whet an appetite. It's worth taking a minute to grate the knobby root rather than substituting ground ginger. Use a hand-held vegetable grater and grate the ginger onto a plate. After you feel confident about measuring ginger by looking at it, you can grate ginger directly into the dishes that you're cooking.

Preparation time: *5 minutes*

Cooking time: *25 minutes*

Yield: *4 servings*

1 tablespoon vegetable oil

1 small red bell pepper, cored, seeded, and diced

1 small red onion, diced

¼ teaspoon crushed red pepper flakes

1 tablespoon grated fresh gingerroot

2 cups diced cooked chicken

1 cup parboiled or regular long-grain rice

2 cups chicken broth

¼ teaspoon salt

¼ teaspoon pepper

¼ cup finely chopped scallion

1 tablespoon Thai fish sauce (nam pla), or 1 tablespoon reduced-sodium soy sauce

Juice of 1 lime, about 2 tablespoons

1 Heat the vegetable oil in a large sauté pan. Add the bell pepper, onion, red pepper flakes, and gingerroot and sauté 2 minutes.

2 Add the chicken, rice, broth, salt, and pepper and stir. Bring the mixture to a boil. Reduce the heat to low, cover and simmer 18 minutes, or until the rice is tender and the liquid is absorbed. Add the scallion, fish sauce, and lime juice and stir in. Serve immediately.

Per serving: *Calories 380 (From Fat 124); Fat 14g (Saturated 3g); Cholesterol 41mg; Sodium 1,129mg; Carbohydrate 46g (Dietary Fiber 2g); Protein 17g.*

Big-Batch Basics: Braised Brisket

Brisket is a beef cut from the breast of beef cattle. Because it's a well-used part of the animal, it's tough. That makes it the ideal cut for cooking in a liquid. Brisket has a coarse texture with muscle running through the cut, but slow-cooking the meat for a long time tenderizes it. Brisket goes from barely chewable to fork tender in 3 to 4 hours.

Braising is the best technique for cooking brisket. This no-fuss method allows meat to soak up the flavors of the braising liquid. By covering the meat for most of the cooking, then uncovering it for the last 30 minutes or so, the brisket turns an appealing brown color. (Check out the "Braising" section, later in this chapter, for the specifics on this technique.)

Buying brisket

Some supermarkets carry fresh brisket the year round; other stores only stock it periodically. Call your supermarket or butcher shop in advance and ask if they sell fresh brisket. If not, ask your butcher to order it. Brisket has two seasons: during the fall, for celebration of Rosh Hashanah, the Jewish holiday, and March 17, St. Patrick's Day. Braised brisket is the pride of many Jewish cooks, who often prepare it in a sweet and sour sauce. Corned brisket is the signature dish of the St. Patrick's Day table.

Don't substitute corned beef for plain brisket. *Corned beef* is cooked in a brine of sugar, pickling spices, and vegetables, and then sold. You can reheat it or cook it more in a broth with vegetables before serving. It's not a different animal, but it's a completely different taste.

The brisket and the mother-in-law

A bride is upset because she can't cook brisket well even though she's using her mother-in-law's recipe. This, of course, is the dish that her groom brags about whenever he mentions his mother's cooking. Wanting to satisfy her new husband, the bride calls the mother-in-law for brisket advice. The mother-in-law suggests that the young woman come over, and they'll make brisket together. Everything seems familiar as the mother-in-law prepares the dish. But then the bride watches as her mother-in-law, the experienced cook cuts the large brisket in half and fits it into a roasting pan.

"Aha!" says the bride. That must be the secret trick I didn't know about. "Why do you cut the brisket in half?" asks the bride, assuming it must do something to improve the taste. "Because my roasting pan is too small to fit the whole brisket in one piece," answers the mother-in-law.

The moral of this story is, if you can't fit a whole brisket in your roasting pan, go ahead and cut it into large pieces. Or, if you can't find one large brisket, buy two smaller ones.

Brisket is a flat piece of meat, about 1½ to 2 inches high. Supermarket cuts weigh from 3 to 6 or more pounds. During the fall, I'm often able to buy 6-pound briskets, which is perfect for my Sweet and Sour Braised Brisket starter recipe. Other times of the year, meat counters only carry 3-pound cuts. Then I do a variation of the version found in "The brisket and the mother-in-law" sidebar in this chapter and piece two small cuts together.

Don't underestimate how much brisket you need for a recipe: A 6-pound purchase can yield 4 pounds of edible beef. Brisket has a high proportion of fat that you should trim away before cooking. Then even more fat melts out during braising.

Storing uncooked brisket

Because brisket is sometimes hard to find, you may have to buy it in advance. You can store uncooked brisket in the refrigerator (at 40 degrees) for three to five days. Storage times for uncooked brisket in the freezer (at 0 degrees) vary widely between 4 and 12 months. If you put three meat experts together, you'll get a variation of 8 months in brisket storage time. Freezing meat isn't an exact science. Much depends on how the meat is stored in the supermarket and in your freezer. But to be on the safe side, stick with the low end of the scale.

Braising

After you have your brisket in hand, a little prep work is necessary before turning on the heat. Looking at the underside of the meat, you see a ¼ to ½-inch thick fat layer. For your health's sake, and even for flavor's sake, that has to go. Place a sharp knife at a 45-degree angle to the fat at one end of the brisket. Work the knife along between the fat and the meat. Lift the fat as you go, making it easier to slice away. Figure 8-2 shows how to make a fat brisket thin.

REMOVING FAT FROM BRISKET

1. WORKING THE POINT OF A SHARP KNIFE UNDER THE STRIPS OF FAT, SLICE HORIZONTALLY TO REMOVE THE FAT IN SHEETS

2. USING YOUR HANDS, PULL THE FAT AWAY WITH ONE HAND AS YOU SLICE WITH THE OTHER.

Figure 8-2:
Slice the fat off the brisket as you go.

Leftovers by any other name

Leftovers have a bad name. If they're good, then why are they left over? Cooks are working on improved language, and maybe Madison Avenue can provide some advice. Until then, you're serving one of the following:

✔ **A repeat** until the sweeps season, just like your favorite TV program.

✔ **The refund dinner.** Just as you get money back after tax time if you plan well, you get a second or third dinner as a reward for careful kitchen planning.

✔ **Version XP.** Microsoft can do it, why not you?

✔ **One of your greatest hits.** It's part of an edible anthology of your best cooking.

Put your braising liquid in a large roasting pan. To braise brisket, cook a large hunk of meat in a covered container in a flavored liquid — such as beef broth, tomato sauce, wine, and herbs and seasonings. You can do this on top of the stove or in an oven. Keep the temperature low, so the meat gradually cooks and doesn't fall apart. I prefer oven-braised brisket; the meat is out of sight, and I'm less likely to fuss with it.

Make sure that the pan accommodates the liquid and the meat. Most roasting pans don't come with matching lids. Use heavy-duty aluminum foil to protect the meat from browning too much. Regular foil is too thin to shield the beef.

Don't peek at oven-roasting meat until the recommended cooking time is close, and the meat's aroma fills the kitchen. When you frequently check on meat in the oven, you lower the temperature, adding to the meat's cooking time. Besides, by jumping up all the time, you could lose your place in that novel that you're reading.

This recipe for Sweet and Sour Braised Beef makes the rounds among my friends. Serve it once, and your family and friends will develop an instant nostalgic need for an encore.

Sweet and Sour Braised Brisket

This recipe doesn't call for browning brisket before braising it. Removing the foil cover from the meat during the last 30 minutes of cooking ensures an inviting deep color.

Brisket is sold whole, which is 10 or 15 pounds, and too much meat for even me to suggest. Instead choose either the first cut (also called the flat), which is a lean and expensive piece of brisket, or the front cut, which is fatty but tasty. I opt for the inexpensive front cut.

Preparation time: *15 minutes*

Cooking time: *3 hours*

Yield: *12 servings*

2 jars (12 ounces each) chili sauce	*2 large cloves garlic, chopped*
¼ cup balsamic or white wine vinegar	*1 large onion, chopped*
¼ cup Dijon-style mustard	*4 cups baby carrots*
1 cup lightly packed brown sugar	*6 pounds brisket, trimmed of outside fat*

1 Preheat the oven to 350 degrees.

2 Spoon the chili sauce into a 15-x-20-inch roasting pan. Fill the chili jars with water and add both jars of water, which is 3 cups of water to the pan. Add the vinegar, mustard, brown sugar, garlic, onion, and baby carrots and stir well.

3 Place the brisket over the vegetables. Add a sheet of heavy-duty foil and cover the roasting pan. Place the pan in the oven and let the beef braise for 2½ hours. Don't be tempted to baste the beef. Let it simmer in it's own juices while you put your feet up.

4 After the 2½ hours, remove the foil and let the beef brown for 30 minutes. Remove the pan from the oven. Remove the beef from the pan liquids and let it stand for 10 minutes to make carving easier.

5 Cut ⅓ of the beef into a serving piece. Slice this portion across the grain into slices ¼-inch thick. Arrange the sliced beef on a serving platter. Spoon 1 cup of the pan juices and the vegetables over the beef.

6 Refrigerate the remaining beef and pan juices and vegetables for two more dinners.

Per serving: Calories 342 (From Fat 126); Fat 14g (Saturated 5g); Cholesterol 100mg; Sodium 909mg; Carbohydrate 20g (Dietary Fiber 1g); Protein 32g.

Brisket Strategy

Braising a 6-pound brisket with all the fat trimmed yields about 4 pounds of cooked beef. Allow about 1½ pounds of beef for the Sweet and Sour Braised Brisket for 4. (When serving brisket, slice it, and other stringy meats, across the grain.) Serve the braised brisket with about 1 cup of the pan juices and 2 cups of the cooked carrots. You have 2½ pounds of beef for two more meals. And as an added bonus you have 2 cups of cooked carrots and 5 cups of leftover pan juices. With this gift, you can cook an old-fashioned Sweet and Sour Cabbage and Beef Soup that makes grandmothers everywhere jealous.

Packaging leftover brisket

When you're ready to pack up your leftover brisket, you can choose between the freezer and the fridge. You can store cooked brisket in the refrigerator (at 40 degrees) for three to four days and in the freezer (at 0 degrees) for two to three months.

Brisket tastes even better the day after it's braised. If you can resist serving it immediately, cover the meat with an airtight wrapping (so it doesn't dry out) and refrigerate it. Don't slice the beef. It will stay fresher if it's unsliced, and cold beef is easier to cut than hot-from-the-oven beef anyhow. Put the beef on a plate and cover with two layers of heavy plastic wrap.

When you're ready to use the beef again, slice up the portion you want for the meal. Take a spoon and lift the hardened fat off the pan sauces. Simmer the sliced meat with some of the pan sauces in a skillet for 5 minutes or until it's heated through.

If you're going the freezer route, divide the leftover beef in half; each half provides enough meat for one recipe. Place the beef in a plastic freezer bag, squeezing out excess air. Then place the meat in a double layer of heavy-duty aluminum foil and seal well. Label the package with the name of the item, the date you freeze it, and the date by which you should defrost and use the beef.

That's using your head . . . of cabbage

This section gives you two completely different recipes for leftover brisket and cabbage. I'm not sure why brisket and cabbage have such a natural affinity. But trust me, they're delicious together.

Sweet and Sour Cabbage and Beef Soup

This is the stick-to-your-ribs kind of soup that usually takes hours to make. Starting with the sweet-sour pan juices reserved from roast brisket, you get tangy-sweet flavors in less than 30 minutes.

Preparation time: *10 minutes*

Cooking time: *15 minutes*

Yield: *4 servings*

2 tablespoons vegetable oil

2 cups finely shredded cabbage

2 cups cooked carrots, from Sweet and Sour Braised Brisket (preceding recipe)

3 cups pan juices, from Sweet and Sour Braised Brisket (preceding recipe)

1 cup beef broth

1½ pounds cooked brisket, cut into 1-inch cubes (about 3 cups)

¼ teaspoon salt

¼ teaspoon pepper

¼ teaspoon crushed, red pepper flakes (optional)

1 Heat the oil in a large Dutch oven. Add the cabbage and sauté over high heat 5 minutes or until limp, stirring frequently. Add the carrots, brisket juices, broth, brisket, salt, pepper, and crushed, red pepper flakes (if desired).

2 Bring the soup to a simmer. Cover and simmer 10 minutes, or until the soup is hot and the cabbage is tender.

Vary It! *In place of the cabbage, add 2 cups of frozen baby lima beans. Eliminate the vegetable sauté step, and instead, combine all the ingredients and simmer for 15 minutes or until the beans are soft. Also, you can pour leftover soup in single-serving portions into freezer containers. Leave about 1 inch of space, because liquid expands as it freezes.*

Per serving: *Calories 735 (From Fat 269); Fat 30g (Saturated 8g); Cholesterol 158mg; Sodium 3,021mg; Carbohydrate 62g (Dietary Fiber 3g); Protein 54g.*

BBQ Brisket 'n Slaw Sandwiches

When Southerners cook barbecue, it's a sun-up-to-sundown ritual. This quick take on the classic is ready whenever the gang clamors for dinner.

Preparation time: 10 minutes

Cooking time: 12 minutes

Yield: 4 servings

1 tablespoon vegetable oil	2 tablespoons mayonnaise
1 medium onion, thinly sliced	2 tablespoons buttermilk
1 pound cooked brisket, sliced across the grain ¼-inch thick	½ teaspoon sugar
	⅛ teaspoon salt
2 cups pan juices, from Sweet and Sour Braised Brisket (recipe earlier in this chapter)	¼ teaspoon pepper
	2 cups shredded cabbage
4 Kaiser rolls or other crusty rolls	¼ cup finely chopped scallions

1 Preheat the oven to 350 degrees to toast rolls (if desired).

2 Heat the oil in a large sauté pan. Add the onion and sauté over high heat 2 minutes or until limp. Add the sliced brisket and the pan juices and simmer 10 minutes or until the meat is hot.

3 Place the rolls in the oven and toast 5 minutes while the meat is heating (if desired).

4 Make the slaw: Stir together the mayonnaise, buttermilk, sugar, salt, and pepper in a medium-size bowl. Add the cabbage and scallions and stir well.

5 To serve, arrange rolls on each of 4 plates. Top with ¼ of the meat and spoon on some of the pan juices. Spoon the slaw over the meat or serve it on the side.

Per serving: Calories 691(From Fat 239); Fat 27g (Saturated 7g); Cholesterol 110mg; Sodium 2,168mg; Carbohydrate 71g (Dietary Fiber 3g); Protein 41g.

Big-Batch Basics: Browned Ground Beef

I rely on ground beef more than anything else when it comes to making a quick dinner. I can practically recite recipes in my sleep: Brown one pound of ground beef; add . . . and I fill in the blanks according to the current favorites. Ground beef is the mainstay for tacos, chili, and spaghetti and meat sauce for starters. It's such a part of my menus, and yours too I bet, that it makes sense to include the meat in this chapter on big-batch cooking.

Browning ground beef isn't difficult as long as you place the beef in a very large pan. You need the large pan surface, so all the chunks of meat get equally and quickly hot. Using a wooden spoon to push the meat around assures that it browns fast. Admittedly, browning beef can be messy as grease splatters onto the stovetop. So, why not brown 3 or 4 pounds of beef instead of one and get three meals for the same clean-up job?

Purchasing ground beef

Ground beef is sold by percentage points. This isn't a popularity contest, but an indication of the amount of lean and fat in the beef. The higher the percentage of lean meat, the fewer grams of fat and calories the package of ground beef has. Table 8-3 contains a few examples.

Table 8-3	Breaking Down 3 Ounces of Ground Beef	
Percentage	*Calories*	*Fat Grams*
95 percent lean	139 calories	5 grams fat
90 percent lean	173 calories	9 grams of fat
85 percent lean	200 calories	11 grams of fat

Ground beef that's between 80 and 90 percent lean is the most popular, according to the meat industry. You won't find ground beef with more than 30 percent fat (which is 70 percent lean), because that's the maximum that's allowed by law. Although I'm all for cutting back on fat and calories, choosing the leanest ground beef doesn't make sense in big-batch cooking. These recipes need a little fat for flavor. Save the 90 to 95 percent lean beef for grilled hamburgers and use 80 to 85 percent lean for the big-batch recipes.

Storing uncooked ground beef

Watching for ground beef sales pays off. It's frequently at a discount in super-markets. Use these instructions that follow for storing ground beef:

- Leave the ground beef in its original package when refrigerating unless you're buying a large amount and only want to use a portion at a time.
- The less you handle it, the less likely you are to contaminate the meat with bacteria.

✔ Ground beef packages can leak, so set the beef in a plastic container in the meat compartment of the refrigerator.

✔ Store ground beef in the refrigerator (at 40 degrees) for one or two days.

To freeze raw ground beef, remove it from the original package and wrap in a double layer of heavy-duty plastic wrap. Then cover in a layer of heavy-duty aluminum foil and date the package. Freeze ground beef (at 0 degrees) for no more than four months for optimal quality.

Browning beef

Ground beef weight shrinks during cooking. How much it shrinks depends on the meat's fat and moisture content and the cooking temperature. The higher the cooking temperature is, the greater the shrinkage; likewise the higher the fat content, the more the meat shrinks. When browning ground beef, use moderate heat.

The ground beef starter recipe is different from the chicken and brisket recipes in this chapter. Because each of the subsequent variations uses such different seasonings — one is savory, one is hot, and one is sweet — I'm keeping the basic recipe simple. You can serve the starter recipe, but the three variations are each much better tasting.

You probably know if you make any dish with ground beef, that onions and garlic are usually part of the package. I add both to my ground beef starter recipe, so you don't have to add them later.

Using a food processor to chop the vegetables for the Master Meat Sauce is a timesaver, though you still have to process the vegetables in batches so you don't turn everything into pulp. Process the garlic and onions together, remove them from the food processor, and then process the carrots and celery.

The skinny on hamburger

Hamburger and *ground beef* mean different things. Hamburger can have beef fat added to it; ground beef cannot. But neither the total fat in hamburger nor in ground beef can be more than 30 percent of the weight.

Master Meat Sauce

Carrots have a sweet flavor that makes for a mild-tasting meat sauce and healthy as well. Serve this thick meaty dish over cooked rice, spaghetti or in a bun. For the ground beef, I use ground chuck because as Goldilocks might say, it's not too fat and it's not too lean.

Preparation time: *10 minutes*

Cooking time: *about 1½ hours*

Yield: *3 quarts; 12 servings*

3 garlic cloves	*4 pounds ground beef*
1 very large onion, or 2 medium onions	*1 can (28 ounces) crushed tomatoes*
1 cup grated carrots	*1 can (6 ounces) tomato paste*
1 large celery stalk, trimmed	*1 teaspoon salt*
2 tablespoons olive oil	*½ teaspoon pepper*

1 Mince the garlic and onion and set aside. Finely chop the carrots and celery.

2 Heat the olive oil in a large Dutch oven. Add the garlic, onion, carrots, and celery and sauté over high heat, stirring frequently, for 5 minutes or until the onions are transparent and lightly browned. The vegetables may give off plenty of liquid, which prevents browning. If this happens, increase the heat to high and continue to cook. Remove the vegetables and set aside.

3 Add the ground beef to the Dutch oven. Brown the meat on all sides, stirring frequently with a wooden spoon. Pour off any accumulated fat. Return the vegetables to the beef. Add the crushed tomatoes, tomato paste, salt, and pepper. Simmer 1 hour.

Per serving: Calories 368 (From Fat 183); Fat 20g (Saturated 7g); Cholesterol 112mg; Sodium 391mg; Carbohydrate 11g (Dietary Fiber 2g); Protein 35g.

Ground Beef Strategy

Cooking the ground beef starter recipe gives you about 3 quarts of meat sauce, enough for 3 recipes. Using one quart and freezing the remaining two, you'll have meat sauce for the next few months.

Zeroing in on freezer guidelines

Refreezing frozen, thawed food can be a risk to your health. Remember this simple rule: Freeze once for raw, and freeze once for cooked. Freezing raw chicken, ground beef, or brisket is fine. After you thaw it, however, don't return it raw to the freezer. Meat and poultry can become contaminated with bacteria. Even if you're careful handling thawed meat or poultry to avoid spoilage, you're diminishing the quality of the food when you freeze, thaw, and refreeze it. Meat and poultry lose their juiciness.

Packing cooked ground beef

One word of caution when you make the starter recipe: Don't cool the meat at room temperature before refrigerating or freezing it. Letting meat sit at room temperature invites bacterial contamination.

Immediately pour the meat into 1-quart portions, so it gets cold faster. A large pot of meat sauce takes longer to chill. If refrigerating, use a plastic food storage container with a lid. You can store cooked ground beef in the fridge (at 40 degrees) for three to four days. If freezing, pour the meat into plastic freezer containers and allow an inch of space for expansion. Cover and freeze. It'll stay good in the freezer (at 0 degrees) for two to three months.

Speedy spaghetti

No one says "No" to spaghetti night. Starting with the Master Meat Sauce from earlier in the chapter, you have a slow-simmered sauce in 30 minutes. You can also use the spaghetti sauce for lasagna. Starting your favorite lasagna dish with no-boil lasagna noodles means trimming 15 minutes off preparation time.

Mom's Spaghetti and Sauce

Stir cooked spaghetti into the pot with meat sauce and let the combination simmer together for a minute, so the pasta is permeated with the sauce. You may prefer to spoon the spaghetti into a serving bowl and top with the sauce.

Preparation time: *5 minutes*

Cooking time: *20 minutes*

Yield: *4 servings*

1 tablespoon olive oil	*1 bay leaf*
2 cups sliced mushrooms	*1 teaspoon crushed, dried oregano*
¼ cup dry red wine	*1 teaspoon salt*
1 quart Master Meat Sauce (from previous recipe)	*½ teaspoon pepper*
1 can (14 ounces) diced tomatoes with liquid	*¼ cup finely chopped fresh basil (optional)*
	½ pound spaghetti, cooked

1 Heat the olive oil in a large sauté pan. Add the sliced mushrooms and sauté over high heat 5 minutes or until tender. Add the red wine and cook over high heat until the liquid is reduced to half of its original volume.

2 Add the Master Meat Sauce, diced tomatoes, bay leaf, oregano, salt, and pepper. Simmer the mixture 10 minutes. Discard the bay leaf. Add the basil (if desired) and cook 2 minutes. Serve the meat sauce over spaghetti.

Per serving: Calories 509 (From Fat 219); Fat 24g (Saturated 8g); Cholesterol 112mg; Sodium 1,100mg; Carbohydrate 33g (Dietary Fiber 6g); Protein 39g.

Fifteen minutes to chili

The evening commuter train is late and traffic is snarled, but you're not snarly. You have a quart of Master Meat Sauce in the fridge and beans in the cupboard. Work a little magic with this combination and, you have a family-pleasing meal in 15 minutes.

Medium-Hot Chili with Beans

With enough seasonings to tantalize adult palates but not too much spice for children, this is the perfect family chili. Either seed and mince a fresh chili or use 2 tablespoons from a can of hot, diced chiles.

Preparation time: *5 minutes*

Cooking time: *10 minutes*

Yield: *4 servings*

1 quart Master Meat Sauce (from recipe earlier in this chapter)

1 can (14½ ounces) diced tomatoes with chiles

1 can (15½ ounces) kidney beans, rinsed and drained

2 tablespoons minced jalapeno chile

1 tablespoon medium-hot chili powder

½ teaspoon salt

¼ teaspoon pepper

2 tablespoons minced fresh cilantro

Place Master Meat Sauce in a large saucepan. Add the tomatoes, kidney beans, chile, chili powder, salt, and pepper. Simmer 10 minutes or until hot. Sprinkle with cilantro.

Per serving: *Calories 453 (From Fat 189); Fat 21g (Saturated 7g); Cholesterol 112mg; Sodium 1,326mg; Carbohydrate 26g (Dietary Fiber 8g); Protein 39g.*

Meat sauce Latin style

Picadillo (peek-ah-*dee*-yoh), made with ground pork or beef, tomatoes, garlic, onion, and sweet aromatic spices such as cinnamon, is one of the pleasures of Cuban and Mexican cuisine. Starting with Master Meat Sauce, you can get this specialty to the table in no time.

Picadillo with Almonds and Rice

Serve picadillo over rice with a side of black beans as Cuban cooks do, or spoon it over corn bread Southwestern style.

Preparation time: *5 minutes*

Cooking time: *10 minutes*

Yield: *4 servings*

1 quart Master Meat Sauce (from recipe earlier in this chapter)

1 can (14½ ounces) diced tomatoes with liquid

¾ teaspoon cinnamon

½ teaspoon ground ginger

1½ tablespoons white wine vinegar

¼ teaspoon crushed red pepper flakes

½ teaspoon salt

¼ teaspoon pepper

½ cup golden raisins

2 cups cooked rice (optional)

¼ cup sliced almonds

1 Place Master Meat Sauce in a large sauté pan. Add tomatoes, cinnamon, ginger, vinegar, red pepper flakes, salt, pepper, and raisins. Simmer 10 minutes or until heated through.

2 Spoon ½ cup rice (if desired) on each of 4 plates. Top each with a portion of picadillo. Sprinkle each serving with 1 tablespoon sliced almonds.

Vary It! *Spoon picadillo into flour tortillas, roll up, and serve.*

Per serving: *Calories 491 (From Fat 211); Fat 24g (Saturated 8g); Cholesterol 112mg; Sodium 818mg; Carbohydrate 33g (Dietary Fiber 6g); Protein 37g.*

Part III
Quick Meals without the Hassle

In this part . . .

You want a bunch of 30-minute meals? Well, you've come to the right part. You can find speedy versions of your favorite recipes along with dishes that you probably never thought you could make given your limited time. Imagine full-bodied soups that go from the pot to the table in 30 minutes or less or skillet dinners — robust combinations of rice or noodles, meat, and vegetables — all ready in less time than it takes your guests to reach your door.

Remember when a salad or sandwich didn't count as a meal, because it wasn't filling enough? You won't hear any complaints about that when you serve the hot and hearty pasta salads and sandwiches that you can whip up in minutes. Finally, just because you're cooking fast doesn't mean that you can't splurge on an occasional dessert, and I've got you covered (or maybe I should say "sauced") with tempting fruity toppings that take only minutes to make.

Chapter 9

Satisfying Soups

In This Chapter

▶ Turning soup into a hearty supper

▶ Simmering soup bases from broth to cream

▶ Adding veggies, pasta, or protein to the mix

▶ Doctoring canned soups with fresh items

Soup is the most improbable yet welcome dish in the 30-minute cook's repertoire for a number of reasons. The fact that a bowl of liquid could be filling enough to serve as a meal is a bit mysterious. Although I never got past Human Anatomy and Physiology 101 in school, I'm convinced the answer is in the volume. All that liquid takes up space in your stomach, so you feel full.

Hot, chunky soup can also offset the effects of a nasty winter evening, and cold soup can cool you off during the hottest summer day. When you're serving a hungry family or a table full of friends, soup is just plain satisfying — especially if you prepare a robust soup with vegetables; meat, poultry, or seafood; and a starch.

Another of soup's surprising and welcome attributes is that some soups can be quick cooking. Most folks wouldn't think that a dish that built its reputation on a slow-simmer process could get to the table in minutes. But it can.

In this chapter, I show you a mouthwatering variety of soups that fit your busy schedule. I also review some tips and tricks that you can use to turn that old pantry standby — the can of condensed soup — into a speedy meal that everyone will love. In the process, I share my favorite recipes for a variety of soups, including old-fashioned chowders, cream soups, can-opener specialties, and broth-based soups.

Introducing the Super Soup Quartet

On long car trips, my family loves to tune in to the oldies stations to listen to vocal quartets like the Four Tops and the Four Seasons. Four also brings harmony to a soup entree. Rib-sticking soups that double as dinner include these components:

- Flavored liquid or *base*
- Vegetable(s)
- Starch
- Protein

Keep on reading for an in-depth explanation of each of these elements. Each one plays a roll in giving soup the body, texture, taste, and nutrients it needs to serve as a meal.

Starting on first base

In the soup world, a *base* is any flavored liquid you eat with a spoon. Some of the most common bases for soups are broths, but the liquid doesn't have to be broth. Depending on the recipe, you can use milk or cream or even leftover vegetable cooking liquid. You can also use the liquid from canned vegetables or a dash of wine.

Basing your soup on broth

Although you don't have to use broth as a base, more often than not, you probably will because it's so versatile and accessible. You can even use chicken broth in soups that you'd never dream of putting an actual chick in — such as some fish and seafood soups.

When I refer to *broth,* I mean a flavored liquid made by cooking meat, fish, chicken, and/or vegetables in water for 30 minutes to an hour. A broth has a fresh taste and isn't thick or heavy. Other folks use *stock* (also a flavored liquid) as the base for their soups, which is great when you have two or three hours to burn: Stocks, which often use meat bones for their intense taste, take hours to cook.

Because you don't have all day to cook, I'm not going to tell you how to make a broth or a stock from scratch. Neither one fits into my lifestyle, and it sure doesn't fit into a 30-minute meal, but don't worry. I stopped being a food snob when my children were born. Racing home from work to be with my infant, I had to let go of something else, and homemade broth and stock was it.

Supermarkets stock an array of chicken and beef broths and stocks in several forms that are acceptable building blocks for making a great, wholesome meal in a bowl. The list that follows provides a look at the broth varieties available in supermarkets.

- **Frozen, concentrated stock:** Find this product in beef and chicken flavors in upscale supermarkets. Keep it in your home freezer and use according to the package directions when you want the full taste of beef or chicken in your soup.

- **Soup base:** This paste or concentrated powder is made from soup stock. Depending on the brand, you can find soup base in a gourmet food store's refrigerated unit or on a store shelf. Flavor choices usually include beef, chicken, vegetable, veal, and turkey. To use, stir a teaspoon of soup base into a cup of boiling water or follow the package directions.

- **Canned broth:** This is the workhorse of the soup line. Every manufacturer has a distinctive formula for making chicken, beef, or vegetable soup broth — but they usually include a bunch of sodium. I prefer brands with less sodium, because I want to add salt and herbs to my own taste, and I don't need all that sodium. Most canned broth is ready to use and doesn't require any water. If you have leftover broth, pour it into a plastic container and refrigerate for a few days.

- **Ready-to-use:** This new entry into the broth category is sold in 1-quart containers in the soup section of your supermarket. Chicken, vegetable, and a vegetarian version of chicken broth are some of the more common flavors. This type of broth is usually lower in sodium and has less of a chemical taste than the canned varieties. But the quality depends on the brand. I recommend you experiment and see what brand you prefer. The broth is convenient, because you don't have to add water — it's ready to go. If you don't use the entire container, store the remainder in the refrigerator.

- **Bouillon:** This powder or cube concentrate is a blend of seasonings with a little flavoring from beef or poultry. One serving of some brands of bouillon equals about half the sodium that you should have in a day. Use bouillon if you must for emergencies, but don't include it in your routine cooking.

Feel free to use one form of broth in place of another when you're cooking. The beauty of soup recipes is that you don't have to follow rigid rules. Just be sure to dilute a concentrated broth.

I prefer reduced-sodium broth in soups that contain salty ingredients, such as Canadian bacon and Parmesan cheese.

Bean and Canadian Bacon Soup

Lean Canadian bacon has a delightful smoky flavor that pairs well with canned beans. Serve this soup with plenty of crusty bread for dunking.

Preparation time: *5 minutes*

Cooking time: *17 minutes*

Yield: *4 servings*

1 tablespoon olive oil	2 cans (14 ounces each) chicken broth, preferably reduced-sodium
1 large carrot, trimmed and diced	¼ teaspoon crushed, dried oregano
1 medium onion, chopped	2 bay leaves
12 ounces Canadian bacon, diced	½ teaspoon salt
1 can (15 ounces) Great Northern beans, drained and rinsed	¼ teaspoon pepper

1 Heat the olive oil over medium heat in a large pot. Add the carrot and onion and cook 5 minutes or until the onion is transparent. Add the Canadian bacon, turn the heat to high, and sauté 1 to 2 minutes, just to lightly brown.

2 Add the beans, chicken broth, oregano, bay leaves, salt, and pepper. Bring to a simmer and cook for 10 minutes for flavors to blend. Remove bay leaves before serving.

Vary It! *If desired, pour the soup into a blender and blend 1 minute, so the ingredients are finely chopped. For a thicker soup, puree the beans in a blender or food processor and then stir them into the soup. Or give the finished soup a few zaps with a wand blender for a bit more body. Also, this soup tastes even better as it gets older. Pour leftovers into single-serve containers and freeze up to one month.*

Per serving: *Calories 218 (From Fat 74); Fat 8g (Saturated 2g); Cholesterol 31mg; Sodium 1,780mg; Carbohydrate 15g (Dietary Fiber 5g); Protein 20g.*

Harvest Vegetable Soup

This simple soup has the flavor and aroma of newly picked vegetables and herbs. Don't skip the bread and cheese topping. It adds crunchy texture to the soup. Finish this soup meal with a simple salad of romaine lettuce and shredded carrots.

Preparation time: *10 minutes*

Cooking time: *15 minutes*

Yield: *4 servings*

2 tablespoons olive oil	*2 cups vegetable juice*
1 small diced red onion	*2 cups vegetable or chicken broth*
2 zucchini, halved lengthwise and thinly sliced	*¼ cup slivered basil*
2 cups sliced oyster mushrooms	*4 thin slices French bread*
4 medium cored, diced tomatoes	*¼ cup grated Parmesan cheese*

1 Preheat the broiler. Heat the oil in a medium-sized pot. Add the onion, zucchini, mushrooms, and tomatoes. Sauté over high heat 10 minutes or until the vegetables are tender and the tomatoes are pulpy. Add the vegetable juice and chicken broth. Simmer 2 minutes or until hot. Stir in the basil and simmer 2 minutes.

2 Meanwhile, place the bread on a cookie sheet and sprinkle with Parmesan. Place the cookie sheet under a broiler, 3 inches from the heat, and broil for 20 seconds or until the cheese browns lightly.

3 Pour the soup into 4 bowls. Cover each serving with a cheese-topped bread slice.

Per serving: Calories 257 (From Fat 94); Fat 10g (Saturated 2g); Cholesterol 4mg; Sodium 1,111mg; Carbohydrate 34g (Dietary Fiber 5g); Protein 10g.

For flavor as close to homemade as possible, read the package label. Does it say *chicken broth,* which means the manufacturer uses some chicken parts, or does the label say *chicken-flavored broth?* The latter means that the broth doesn't contain any chicken, but it contains substances that approximate the taste of poultry. Make sure the ingredient list contains the foods that you're paying for.

Doing the dairy thing

Chowders, with the notable exception of Manhattan clam chowder that uses tomatoes, are made with milk as the base instead of broth. Chowders deliver romance with every spoonful. The dish originated with French fishermen who made stews from their catch of the day. But if your fish comes from a can, and not the net, you can still make great chowder. Add a little lemon zest, the grated outer rind of the lemon, to bring a fresh accent to the soup.

You can make soup with fat-free milk if you're cutting back on your fat and calorie intake. The soup won't have the same body or flavor, however, as it would if you used whole milk.

Salmon and Bell Pepper Chowder

Your supermarket produce department carries cooked potatoes in the refrigerated aisle. Take advantage of the convenient spuds to make a robust entree soup. Add the Mango-Rum Sauce from Chapter 14 over store-bought pound cake as a luscious finish to the meal.

Preparation time: *6 minutes*

Cooking time: *15 minutes*

Yield: *4 servings*

1 tablespoon butter	*1 can (15 ounces) salmon, drained and flaked*
2 red bell peppers, cored, seeded and cut into thin strips	*¼ cup chopped scallions*
¼ cup chopped red onion	*¼ teaspoon crushed red pepper flakes*
2 tablespoons flour	*1 teaspoon grated lemon zest*
3 cups milk	*½ teaspoon salt*
2 cups refrigerated diced potatoes	*½ teaspoon pepper*

1 Melt the butter over medium heat in a medium-size pot. Add the peppers and onion and cook 2 to 3 minutes or until the peppers are tender. Stir in the flour to form a paste with the butter. Slowly add the milk to avoid lumps and cook the soup over medium heat, stirring constantly, or 3 to 5 minutes or until the mixture is smooth and slightly thickened.

2 Stir in the potatoes, salmon, scallions, crushed red pepper flakes, lemon zest, salt, and pepper. Simmer 5 minutes or until the ingredients are hot.

Per serving: *Calories 364 (From Fat 144); Fat 16g (Saturated 7g); Cholesterol 87mg; Sodium 752mg; Carbohydrate 33g (Dietary Fiber 3g); Protein 25g.*

Taking your lumps

Curdling is one of the culprits when it comes to lumps in your soup. Milk and cream curdle if you add an acid. However, you can prevent milk-based soups from separating by stabilizing the milk before adding the acid. To stabilize the milk, add a white sauce (see the "Thickening with white sauce" section in this chapter for directions on making a white sauce) or a French *beurre manié* (*brrr* man-ay) — butter and flour mashed together into a paste. Using your fingers, work 3 tablespoons of butter together with 2 tablespoons of flour until the mixture is a smooth paste. Gradually pull off small pieces and add them to the simmering soup. Or you can whisk the beurre manié into the soup, bit by bit until the liquid looks smooth. Then simmer the soup for 5 minutes to thoroughly cook the flour. After the soup thickens, add the lemon juice, vinegar, or other acid.

And you don't want to boil milk-based soups, either. If you do, the liquid separates, leaving you with a lumpy mess. If you do get carried away, however, you can rescue your soup with a beurre manié.

Believe it or not, you may actually want lumps sometimes, such as when a recipe calls for buttermilk, and you're fresh out. For every cup of buttermilk that's called for in the recipe, substitute a tablespoon of lemon juice mixed with a cup of low-fat or whole milk.

Adding vegetables to the mix

Vegetables add taste, texture, and color to soups. Because vegetables are key to fabulous, quick-meal soups, I have a bunch of tips that you can use when you're following a recipe or going at it alone:

- ✓ **Choose vegetables that cook in the same length of time.** You don't want to have some ingredients that are tough and others that are mushy. For example, combine carrots, parsnips, and potatoes for one soup, or broccoli, onions, and cauliflower in another.

- ✓ **Think color.** The fashion police won't arrest you for serving a bowl of beet soup with spinach, but you may have a hard time selling that color combo to your dinner guests.

- ✓ **Chop or dice firm vegetables into ½-inch pieces.** They cook faster this way. To save even more time, partially cook vegetables, such as carrots and parsnips, in a separate pot. Add the vegetables to the soup during the last 5 minutes of cooking, so they soak up the seasonings in the soup.

- ✓ **Think frozen.** Frozen vegetables are a boon for busy soup makers. Buy vegetables that are separately frozen in bags and pour what you need into the soup pot. Avoid frozen vegetable blocks that dilute soup.

- ✓ **Don't cook raw potatoes in a broth-based soup that should remain clear.** The potatoes give off starch that clouds the soup. Instead, partially or completely cook potatoes in a separate pot and add them to the soup for 5 to 10 minutes at the end. My favorites for soup, New potatoes and Yukon Gold, are fast-cooking and keep their shape.

Most recipes tell you to sauté aromatic vegetables, such as onions and garlic, at the start of soup preparation. Sautéing brings out the sweetness in vegetables, so they taste better. It also colors the vegetables golden brown, so your soup looks more appetizing. You're also filling the house with an incredibly tempting aroma, so you don't have to call the troops to dinner.

Corn and Bacon Chowder

Chowder doesn't have to use seafood. This land-lover's pot of bacon, corn, and mushrooms makes a smoky and sweet-tasting soup. Don't use extra-lean bacon in this recipe, or you won't get enough fat. Buy corn bread at your supermarket bakery department to serve with the chowder.

Preparation time: *5 minutes*

Cooking time: *20 minutes*

Yield: *4 servings*

4 bacon strips	½ teaspoon ground cumin
2 cups sliced mushrooms	1 cup milk, or ½ cup milk and ½ cup half-and-half
1 garlic clove, minced	
2 tablespoons flour	¼ teaspoon hot red pepper sauce
2 cups chicken broth, preferably reduced-sodium	½ teaspoon salt
	½ teaspoon pepper
2 cups canned or frozen corn kernels	2 tablespoons chopped cilantro (optional)

1 Place the bacon strips in a medium-size pot and brown over medium-high heat 2 to 3 minutes per side or until crisp. Remove the bacon and place on a dish lined with paper towels to drain. Crumble the bacon.

2 Pour off and discard all but 2 tablespoons of the bacon fat. Add the mushrooms and garlic and sauté for 3 minutes over high heat. Sprinkle the flour over the mushrooms and stir for 30 seconds or until the flour is lightly browned and forms a paste with the bacon fat.

3 Stir in the chicken broth, mixing until the flour is without lumps. Add the corn, cumin, milk, hot red pepper sauce, salt, and pepper. Simmer 5 minutes or until the ingredients are hot. Do not let the mixture come to a boil or the soup can separate. Sprinkle on the crumbled bacon and the cilantro (if desired).

Per serving: Calories 239 (From Fat 105); Fat 12g (Saturated 4g); Cholesterol 20mg; Sodium 1,191mg; Carbohydrate 25g (Dietary Fiber 3g); Protein 8g.

Stirring in starches

Rice, noodles, quick-cooking barley, toasted couscous, or stale bread cubes give a soup body. These starches are also fun. Did you pick out the letters of your name when you ate alphabet soup as a child? I did. The song "Chicken Soup with Rice" runs through my head whenever I make chicken soup. I can't help but smile when I put it on the table.

Soups are a wonderful way to use up leftover starches. Add a scoop of rice from last night's stir-fry to a chicken soup or stir cooked noodles into a beef soup. Whenever you cook rice or other starches, make extras to have on hand for a soup recipe.

When you include a starch, such as rice or pasta, in a soup cook the starch in one pot and everything else in a separate pot. That way the starch doesn't make the soup too cloudy or, well, starchy. Then add the cooked starch, such as noodles or rice, to the soup and let it simmer 3 to 5 minutes before serving so the soup flavors the starch. (For more info on starches like rice and pasta, check out Chapter 3.)

Packing in protein

Protein is a meal soup's centerpiece. Any food you that you regularly serve as an entree on its own, including cheese, fish, seafood, chicken, or pork can give a tasty, nutritional boost to a soup. Match your protein to the soup style that you're making: Enhance the velvety consistency of a cream soup with cheese or pump up a chunky vegetable soup with pieces of beef. See the list that follows for the lowdown on a number of soup-friendly proteins:

- ✔ **Meat:** Cut beef, chicken, or pork into small pieces of the same size. Select the more tender beef cuts, such as flank steak instead of bottom round steak or pork tenderloin instead of pork shoulder.

- ✔ **Fish and seafood:** Fish cooks so quickly that the problem isn't how to make it tender but how to keep it from falling apart. Chunks of fish steak hold together better than fish fillets. Firm tuna, swordfish, or salmon have the best texture for soups. Shrimp can work well, too. Add shrimp during the last 10 minutes of cooking so the delicate seafood doesn't overcook and get tough. Try the Tomato, Zucchini, and Shrimp Bisque recipe in the "Transforming Condensed Soup into Can-Do Cuisine" section, later in this chapter.

✔ **Cheese:** Cheddar is my favorite cheese for soup because of its sharp flavor, golden orange color, and creamy texture. To cook with cheddar cheese, you first make a white sauce. (See the "Thickening with white sauce" section, later in this chapter, for directions on making a white sauce.) Sprinkle grated cheddar cheese into the white sauce by the handful, so the cheese melts slowly and evenly. If you just add grated cheese to a hot broth, it clumps up into a rubbery mess.

Natural cheese makes the best soup. It tastes great and melts evenly. Processed cheese doesn't have the complex nutty and tangy flavor of natural cheese, but you can use it in an emergency. Avoid fat-free cheese, because it doesn't melt well.

The souper dictionary

From soup to nuts, some of the terms that you come across as you make *potage* — that's French for *soup* — are as follows:

✔ **Bisque:** This is a soup that's thickened with a vegetable puree. Most bisque recipes call for seafood, such as shrimp, lobster, or mussels. However, you can find vegetarian tomato bisque on most grocers' shelves.

✔ **Bouillon:** A clear broth made from poultry, vegetables, beef, or fish cooked in water and seasonings. It's easy to confuse this with the bouillon cubes that I discuss in the "Basing your soup on broth" section in this chapter, but don't tell that to a French chef. They're two different things.

✔ **Chowder:** A thick, chunky soup that usually includes fish or seafood and is usually made with milk. Vegetable chowders are made without fish or seafood.

✔ **Condensed soup:** A soup that's cooked down, so it can be packed in a smaller container. Many condensed soups are sold canned and should be reconstituted with water or milk before serving as a soup.

✔ **Consommé:** To eliminate any solid particles, cooks strain the broth through layers of cheesecloth before serving it.

✔ **Cream soup:** When commercially made, this soup may have cream, but it's just as likely to contain flour or cornstarch for its creamy texture. Cream soups are usually condensed. Either use the soup straight from the can as a sauce or reconstitute it with water or milk and serve as a soup.

✔ **Dehydrated soup mix:** A blend of freeze-dried vegetables, seasonings, and broth. Combine it with water and simmer it for a soup. You can also use dehydrated soup mixes as flavorings, such as that perennial favorite, onion soup-sour cream dip.

✔ **Puree:** A soup that's blended to a fine consistency in a food processor or blender.

✔ **Ready-to-serve:** A canned, frozen, or packaged soup that doesn't require the addition of any liquid.

☞ Cheddar Cheese Soup

By cooking vegetables in one pot while you prepare a white sauce in a second pot, you cut cooking time by half. You deserve a reward for your efficiency, so get someone else to do the cleanup. Serve this soup with baby carrots and a dipping sauce from your supermarket's deli or produce section.

Should you have any leftover soup, you'll find that this soup freezes well but should be reheated at a low temperature. Store the soup in freezer containers up to one month. Thaw the soup in the refrigerator overnight and reheat at medium speed in a microwave oven or on the stove over low heat.

Preparation time: *10 minutes*

Cooking time: *20 minutes*

Yield: *4 servings*

1 cup pared, diced carrot	¼ cup whipping cream, preferably heated
2 medium Yukon Gold potatoes, peeled and diced	3 cups milk, preferably heated
1 tablespoon butter	1½ cups grated sharp aged cheddar cheese (6 ounces)
1 small onion, diced	¼ teaspoon salt
1 jalapeno chile, cored, seeded, and minced	¼ teaspoon pepper
1 tablespoon flour	

1 Combine the carrots and potatoes in a small pot and add water to cover the vegetables. Bring the water to a boil and cook 10 to 15 minutes or until the vegetables are tender.

2 While the vegetables are cooking, melt the butter in a medium-size pot. Add the onion and chile and cook over medium heat for 2 minutes. Stir in the flour to form a paste. Add the cream and cook, stirring constantly, for 1 minute or until the mixture is smooth and thick. Add the milk and heat through, about 1 minute.

3 Add the cheese ¼ cup at a time, stirring constantly, until cheese melts and mixture is thick. Drain the vegetables and stir into the cheese soup. Simmer for 5 minutes. Season with salt and pepper.

Per serving: *Calories 446 (From Fat 257); Fat 29g (Saturated 18g); Cholesterol 97mg; Sodium 526mg; Carbohydrate 28g (Dietary Fiber 2g); Protein 19g.*

Simmer protein-based soups. Vigorous boiling toughens proteins, such as beef, poultry, and pork.

Body-Building Options

Body is essential to a dinner soup. If you're serving a bowl of soup as a meal, the dish should look thick and robust enough to quell your hunger pangs. You don't have to use your muscles — or your valuable time — to give a soup body. In this section, I share a few quick bodybuilding techniques with you.

Thickening with white sauce

White sauce gives soups the body to stand up to big appetites. White sauce is a combination of a fat and flour cooked together and mixed with milk. The fat can come in the form of butter, margarine, or fat drippings from bacon, for example. For most recipes, I prefer butter, which has a sweet, creamy flavor. Vary the proportions of fat, flour, and liquid, and you change the consistency of the sauce.

Use a white sauce when you want to prepare a hot soup with a creamy texture. If soups are your comfort food, you'll love how white sauce transforms soup into the meal equivalent of a favorite blanket. Prepare a white sauce toward the beginning of soup preparation. Then add your liquid base, vegetables, starch, and protein. Simmer the soup, and you've got a robust meal.

For a basic white sauce that gives soup a little oomph, check out Figure 9-1 in combination with these steps:

1. Melt 1 tablespoon butter or other fat in a pot.

2. Stir in 1½ teaspoons of flour and cook the mixture to a paste, stirring constantly.

3. Gradually add 1 cup of hot milk, stirring constantly. You could use cold milk, but hot milk blends into the flour mixture more easily.

For a couple of consistency options for this white sauce, you may want to consider the following:

✔ For a basic thin white sauce, use 1 tablespoon each of fat and flour with 1 cup of milk.

✔ If you want a spoon to practically stand on its own, combine 2 tablespoons each of fat and flour with 1 cup of milk.

Changing the consistency is one way to play with this sauce, but I have a couple of ideas to vary the taste as well:

✔ When you're sautéing a vegetable for soup, don't clean out the pot to make a white sauce. The leftover vegetable essences provide a more intense flavor for the sauce. Cook the vegetable and remove it from the utensil. Add more fat to the leftover sauté fat and proceed with the steps for a basic white sauce.

✔ White sauce with cheese is also called *Mornay sauce.* A typical recipe for Mornay sauce uses grated *Gruyere* (groo-*yer*) a nutty-tasting cheese similar to Swiss cheese and also from Switzerland.

✔ You don't have to use milk to make a white sauce. Substitute cream or half-and-half for part of the liquid. When you use a broth instead of milk, you're making a velouté (vel-*oo*-tay) sauce. It's easy to do, but these French words sound so sophisticated and complex.

Cream of Mushroom Soup

Shiitake mushrooms, which have a meaty and succulent texture, and oyster mushrooms that have a delicate herbal taste are delicious in this soup. Serve this soup with the Asian Greens and Radish Salad in Chapter 5 and a crusty French bread.

Preparation time: *5 minutes*

Cooking time: *17 minutes*

Yield: *4 servings*

2 tablespoons butter	*2 cups chicken broth*
4 cups of coarsely chopped mushrooms	*2 tablespoons minced scallions*
1 celery stalk, trimmed and chopped	*1 teaspoon minced fresh dill*
2 tablespoons flour	*¼ teaspoon salt*
2 tablespoons brandy or dry sherry (optional)	*¼ teaspoon pepper*
¼ cup half-and-half	

1 Melt 1 tablespoon of the butter in a medium-size pot and set the remaining butter aside. Add the mushrooms and celery and cook for 10 minutes over medium heat or until the celery is tender. Add the remaining tablespoon of butter and melt. Sprinkle on the flour and cook, stirring constantly, for 1 minute or until the butter and flour form a paste.

2 Add the brandy (if desired) and stir in. Pour in the half-and-half and the broth. Simmer the soup for 5 minutes or until it is smooth. Stir in the scallions, dill, salt, and pepper and simmer another minute.

Vary It! *For an elegant yet fast presentation sure to be a hit when you're entertaining, pour the soup into 4 small ovenproof bowls. Thaw a sheet of frozen puff pastry and cut out four circles, each the diameter of the top of the soup bowls. Place a circle of puff pastry over each bowl and make 2 to 3 slashes for steam to escape. Place the bowls on a cookie sheet and bake in a preheated 400-degree oven for 10 minutes or until the puff pastry is golden brown.*

Per serving: *Calories 128 (From Fat 87); Fat 10g (Saturated 5g); Cholesterol 23mg; Sodium 668mg; Carbohydrate 7g (Dietary Fiber 1g); Protein 4g.*

MAKING A WHITE SAUCE

Figure 9-1:
Make
a white
sauce in
three easy
steps.

1. MELT BUTTER IN A POT.

2. STIR FLOUR INTO THE BUTTER.

3. POUR MILK OR OTHER LIQUID INTO THE FLOUR-BUTTER PASTE.

Blending in with the cool crowd

Chopping the soup's ingredients to a fine puree in a blender or food processor gives soup more body and texture. White sauces are excellent for hot soups, but when you want to take a break from the heat, nothing beats a chilled blender soup.

Blender soups have several advantages, because you can

- ✔ Add big vegetable chunks to a blender and let the machine do all the work.

- ✔ Get your kids to eat more vegetables. Tell them you're serving a smoothie for the main course.

- ✔ Serve raw fresh-from-the-market summer vegetables and herbs in a soup, so you save a cooking step. But you can also cook vegetables first and then puree them if you prefer.

Vegetables with high-water content, such as bell peppers, cucumbers, sweet Vidalia or Maui onions, and tomatoes, make the best blender soups. If your vegetables are juicy enough, you don't have to add any additional liquid. But I usually like to add a little liquid to thin the vegetable mixture. Check out the following few suggestions:

- ✔ Tomato juice tastes good in gazpacho, a Spanish chopped vegetable soup.

- ✔ Broccoli has a pronounced flavor that needs a subtle liquid, such as vegetable broth.

- ✔ Use buttermilk for an old-fashioned, tangy cucumber, leek, or potato soup.

Blender soups that use raw vegetables should be served the day that they're prepared. Raw vegetables develop a slightly unpleasant, sour taste after a day.

☺ *Broccoli-Scallion Soup*

The floral tops of a head of broccoli are the most tender and sweet part of the vegetable. If your supermarket doesn't sell the heads separately, buy the entire stalks. Dice and steam the thick stalks for another dish (I provide suggestions in Chapter 6) or use a 10-ounce package of frozen broccoli florets. Although this recipe cooks in minutes, make it at least 2 hours in advance to chill. For a real convenience, how about making this soup after dinner for an instant meal the next night? Biscuits from your supermarket's bakery round out the meal.

Preparation time: *5 minutes*

Cooking time: *15 minutes*

Yield: *2 servings*

1 tablespoon vegetable oil	*½ cup milk*
1 shallot, chopped	*½ cup whipping cream*
½ cup coarsely chopped scallions	*¼ teaspoon pepper*
2 cups broccoli florets	*Salt to taste*
1 cup vegetable broth	*⅛ teaspoon ground nutmeg*

1 Heat the oil in a 3-quart pot. Add the shallot and scallions and cook over medium heat for 1 minute. Add the broccoli and vegetable broth. Cover and cook until the broccoli is tender, about 15 minutes.

2 Pour the broccoli mixture into a blender and puree. Place the broccoli mixture in a pitcher. Add the milk, cream, pepper, salt, and nutmeg. Chill the soup from 2 to 24 hours. Serve cold.

Vary It! *Substitute 1 cup of buttermilk for the milk and cream in the recipe for a tangy and lower-fat soup.*

Per serving: *Calories 351 (From Fat 287); Fat 32g (Saturated 16g); Cholesterol 90mg; Sodium 868mg; Carbohydrate 14g (Dietary Fiber 3g); Protein 7g.*

 **Three-Herb Gazpacho**

When you're weighed down with fresh tomatoes from your farmers market, haul out your blender and make this tangy, fresh-tasting soup. Gazpacho doesn't keep well, so make and serve it the same day. *Brie* (bree), a soft, creamy French cheese, spread on crusty bread is heavenly with this vegetable soup.

Preparation time: *10 minutes*

Yield: *4 servings*

1 medium red onion, coarsely chopped	*2 tablespoons olive oil*
1 cucumber, peeled, seeded and coarsely chopped	*2 teaspoons fresh lemon juice*
	¼ teaspoon salt
4 ripe tomatoes, cored and coarsely chopped	*⅛ teaspoon pepper*
1 cup tomato juice	*2 tablespoons finely chopped parsley*
¼ cup chopped basil	*½ cup garlic croutons (optional)*
1 tablespoon chopped chives	

1 Place the red onion, cucumber, tomatoes, tomato juice, basil, and chives in a blender. Turn on and off in quick motions until the mixture is finely chopped but not pureed.

2 Remove the vegetables to a serving bowl. Stir in the oil, lemon juice, salt, pepper, and parsley. Pour into bowls and top each serving with 2 tablespoons croutons (if desired).

Vary It! *Use spicy tomato juice or add a pinch of crushed red pepper flakes to the blender.*

Per serving: *Calories 112 (From Fat 66); Fat 7g (Saturated 1g); Cholesterol 0mg; Sodium 374mg; Carbohydrate 11g (Dietary Fiber 2g); Protein 2g.*

 Cucumbers are a great ingredient for cool, blender soups. I use them in Three-Herb Gazpacho and Cucumber-Buttermilk Soup in this chapter. Cucumber seeds are edible, but they give cucumber-based soups a coarse feel. Seed the cucumbers for a silken texture. (See Figure 9-2 for the particulars.) You can also buy foot-long seedless cucumbers in most supermarkets. Inch for inch, seedless varieties cost about double what you pay for seeded cucumbers.

ᗡ *Cucumber-Buttermilk Soup*

Cool as a cucumber isn't just a saying, it's the experience you have when you taste this refreshing summer soup. If you have the time, chill this soup for 30 minutes, so the mint flavor comes through. A side of whole wheat bread makes this simple meal very nourishing.

Preparation time: *10 minutes*

Yield: *2 servings*

2 medium cucumbers, peeled, quartered lengthwise, and seeded

1 small shallot, trimmed and halved or 2 scallions, trimmed and coarsely chopped

1 tablespoon coarsely chopped fresh mint leaves

1 small garlic clove

1 cup low-fat buttermilk

¼ teaspoon salt

¼ teaspoon pepper

1 Cut the cucumbers into large chunks and place in a blender. Add the shallot, mint leaves, garlic, buttermilk, salt, and pepper.

2 Turn the blender on/off at the puree setting for 1 minute or until the mixture is finely minced.

Vary It! *Add ¼ cup heavy cream with the buttermilk.*

Per serving: *Calories 85 (From Fat 13); Fat 1g (Saturated 1g); Cholesterol 5mg; Sodium 426mg; Carbohydrate 14g (Dietary Fiber 2g); Protein 6g.*

How to Seed a Cucumber

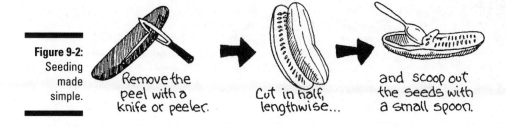

Figure 9-2: Seeding made simple.

Remove the peel with a knife or peeler.

Cut in half, lengthwise...

and scoop out the seeds with a small spoon.

Transforming Condensed Soup into Can-Do Cuisine

A hungry clan leads me to the wonders of canned soup. Yes, I admit it. I like canned condensed soups. Few other products have the same versatility. Condensed soup is concentrated. Serve it straight from the can, and it's a sauce. Add a base, such as milk or water, and it's a soup. Condensed soup is also a flavor booster you can add to your favorite from-scratch soup recipes. I recommend adding canned condensed soup to your dinner repertoire.

If you hated these soups and the recipes that they conjure up from your childhood (shame on you!), don't worry. Canned, condensed soups have improved over past versions. Manufacturers frequently upgrade their formulations. For example, canned cheese soup comes in nacho flavor; mushroom soup uses classy wild mushrooms.

Use canned condensed soup as a fast alternative to making a white sauce base. Then add vegetables and poultry or meat to round out the dish. Most canned condensed soups contain a starch or taste starchy enough without adding rice or pasta. Check out the following uncanny recipes (I couldn't resist that one) to get the hang of these makeovers.

Keeping two canned condensed soups on hand covers most emergencies: Keep a canned cream soup, such as mushroom, celery, or chicken, and a tomato or tomato bisque (which is a chunky tomato soup) in your pantry for when you really need it.

Demonstrating the power of dairy

You can use dairy products to enhance a variety soups. Just follow these guidelines:

✔ **Milk:** Use whole milk in chowders, cheese soups, or cream soups, such as cream of celery soup. Combine milk, not water, with condensed canned cream soups for a creamier taste.

✔ **Half-and-half:** When a recipe calls for milk, substitute half-and-half (which is half cream and half milk) for half the milk. The resulting taste is rich and smooth.

✔ **Heavy cream:** Use this product sparingly when you want a rich finish to a soup. For example, add a couple tablespoons of heavy cream to a soup made with mussels or a cheese chowder.

Cream of Celery, Mushroom, and Chicken Soup

Buy raw chicken breast strips for stir-fry or cubed chicken, so you don't have to cut up the chicken. Using sliced mushrooms also eliminates a cooking step. Heat a package of frozen broccoli or asparagus spears to serve with the soup.

Preparation time: *5 minutes*

Cooking time: *15 minutes*

Yield: *4 servings*

2 tablespoons unsalted butter

1 pound boneless chicken breast, cut into bite-size strips or chunks

1 medium onion, diced

1 package (4 ounces) sliced wild mushrooms (3 cups sliced)

2 cans (10¾ ounces each) condensed cream of celery soup

¼ teaspoon crushed, dried thyme

1 Melt the butter in a medium-size pot. Add the chicken breast and onion and cook over medium-high heat 3 minutes or until the pieces turn white. Add the mushrooms and sauté 5 minutes or until they give off liquid.

2 Stir in the soup and mix well. Add 2 soup cans of water and the thyme. Simmer the soup 5 minutes or until it's hot.

Vary It! *Add 2 cans of milk instead of water for a creamier soup.*

Per serving: *Calories 297 (From Fat 137); Fat 15g (Saturated 6g); Cholesterol 95mg; Sodium 1,211mg; Carbohydrate 14g (Dietary Fiber 2g); Protein 26g.*

Substitute your favorite cream soup for the celery soup in the Cream of Celery, Mushroom, and Chicken Soup recipe in this chapter. Nacho cheese soup with its velvety smooth texture and steamy taste is a welcome antidote to winter's blast and is delicious with the mushrooms. Cream of asparagus soup is another natural. Substitute 3 cups of steamed, chopped asparagus for the mushrooms. Enhance the soup's richness by using milk in place of water.

Nacho Cheese and Sausage Soup

The same ingredients — sausage, cheese, and chiles — that make nachos so appetizing, make this soup delicious, too. I like to serve low-fat baked tortillas for crumbling into the soup.

Preparation time: *5 minutes*

Cooking time: *10 minutes*

Yield: *4 servings*

1 pound bulk pork sausage

1 small onion, chopped

1 can (11 ounces) condensed nacho cheese soup

1 can (14½ ounces) diced tomatoes with roasted garlic and onion

2 tablespoons minced cilantro (optional)

1 Take sausage out of the wrapper and place the sausage in a 3- to 4-quart pot. Break the meat into small pieces, using a wooden spoon. Add the onion. Cook over medium-high heat, stirring frequently, for 5 minutes or until all the sausage is browned. Pour off any accumulated fat.

2 Add the nacho cheese soup to the pot. Add 1 soup can of water and stir well. Add the canned tomatoes with the liquid and simmer 5 minutes or until the soup is hot. Stir in cilantro (if desired).

Vary It! *Substitute sage-flavored or hot pork sausage if you prefer. If you really appreciate a soup with bite, try chorizo, a zesty Mexican sausage that you'll find in many supermarkets.*

Note: *This is a soup that you can freeze for later enjoyment, too. You can pour leftover soup into single-serve plastic containers. Add a piece of freezer tape to the lid and mark it with the name of the dish and the date you freeze it. Store the soup in the freezer up to one month. Thaw the soup in the refrigerator overnight before you reheat it.*

Per serving: *Calories 354 (From Fat 241); Fat 27g (Saturated 10g); Cholesterol 51mg; Sodium 1,473mg; Carbohydrate 16g (Dietary Fiber 2g); Protein 13g.*

Tomato, Zucchini, and Shrimp Bisque

This dish has such a heady aroma of basil and scallions that you'd never know it starts with canned soup. Fresh herbs make a significant improvement in the color and flavor of this soup, so I don't recommend using dried basil as an alternative. Add bread sticks and a glass of wine for a feast.

Preparation time: *2 minutes*

Cooking time: *15 minutes*

Yield: *4 to 6 servings*

1 tablespoon olive oil	*¼ cup chopped fresh basil*
2 small zucchini, trimmed, and diced	*¼ cup chopped scallions*
2 cans (11 ounces each) condensed tomato bisque	*¼ teaspoon pepper*
2 packages (8 ounces each) individually frozen, cooked, peeled medium-size shrimp	

1 Heat the olive oil in a 4- to 5-quart pot. Add the zucchini and sauté over high heat 3 to 4 minutes or until golden, stirring occasionally. Add both cans of tomato bisque and 2 soup cans of water. Bring the soup almost to the boil, but do not boil.

2 Add both packages of shrimp. It isn't necessary to thaw the shrimp first. Add the basil, scallions, and pepper and simmer 5 minutes or until the soup is hot.

Per serving: Calories 202 (From Fat 47); Fat 5g (Saturated 1g); Cholesterol 152mg; Sodium 1,020mg; Carbohydrate 21g (Dietary Fiber 2g); Protein 18g.

Chapter 10

Salad Selections

Salads are like the get-out-of-jail card in the Monopoly game. Passing the stove and going right to the table makes you a winner in the dinner-hour game. Stocking a selection of fresh vegetables, bits of leftover meat, poultry, or seafood that you can add to your salad means that you have a filling meal without spending much time preparing it. In this chapter, you can discover how easy it is to combine a handful of vegetables with some dinner leftovers or eggs and cheese to create a salad meal.

But speed isn't the only reason to make a meal of salad. Nutrition is another great incentive. Sneaking more vegetables into the dinner menu is a time-honored tradition among moms, dads, and other health-minded folk, and salads offer the perfect opportunity to eat healthy. Some people would rather wash dishes for a month than eat a serving of cooked spinach, but hiding those greens in a coating of dressing with a sprinkling of croutons and grated cheese will have them picking the last scrap from the salad bowl. And during the summer when you don't want to heat up the kitchen, salads are the healthful, cool, and refreshing alternative to a hot meal.

In this chapter, I present a number of leafy meal recipes and suggestions. I also provide you with hints, tips, and tricks for dealing with dressings — homemade and bottled. And who says salads have to be green? So I show you how to use cupboard ingredients, such as bread, beans, pasta, and whole grains, as the base for robust salad recipes.

Breaking the Ice

I'm a big fan of gourmet greens (which I discuss in Chapter 5, where you can also find a ton of tips about incorporating other veggies into your 30-minute meals). They're a great way to really jazz up both the taste and presentation of salads. However, I'm definitely not an iceberg-disparaging snob. In fact, when you're talking about salads, I think that you have to start with the old standby. A head of iceberg lettuce is the ideal building block for a super-size salad.

Iceberg lettuce has several qualities that make it a good salad ingredient:

✔ **Long-lasting:** Store iceberg lettuce in the crisper department of your refrigerator for a week or more.

✔ **Economical:** A head of lettuce sells for about a dollar in season and serves 4 to 6 in an entree salad.

✔ **Mild-tasting:** It goes with any kind of dressing, vegetable, or meat you want to add.

✔ **Low-cal:** Iceberg lettuce has a high-water content and few calories. Each leaf has 3 calories, which is about as low as you can limbo.

✔ **Bulk:** Iceberg lettuce bulks up a salad. When you want a little bit of greenery to go a long way, choose iceberg lettuce.

Check out Figure 10-1 for a step-by-step guide to shredding iceberg lettuce. The cut edges of lettuce brown quickly, so perform this part of the salad-making process just before assembling the salad.

Consider the following factors the next time that you shop for iceberg lettuce:

✔ Choose heads that are green with firm, crisp-textured leaves.

✔ Avoid lettuce heads with dark green limp leaves. These are past their prime.

✔ When you're paying by the head and not the pound, select large heads. However, don't pick the heaviest heads for their size. These heavy heads have small, compact leaves that may wither sooner.

✔ If possible, buy lettuce that isn't prepackaged, so you see what you're getting.

Check the label when you buy lettuce and other salad greens in packages. If the label says *prewashed,* you don't have to wash the greens again at home.

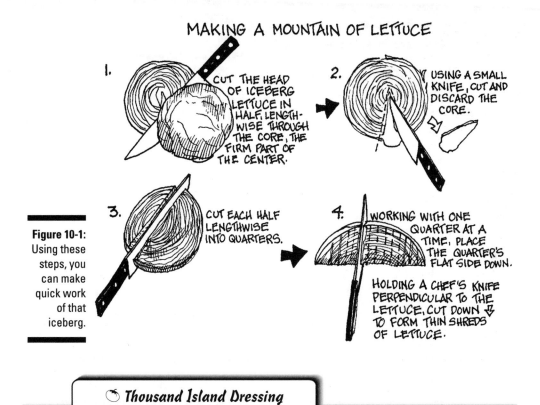

MAKING A MOUNTAIN OF LETTUCE

1. CUT THE HEAD OF ICEBERG LETTUCE IN HALF, LENGTH-WISE THROUGH THE CORE, THE FIRM PART OF THE CENTER.

2. USING A SMALL KNIFE, CUT AND DISCARD THE CORE.

3. CUT EACH HALF LENGTHWISE INTO QUARTERS.

4. WORKING WITH ONE QUARTER AT A TIME, PLACE THE QUARTER'S FLAT SIDE DOWN.

HOLDING A CHEF'S KNIFE PERPENDICULAR TO THE LETTUCE, CUT DOWN TO FORM THIN SHREDS OF LETTUCE.

Figure 10-1: Using these steps, you can make quick work of that iceberg.

❍ Thousand Island Dressing

Use Thousand Island dressing with iceberg lettuce or as a change from plain mayonnaise on a sandwich. Leftover dressing will keep if covered in the refrigerator for a few days.

Preparation time: *5 minutes*

Yield: *1½ cups; about 6 servings*

1 cup commercially prepared mayonnaise	2 tablespoons minced, fresh chives
¼ cup bottled chili sauce	1 teaspoon fresh lemon juice
2 tablespoons sweet pickle relish	¼ teaspoon pepper

Place the mayonnaise in a small bowl. Stir in the chili sauce, pickle relish, chives, lemon juice, salt, and pepper.

Vary It! *Add a dash of hot red pepper sauce to give the dressing a little zing.*

Per serving: *Calories 285 (From Fat 263); Fat 29g (Saturated 4g); Cholesterol 22mg; Sodium 571mg; Carbohydrate 6g (Dietary Fiber 0g); Protein 1g.*

Mountain of Lettuce Special

Serve this heaping platter of iceberg lettuce, meat, and cheeses with a pitcher of lemonade and breadsticks for a quick lunch or light dinner.

Preparation time: *10 minutes*

Yield: *4 servings*

1 head iceberg lettuce

2 hard-cooked eggs, peeled and quartered

2 plum tomatoes, cored and quartered

½ pound ham, cut into thin strips, or ¼ pound ham and ¼ pound roasted, sliced chicken breast, cut into thin strips

8 ounces sliced Swiss cheese, cut into thin strips

Thousand Island Dressing (see recipe in this chapter)

1 Cut the head of lettuce lengthwise in half. Remove the core; then cut the lettuce into quarters and shred as shown in Figure 10-1. Mound the lettuce on a serving platter.

2 Arrange the egg quarters on the platter at the base of the salad, alternating with the tomato wedges. Place the ham strips vertically across the mount of lettuce; then cross the ham with horizontal cheese strips.

3 Drizzle enough Thousand Island dressing over the salad to give it a strong, pink color. Then pass the remaining dressing separately.

Vary It! *Don't be tempted to turn this into a fancy salad but add pitted ripe olives if you like.*

Speed It Up! *Use the bottled version of Thousand Island Dressing. To perk up the flavor and make bottled taste more like fresh, pour ¼ cup of dressing into a bowl and add a dash of lemon juice. If you have a scallion in the fridge, chop it up and add it to the dressing as well.*

Per serving: *Calories 620 (From Fat 451); Fat 50g (Saturated 16g); Cholesterol 207mg; Sodium 1,510mg; Carbohydrate 14g (Dietary Fiber 3g); Protein 32g.*

Developing a sense of good taste

I quickly developed an appetite for salad when I started my first job out of college. Once a week, I celebrated my meager paycheck with an awesome salad — the *Field's Special* at Marshall Field's in Chicago — roast turkey slices spread over a half-head of iceberg lettuce, smothered in Thousand Island dressing and topped with tomato and egg wedges. Heads turned as the waitress brought it to my table. Serve a version of the Field's Special (may I suggest my Mountain of Lettuce Special in this chapter) during the summer when you want a meal that's both cooling and filling.

Turning fresh bread stale in seconds

Most salads that list bread as an ingredient call for stale bread, but you don't need stale bread if you toast it instead:

1. Rub a half garlic clove on 1-inch thick bread slices.

2. Place the bread on a cookie sheet and place in a preheated broiler 4 inches from the heat source until the bread browns, about 30 seconds per side.

If you're planning an outdoor grill menu and the grill is hot, place the bread directly on the grill rack and toast it for 1 to 2 minutes per side, depending on the grill heat.

Leafing through Two International Favorites

The French usually prefer salad with a meal, not in place of one. But they make an exception for an attractively composed salad of vegetables and tuna. If you think canned tuna isn't for company, read on. And while I'm on the subject of international salads, I've included one with Mexican roots, the Caesar Salad.

Saluting the French

Salade Niçoise (sal-*ahd* nees-*waz*), a pretty arrangement of potatoes, green beans, tuna, tomatoes, olives, and onions, hails from the city of Nice on the French Riviera. The French point to it as proof that not all their dishes are cream-coated.

Making a Salade Niçoise is almost as tantalizing as that fantasy of escaping to the French countryside. One bite, and you can almost feel the Mediterranean breezes. This assortment of textures and flavor is second to none for delivering summer's garden colors to the dinner table. My staple Niçoise recipe takes a few tasty liberties with the original:

 ✔ **Substituting canned salmon for the tuna:** For great looks and outstanding nutrition, canned salmon has a lovely coral color that brightens a salad. The small soft bones in the salmon are packed with calcium, a mineral that your body needs to strengthen your bones.

✔ **Substituting Boston or Bibb lettuce for romaine lettuce:** Lining the platter with these lettuces makes your salad more substantial and attractive. Both have their strong points:

- **Boston lettuce** has delicate, light green leaves about the size of a woman's hand. The lettuce tastes sweet and mild. A head of Boston lettuce lines 2 to 4 dinner plates.

- **Bibb lettuce** is similar to Boston, but it's about the size of a baseball and even more delicately textured. A head of Bibb lettuce covers 1 or 2 plates.

Salmon Salade Niçoise

If you prefer to use tuna in this salad, choose oil-packed tuna, which tastes more like the tuna in Nice.

Preparation time: *10 minutes*

Cooking time: *15 to 20 minutes*

Yield: *2 servings*

8 small red potatoes, scrubbed with the skins on	¼ teaspoon salt
½ teaspoon salt	¼ teaspoon pepper
1 cup green beans, trimmed	1 small shallot, minced
1 head Boston, or 2 heads Bibb lettuce	2 hard-cooked eggs, peeled and quartered
¼ cup olive oil	1 cup grape tomatoes, halved lengthwise
1 teaspoon Dijon-style mustard	1 can (8 ounces) salmon
1 tablespoon white wine vinegar	¼ cup Niçoise olives

1 Place the potatoes in a small pan with the ½ teaspoon of salt. Bring the water to a boil, and cook the potatoes at high heat for 10 minutes or until almost tender.

2 Meanwhile, cut the green beans into 1-inch lengths. Add the green beans to the potatoes and cook another 5 minutes or until the potatoes are tender and the green beans are crisp-tender. Drain the vegetables well.

3 While the potatoes are cooking, separate the lettuce into individual leaves, rinse under cold running water, and pat dry.

4 Also prepare the dressing while the potatoes cook. Whisk together the olive oil, mustard, vinegar, ¼ teaspoon each salt and pepper in a cup or small bowl. Stir in the shallot.

5 Arrange the lettuce leaves on 2 serving plates. Cut the potatoes into quarters. Place half the potatoes on each of the two plates in a wedge to take up one quarter of the plate. Place half the green beans on each plate taking up a second quarter. Then add the egg pieces to each plate for a third quarter. The tomatoes take the last quarter. Spoon half the salmon in the center of each plate, over the vegetables and eggs. Sprinkle half the Niçoise olives over each serving.

6 Pour the dressing over each salad or pass separately.

Vary It! Substitute cooked, leftover salmon or tuna steak for the canned salmon. A half to one cup of fresh salmon or tuna makes one serving.

Per serving: Calories 341 (From Fat 201); Fat 22g (Saturated 4g); Cholesterol 135mg; Sodium 782mg; Carbohydrate 22g (Dietary Fiber 3g); Protein 15g.

Hailing Caesar

Caesar salad is so yummy, elegant, and quick, I recommend including it in your salad repertoire. (See the sidebar, "As American as apple pie," in this chapter, for more on the origins of this tempting salad.) Traditional Caesar salad uses the long, crisp, sweet leaves of romaine lettuce.

Coddled eggs, a standard ingredient in Caesar salads, are cooked for a shorter time than the usual hard cooked eggs, so the yolk remains slightly runny. The contrast of the creamy egg yolk and crisp romaine lettuce leaves is what makes Caesar salad so delicious. Unfortunately, coddling, which calls for gently boiling an egg for 2 minutes, doesn't assure that harmful bacteria, such as salmonella, are killed. The Caesar recipe in this chapter, though, uses a safe alternative.

For a dramatic look, use whole uncut leaves in a Caesar salad. The finest Caesar salads exclude the outer leaves of a head of romaine lettuce and go right to the heart to find the smaller, more delicate leaves. Check out Figure 10-2 for a step-by-step guide.

The naturally darker the lettuce leaves, the more vitamins that the vegetable has. Romaine lettuce, with its long leaves, distinctive thick rib, and bright green color has about 10 times the vitamin A and twice the folate of iceberg lettuce. Eating foods high in folate may reduce your risk of heart disease.

Caesar Salad

If you prefer to use the whole romaine lettuce leaves, buy 1 large or 2 medium heads for this recipe; if you use only the hearts, buy 4 heads. Last night's grilled chicken breast or leftover steak can enhance this dinner salad. Cut the chicken or meat into thin strips and arrange over the salad after it's dressed. Caesar is an excellent first course for a dinner party, or you can serve it as a side dish or a light entree.

Preparation time: *15 minutes*

Cooking time: *4 minutes*

Yield: *4 servings*

1 egg	*¼ cup grated Parmesan cheese*
2 tablespoons water, milk, or chicken broth	*1 tablespoon white wine vinegar*
1 garlic clove	*5 tablespoons extra-virgin olive oil*
½ teaspoon Worcestershire sauce	*½ teaspoon pepper*
1 tablespoon anchovy paste, or 3 anchovies, finely minced	*6 cups romaine lettuce leaves, whole or torn*
	1 cup salad croutons

1 To provide a safe alternative to a coddled egg (a Caesar standard), beat the egg and combine it with water in a small, heavy pan. Cook the mixture over low heat, stirring constantly with a spoon for about 4 minutes or until the egg thickens into a foamy mass and coats a metal spoon with a thin egg layer.

2 Remove the egg from the pot and place it in a blender with the garlic clove, Worcestershire sauce, anchovy paste, 1 tablespoon of Parmesan cheese, vinegar, oil, and pepper. Turn the blender on and process about 30 seconds or until the mixture is creamy.

3 Place the lettuce leaves in a large serving bowl and toss with the croutons. Pour on the dressing and toss gently but well. Sprinkle the remaining 3 tablespoons of Parmesan cheese over the salad.

Per serving: Calories 240 (From Fat 183); Fat 20g (Saturated 4g); Cholesterol 59mg; Sodium 720mg; Carbohydrate 9g (Dietary Fiber 2g); Protein 7g.

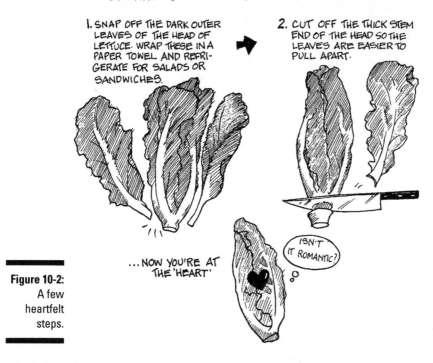

GETTING TO THE HEART OF ROMAINE LETTUCE

1. SNAP OFF THE DARK OUTER LEAVES OF THE HEAD OF LETTUCE. WRAP THESE IN A PAPER TOWEL AND REFRIGERATE FOR SALADS OR SANDWICHES.

2. CUT OFF THE THICK STEM END OF THE HEAD SO THE LEAVES ARE EASIER TO PULL APART.

...NOW YOU'RE AT THE 'HEART'

ISN'T IT ROMANTIC?

Figure 10-2:
A few
heartfelt
steps.

The Well-Dressed Salad

If a salad were complete in itself, it wouldn't have a need for dressing. Dressing adds spark and fire to any salad. It's the perfect tie with the suit — the right scarf with a dress.

And don't think manufacturers haven't figured out how important salad dressing is. Supermarket salad dressing sales come to more than a billion dollars a year, according to food industry statistics. Yes, that's *billion* with a *B*. Rows and rows of dressing vie for your attention in both the supermarket produce section and in the aisles with staples.

Starting with the classics, such as French and Italian, new flavors, including balsamic vinegar, roasted garlic, Parmesan vinaigrette, and toasted sesame, beckon. For those times when you opt for bottled convenience, see the "Adding Pizzazz to Bottled Dressings" section, later in this chapter.

But you don't have to walk the supermarket aisles to find the right dressing for your salad. With all the convenience products available, you may think that making your own dressing isn't worth the expenditure of your time and energy, but let me describe the advantages:

- ✔ Homemade dressings don't contain additives, preservatives, or artificial colors. You make salad dressing fresh each time you use it.

- ✔ Homemade dressings let you use healthy olive oil or canola oil — not cheap oil that the producer chooses.

- ✔ You can fine-tune the seasonings. Add a dash of curry powder, cayenne pepper, ginger, or horseradish for a dressing with a unique flavor.

- ✔ Making your own salad dressing is almost as fast as opening a bottle.

Mixing oil and vinegar

All salad dressings are a mixture of an oil or other form of fat (such as sour cream) and an acid. The oil or fat coats the vegetables and the acid gives the dressing a balance of tastes. A dressing can be a simple mixture of olive oil and vinegar (or lemon juice), as you find in several of the recipes in this chapter. As long as you have a bottle of oil and vinegar in the cupboard, you don't have to juggle bottles of store-bought dressings.

Whisking together 1 part lemon juice or vinegar to 5 parts olive oil gives you a dressing that's mild and suitable for delicate-tasting greens. To make the dressing stronger, increase the proportions to 1 part lemon juice to 4 parts olive oil for most salads or choose the blend that suits your taste buds (but start with the 1 to 4 formula before you experiment further). Oil and vinegar is a great start, but how about honing your skills as a salad virtuoso. Let loose with the seasonings:

- ✔ **Add mustard to spice up salad dressing.** Mustard acts as an *emulsifier,* a substance that helps other ingredients, such as case oil and vinegar in this case, stay blended. Not only does it improve the mix, but it enhances the flavor as well.

- ✔ **Add herbs.** Fresh tarragon gives salad dressing a slight licorice taste. Rosemary is a woodsy flavoring. When you add fresh herbs to a dressing, only make enough for one meal. The herbs spoil quickly.

- ✔ **Add spices.** Curry powder and ginger are two hot-sweet seasonings that give dressing a lively taste. And if you want your taste buds to shout, add a pinch of cayenne pepper . . . but not too much or your guests will scream, and that isn't pleasant.

⏍ Mint Vinaigrette Dressing

A salad side should refresh your palate. Using this mint and citrus juice combination will leave you breathless. The combination of mint, lemon, and orange juice is especially good with spinach, onions, and radishes or with a chicken or tuna salad.

Preparation time: *10 minutes*

Yield: *about 1 cup; 8 servings*

1 teaspoon fresh lemon juice

2 tablespoons fresh orange juice

½ cup coarsely chopped mint, preferably spearmint

½ cup olive oil

2 tablespoons white balsamic vinegar, or white wine vinegar mixed with ¼ teaspoon sugar

½ teaspoon salt

¼ teaspoon pepper

Combine the lemon juice, orange juice, mint, olive oil, vinegar, salt, and pepper in a blender. Blend the ingredients until the mint is minced and the mixture is well combined.

Per serving: *Calories 127 (From Fat 122); Fat 14g (Saturated 2g); Cholesterol 0mg; Sodium 148mg; Carbohydrate 2g (Dietary Fiber 0g); Protein 0g.*

Balsamic vinegar, a great vinegar to use in salad dressings, is a barrel-aged vinegar from Italy. It has a slightly sweet flavor that comes from the wood barrels. Most balsamic vinegar is red, but white balsamic vinegar has a lighter flavor and is also available in many supermarkets. If you can't find balsamic vinegar, add ¼ teaspoon sugar for every tablespoon of vinegar that a recipe calls for.

Dressing up with dairy

Don't limit dressings to oil and vinegar. Buttermilk, yogurt, sour cream, and whipping cream make rich and luscious dressings. A hefty Chef salad topped with buttermilk dressing is a refreshing combination.

If you're watching your weight, choose low-fat buttermilk and fat-free yogurt and sour cream for that thick consistency that fools your taste buds, so you're satisfied with fewer calories.

⏱ Buttermilk-Garlic Salad Dressing

The tangy, dairy taste of buttermilk is wonderful on potato salad, green bean salad, or on a bed of mixed greens.

Preparation time: *10 minutes*

Yield: *about 1 cup; 8 servings*

¼ cup fat-free plain yogurt

⅔ cup reduced-fat buttermilk

2 tablespoons reduced-fat mayonnaise

½ teaspoon Dijon-style mustard

1 small garlic clove, minced

2 tablespoons minced scallions

¼ teaspoon pepper

Combine yogurt, buttermilk, mayonnaise, mustard, garlic, scallions, and pepper in a bowl, and stir.

Per serving: *Calories 27 (From Fat 14); Fat 2g (Saturated 0g); Cholesterol 3mg; Sodium 65mg; Carbohydrate 2g (Dietary Fiber 0g); Protein 1g.*

Adding pizzazz to bottled dressings

Bottled dressings are as essential as canned chicken broth when you're pressed for time, but you can still quickly add fresh ingredients for that little something extra. Adding fresh herbs, spices, cheese, mustard, and soy sauce are some of the ways to freshen the taste of bottled dressings. See the list that follows for the details:

- ✔ Stir 1 tablespoon of capers into a half-cup of vinaigrette dressing.

- ✔ Mix 1 teaspoon of Dijon mustard into a half-cup of vinaigrette dressing.

- ✔ Crumble 2 tablespoons of Stilton or Roquefort cheese into a half cup of blue cheese or buttermilk dressing.

- ✔ Finely chop 1 scallion and mix into a half cup of ranch dressing.

- ✔ Blend 1 tablespoon pickle relish and ¼ teaspoon crushed red pepper flakes into a half cup of Thousand Island dressing.

- ✔ Add 1 tablespoon of soy sauce to 1 cup of balsamic vinegar dressing.

- ✔ Combine ½ cup mayonnaise, ¼ cup sour cream, and 1 tablespoon white horseradish in place of plain mayonnaise for potato salad.

✔ Add ¼ teaspoon of curry powder to ½ cup of a sweet and sour dressing, such as the orange-colored French dressing.

✔ Stir 1 finely chopped shallot into 1 cup of vinaigrette or balsamic vinaigrette dressing.

✔ Blend 1 tablespoon of fresh chives and 1 teaspoon minced fresh dill into a creamy garlic dressing.

As American as apple pie

Entree salads — humongous bowls of lettuce, meats, cheese, and vegetables — are an all-American institution. Most American restaurants list Chefs salad, Cobb salad, and Green Goddess salad (to name a few) on their menus. Many of these grand and glorious salads have their roots in the United States, but even when they've originated elsewhere, American menus have come to call them their own. Make these your house specials as well, or improve, changing the ingredients to your taste. Who knows, maybe you'll have a salad named after you.

✔ **Blackhawk Spinning Salad Bowl:** It got its start at the former Celebrity restaurant in Chicago; this fresh feast is a combination of romaine and iceberg lettuce, spinach, beets, hard-cooked eggs, tomatoes, and croutons. The cook gives the salad bowl a twirl and slowly pours in dressing while the bowl is spinning.

✔ **Caesar:** A treat that hails from Tijuana, Mexico, it bears the name of its creator, Chef Caesar Cardini, who originally put together this happy mix of romaine lettuce, croutons, anchovies, grated Parmesan cheese, and coddled egg. Garlic, Worcestershire, lemon juice, and olive oil are the ingredients in the traditional dressing. Restaurants often top Caesar salads with strips of grilled chicken or turkey, but that's not in the original recipe.

✔ **Chef:** Tossed greens, usually iceberg lettuce, are topped with strips of ham (often chicken as well), cheddar and/or Swiss cheese strips, and hard-cooked egg slices. It's served with the salad dressing of your choice.

✔ **Green Goddess:** During the summer when you don't want to heat up the kitchen, salads are the cool and refreshing alternative to a hot meal. The chef of the Palace Hotel honored *The Green Goddess,* a play that opened in San Francisco in the 1920s, with his creation of lettuce, artichoke bottoms, shrimp (sometimes chicken or crab), and tomatoes. The green dressing is the real star of this dish. Green goddess dressing is a blend of mayonnaise, anchovies, parsley, chives, scallions, garlic, and vinegar.

✔ **Waldorf:** At New York's Waldorf-Astoria Hotel in the late 1800s, Chef Oscar Tschirky made a hit with diced apples, celery, walnuts, and grapes mixed with mayonnaise. Some contemporary versions add diced chicken for a main-course salad.

Exchanging Greens for Grains

Greens aren't the only ingredients that make salad a meal. Dressing cooked spaghetti, rice, bulgur, toasted couscous, or even stale bread, transforms the ordinary grain into a marvelous salad. In fact, whenever you have bits of left-over grains from dinner, you've got the base for a salad that takes almost no preparation time. Vegetables are essential to nonlettuce salads, too, but keep reading to discover the wonderful textures of grain-based salads.

Grain salads are a nice change of pace, and they're durable. You know how easily a lettuce salad wilts. You wouldn't pack a Bibb lettuce salad for a potluck, but no such limitations prevent you from making grain salads. When you want to make a salad in advance, make it grains. The flavors actually improve on standing as the grains soak in the dressing and seasonings.

Although I'm usually not a rigid cook, I have some strong opinions about using grains in salads. I'm a big fan of grains, if they're used appropriately. Check out some general tips based on my experience.

✔ **Type:** Select a chunky pasta, such as the tube-shaped penne or farfalle (see Chapter 3), for a hearty, rustic salad, say one with chunks of salami, artichoke hearts, and olives. Use the rice-shaped orzo (see Chapter 3) for a refined salad, such as one with goat cheese, diced tomatoes, and basil.

✔ **Temperature:** Pour dressing on warm or room-temperature grains, so the flavors are absorbed. And serve a grain salad lukewarm or at room temperature but not chilled. Cold rice doesn't taste good. Cold pasta is no better. If you wouldn't eat plain cold pasta, don't eat it as a salad. Besides, grains, such as rice and pasta, get unpleasantly hard when they're cold.

✔ **Presentation:** Choose a selection of vegetables and herbs that add color to a grain salad. Brown and beige salads went out in the '60s.

✔ **Texture:** You want to retain some of the grain's chewy texture so don't overcook grains for salad. That's part of what makes a grain salad so delicious.

Most people overlook several grains when they think of salads. But you can change an old favorite — a basic pasta salad — according to the ingredients that you have on hand. Be sure to use fresh herbs to enliven the salad with flavor and color.

○ *Garden Pasta Salad*

It used to bother me that beets would bleed their red color into other ingredients that they touch, and I omitted beets from my salads for a long time. How much I missed the sweet taste. Now I accept the running colors as a trade-off. You can sprinkle diced beets on top of a salad just before serving to keep the other ingredients from discoloring. I like penne in this salad, but if you have other cooked pasta in the fridge use it instead.

Preparation time: *10 minutes*

Yield: *4 servings*

½ cup chopped Greek olives	*4 ounces (1 cup) crumbled goat cheese*
6 cups cooked penne, or similar pasta	*¼ cup olive oil*
2 medium tomatoes, cored and chopped	*1 to 2 tablespoons lemon juice*
2 cups canned beets, diced	*Pepper to taste*
2 tablespoons chopped fresh oregano, or thyme, or a combination	

1 Combine the olives, pasta, tomatoes, beets, and oregano in a large bowl. Add the cheese.

2 In a cup, stir together the oil, lemon juice, and pepper and stir into salad mixture. Toss gently but well.

Per serving: *Calories 594 (From Fat 253); Fat 28g (Saturated 8g); Cholesterol 22mg; Sodium 581mg; Carbohydrate 68g (Dietary Fiber 5g); Protein 17g.*

Bulgur: The salad grain

Bulgur is also called *cracked wheat*. The chewy, meaty-tasting grain is wonderful in tabbouleh (tah-*boo*-leh), a popular salad or side dish in Middle Eastern countries. Each household knows "the best" way to make this salad. So I don't worry if mine isn't authentic. Try the recipe in this chapter and then make changes for the version that you like best. But don't omit the mint or scallions (which are key flavoring ingredients) when making this dish for the first time. Mint gives tabbouleh a delightful and refreshing taste. It's also a breath-cleanser for the scallions and onions in the recipe.

To cook bulgur, combine 1 cup of the grain with 2 cups water or broth and ¼ teaspoon salt. Bring to a boil, stir, reduce heat, and cover. Simmer 15 minutes or until tender. Scrape bulgur to fluff up. Makes 3 cups.

Tabbouleh is usually served as a salad or side dish, but I prefer to top the salad with cooked chicken strips or frozen, thawed cooked baby shrimp to make it a meal. My basic tabbouleh recipe is ready to top with chicken, fish, or shrimp.

℧ Tabbouleh

Years ago, I developed a passion for mint and planted it in patches around my garden. Peppermint, spearmint, and lemon-scented mint have taken over like weeds. But unlike most weeds, they're delicious in tabbouleh.

Preparation time: *10 minutes*

Yield: *4 servings*

3 cups cooked bulgur	*½ cup finely chopped scallions*
4 plum tomatoes, cored and diced	*¼ teaspoon salt*
1 small cucumber, peeled and diced	*½ teaspoon pepper*
½ cup chopped fresh mint leaves	*¼ cup olive oil*
½ cup chopped red onion (optional)	*3 tablespoons fresh lemon juice*

1 Combine the cooked bulgur, tomatoes, cucumber, mint, red onions (if desired), and scallions in a serving bowl.

2 In a cup stir together the salt, pepper, olive oil, and lemon juice. Pour the dressing into the bulgur mixture and toss well to coat.

Vary It! *Tabbouleh, being one of those sturdy grain salads, can stay in the refrigerator a day or two. Make an extra batch to serve with the elegant salmon recipe that follows.*

Per serving: *Calories 263 (From Fat 128); Fat 14g (Saturated 2g); Cholesterol 0mg; Sodium 164mg; Carbohydrate 32g (Dietary Fiber 8g); Protein 6g.*

Basil-Scented Salmon

This dish of salmon is unusual yet so flavorful; it's a hit when I serve it to company. It's especially good when you pair it with tabbouleh. If you're entertaining guests on a rushed schedule, reach for this recipe. Spread leftover tabbouleh on a platter and set the basil-scented salmon fillets at a diagonal over the grains.

Preparation time: *2 minutes*

Cooking time: *10 minutes*

Yield: *4 servings*

4 pieces (6 ounces each) salmon fillets

1 teaspoon salt

1 teaspoon pepper

1 cup basil leaves

2 tablespoons olive oil

5 cups prepared Tabbouleh (see recipe in this chapter)

1 Season the pink flesh side of each salmon fillet with ¼ teaspoon each of salt and pepper. Press the basil leaves onto the flesh side of the salmon fillets. Heat the olive oil in a large sauté pan over high heat. Carefully add the salmon, basil-side up and cook over medium-high heat about 10 minutes or until the fish is done.

2 Run a spatula or thin knife between the salmon fillets and the salmon skin and separate the two. Discard the salmon skins. Set the salmon aside for 1 minute for the fish to firm up.

3 To serve, spread the tabbouleh on a large platter. Arrange the salmon fillets diagonally over the tabbouleh. Serve immediately.

Vary It! *You can also serve the salmon without the tabbouleh. Add lemon wedges and a small, mixed green salad on the side.*

Per serving: *Calories 542 (From Fat 247); Fat 27g (Saturated 4g); Cholesterol 97mg; Sodium 871mg; Carbohydrate 33g (Dietary Fiber 9g); Protein 43g.*

Bread: It's not just for buttering

Thrifty Italian cooks use day-old bread in a salad with vegetables and herbs. You have to start with a thick, coarse-textured bread that you slice yourself, not sandwich bread. If your bakery or supermarket carries whole loaves of sourdough, French, or Italian bread, reserve half a loaf for *panzanella*, the Italian bread and tomato salad. My take on this dish combines two of my favorite foods, garlic bread and chicken salad.

Garlic Bread and Chicken Salad

Set this salad aside for 15 minutes if you're not pressed for time to allow the tomato juices, oil, and vinegar to thoroughly soak into the bread.

Preparation time: *10 minutes*

Yield: *4 servings*

6 large slices day-old French bread	*1 small red onion, finely chopped*
1 garlic clove, halved	*5 tablespoons olive oil*
¼ cup chopped fresh basil	*3 tablespoons red wine vinegar*
4 large ripe tomatoes, cored and chopped	*½ teaspoon salt*
2 cups diced, cooked chicken breast	*½ teaspoon pepper*

1 Rub the bread on both sides with garlic clove half. Cut each bread slice into 1-inch cubes.

2 Place the bread cubes in a serving bowl. Discard any remaining garlic. Add the basil, tomatoes, chicken breast, and red onion to the bread and toss well. Set aside while making the dressing.

3 Stir the oil, vinegar, salt, and pepper together in a cup. Pour the dressing over the salad and toss again. Let the salad stand for 3 to 5 minutes, so the bread absorbs the dressing.

Vary It! *Olives, goat cheese, feta cheese, and capers add a delightful piquant flavor to bread salad. Add any or all these ingredients in small amounts. But if you do, taste before adding salt.*

Per serving: *Calories 707 (From Fat 220); Fat 24g (Saturated 4g); Cholesterol 60mg; Sodium 1,233mg; Carbohydrate 85g (Dietary Fiber 7g); Protein 37g.*

Side Salads Gone Wild

My household dinner is complete if I say, "Don't forget to eat the salad." It's a long-standing joke, because my family loves salad. When salad isn't the complete meal, I often serve it as a side dish. You, too, can discover how quick and easy it is to use a salad to balance a meal with additional delicious flavors and textures.

If you're looking for a fast and easy side, look no further than the bag of lettuce in the fridge. In the time it takes to rip open a bag of greens and toss in a few grape tomatoes, you've got a nutritious and tasty addition to a meal.

And, if you don't have that bag of lettuce, it's no problem. Rummage through the refrigerator or even the cupboard, and you're sure to find fresh or canned ingredients for a salad. If you were to take a peek into my refrigerator, you'd find the following in the vegetable crisper:

- Broccoli florets
- Cucumber
- Green bell pepper
- Iceberg lettuce
- Radishes
- Red and/or green cabbage
- Red bell pepper
- Mixed baby greens
- Prewashed baby spinach leaves for salad

But that's not all, I don't know of any rule against using fruit in a savory salad, so I also stock apples, oranges, and grapes. With all these possibilities at my fingertips, I can always put a salad on the table.

This is where I share a recipe for one fabulous side-dish salad that uses readily available fruits and vegetables.

➲ *Orange and Radish Salad*

This salad tastes just as delicious if you substitute baby spinach leaves for the salad greens. Serve this salad with a simple chicken entree, such as the Chicken Breasts with Brandy and Mustard Sauce in Chapter 13.

Preparation time: *10 minutes*

Yield: *4 servings*

4 cups mixed salad greens

2 large seedless oranges, peeled and sliced horizontally ¼-inch thick

4 radishes, trimmed and sliced ⅛-inch thick

2 tablespoons orange juice

4 teaspoons red wine vinegar

2 teaspoons honey

1 tablespoon olive oil

¼ teaspoon salt

¼ teaspoon pepper

1 Arrange the salad greens on a serving platter. Top with the orange and radish slices.

2 Stir together the orange juice, vinegar, and honey in a cup, blending well to dissolve the honey. Add the olive oil, salt, and pepper. Drizzle the dressing over the vegetables and serve immediately, so the salad greens won't wilt.

Per serving: *Calories 88 (From Fat 32); Fat 4g (Saturated 1g); Cholesterol 0mg; Sodium 164mg; Carbohydrate 14g (Dietary Fiber 3g); Protein 2g.*

Chapter 11

Sandwich Entrees

Sandwiches are the ultimate convenience food. Layer fillings between two slices of bread or tuck your favorite foods into a pita bread pocket, and you have a meal. I love sandwiches. The contrast of a crusty slice of bread and creamy Brie cheese or chunky peanut butter is heavenly.

You don't have to pack the sandwich bread away after lunch. You're shortchanging yourself if you don't add sandwiches to your brunch, dinner, and even snack repertoire.

Leftovers are excellent in sandwiches, but don't let sandwiches become a dumping place for all the limp, tired food in your refrigerator. A mouthwatering sandwich is a masterpiece. The best-tasting sandwiches contrast textures — chewy bread and tender fillings — bring together colors — red tomatoes, green olives, and yellow bell peppers — and present lively flavors — the salty-sweet taste of ham or the tangy freshness of goat cheese.

In this chapter, I describe all the ingredients that you can use to make outstanding sandwiches. As you discover how many satisfying varieties of breads you can use, your sandwich enthusiasm builds. But fillings are just as important, and you may be surprised at the wide range of choices you have. While I don't overlook the basics, such as ham, chicken and beef, I suggest that you also include vegetables, cheeses, nut spreads, fruity chutneys, and even sliced fruit. Your sandwich can be a balanced meal, and I show you how to accomplish that.

And could a sandwich achieve greater glory than when it's a juicy, plump hamburger sitting on a bun? I suspect you're also a hamburger fan. Few people can resist the aroma, the look, or the taste of a well-made hamburger. I wrap this sandwich chapter up with my tips on making a hamburger fantasy a reality.

When the meal hour approaches and life gives you two slices of bread, celebrate. It's sandwich time.

Sandwiching in a Meal

Sandwiches are great for sit-down dinners, but they're also an unbeatable convenience when you're in a rush. In this section, I provide a few suggestions on letting sandwiches play their traditional role of a convenience meal in your life.

In the following list, I outline ways in which sandwiches can get you out of a jam, or into one if you're a fan of PB&J — that's peanut butter and jelly.

- ✔ **On the road.** Make sandwiches for in-the-car meals when you're going from one evening activity to another. You can make sandwiches that are healthier, less expensive, and less time-consuming than what you buy in a fast-food operation.

- ✔ **In the office.** Pack sandwiches for office lunches when you know you don't have time for a break. Instead of grabbing a candy bar from the office machine, you can have a satisfying lunch.

- ✔ **On the run.** If you skip breakfast, pack breakfast sandwiches the night before and grab a portable breakfast to eat as you run out the door. Cream cheese and jelly or peanut butter and jelly taste delicious in the a.m.

- ✔ **After school.** Keep sandwich ingredients available for after-school snacks. You don't have to worry about your children getting adequate nutrition when they have sandwiches to eat.

- ✔ **On deadline.** The meat didn't thaw as you anticipated, and the family is hungry. As long as you have bread and some staples, such as eggs, tuna, bacon, salad greens, and vegetables, you can whip up a fun and savory dinner. When I'm facing a dinner disaster, I don't broadcast it. I simply switch to sandwiches and no one complains.

PB&J

As sure as peanut butter sticks, you can bet it's one half of the filling that children often ask for in their sandwiches. Jelly is the natural partner to peanut butter. But who invented this unlikely combination of slippery and sticky or salty and sweet or fruity and nutty? Sorry, but I can't track down the name of the clever inventor.

I can tell you, however, that home cooks have been making some form of jelly for a long time. Peanut butter, invented in the late 1800s, was quite a sensation during the 1904 World's Fair in St. Louis — at least among fair goers who could open their mouths to talk about it — but it took a few more decades to meet up with jelly. Some

historians date the marriage of peanut butter and jelly to World War II. American soldiers included both ingredients in their rations and probably created the first PB&J sandwiches.

As any 6-year-old attests, eating peanut butter with jelly is a heck of a lot easier than eating plain peanut butter sandwiches. But peanut butter isn't the only nut butter that you can spread on bread. Look for cashew, almond, or hazelnut butter in gourmet food stores. If you or a loved one has an allergy to peanuts and tree nuts, then try soy butter. It has a flavor similar to peanut butter but without the allergen.

Sandwich with Style

The beauty of sandwiches is that you start with bread and filling, yet you can create so many variations on the same theme. You can make sandwiches using with one, two, or even three slices of bread. You can serve cold sandwiches or hot ones.

Classic sandwich recipes present a tempting glimpse of what you can do. In this part, I introduce you to some of the most popular sandwiches you can make. I hope they inspire you to use your imagination when putting together bread and fillings.

- ✔ **Club sandwich:** This dish is a cold sandwich of chicken, bacon, tomatoes, and iceberg lettuce layered between two or three slices of toasted bread, preferably sliced white bread, with mayonnaise. Cooks have their own arrangements of meat and vegetables, but as a general rule, you can start with mayonnaise-topped bread, tomato slices, bacon slices, another layer of the bread, chicken slices, lettuce slices, and end with the top layer of bread. Use toothpicks to keep the tower from toppling.

- **Croque Monsieur:** Give the French credit for making a grilled ham and cheese sandwich sound, and taste, like more than just a ham and cheese sandwich. A croque monsieur (croak mis-*uyr*) is often served as a snack or light lunch.

- **French dip sandwich:** This hot roast beef sandwich on a French baguette is served with pan juices. Dip the sandwich into the pan juices — which is known as *au jus* (aw *joo*) if you want to get fancy — as you take a bite. You can substitute roast beef from the deli for leftover, homemade pot roast. Buy a can or package of gravy mix for dipping.

- **Italian beef sandwiches:** A Chicago specialty, an Italian beef sandwich is thin slices of rump roast packed on a thick wedge of Italian bread and garnished with hot peppers.

- **Monte Cristo:** The Monte Cristo (*mon*-tee *kris*-toe) sandwich is similar to a Croque Monsieur. It's a combination of ham and cheese, dipped in an egg batter and sautéed in melted butter. It's usually sprinkled with confectioners' sugar and served with jam or a similar sweet dipping sauce. The Monte Cristo makes a delicious brunch sandwich or children's lunch.

- **Muffuletta:** A New Orleans prize sandwich, the muffeletta (muff-uh-*let*-uh) starts with a long piece of Italian bread. Then it's split open and filled with layers of cheese, salami, and ham. A zesty relish of chopped olives, garlic, herbs, olive oil, and vinegar covers the filling. Check out my Olive Relish recipe in the "Relishing the opportunity" section, later in the chapter.

- **Panini:** In Italian panini (pah-*nee*-nee) means small breads or the sandwiches you make from the breads. Panini is a generic term and doesn't refer to a specific filling. However, a panini sandwich is usually made with a flat roll and is grilled and heated in a sandwich press. Fontina cheese with a little prosciutto, an Italian salt-cured, air-dried ham, makes an incredibly delicious filling.

- **Philadelphia Cheese Steak:** A cheese steak sandwich combines thin strips of economical beef cuts, grilled and packed into long rolls. Cheese steaks are topped with cheddar or American cheese, sautéed onions, and bell peppers if you want to eat healthy.

- **Reuben:** This grilled sandwich made with corned beef, Swiss cheese, sauerkraut, and Russian dressing is a prized deli dish. Although some sources say you have to use rye bread for an authentic Reuben, I've only had pumpernickel, and have to say I like the contrast of dark brown pumpernickel with the light-colored cheese and sauerkraut.

- **Sloppy Joe:** This cousin to a hamburger features browned ground beef, tomato sauce, a hint of brown sugar, and vinegar for a sweet and sour flavor. To serve, spoon the meat sauce on a hot roll.

Is this a sandwich or a boat?

Heroes, hoagies, poor boys, grinders, torpedos, and *submarines* all refer to a sandwich consisting of a long roll split and filled with sliced deli meats, cheeses, tomatoes, lettuce, and often peppers, olives, and herbs. Some recipes call for a sprinkling of olive oil and maybe vinegar as well. There are regional, even local differences. For example, a New Orleans poor boy is filled with fried oysters or other fried seafood. If you ask for one in the Crescent City, call it a po' boy. As the names suggest, these are very robust sandwiches.

Bread Makes the Sandwich

Biting into a sandwich, bread makes the first impression. If the bread is too soft, too stale, or just bland, your sandwich isn't delivering as much eating pleasure as you should be getting. Thanks to bakeries' innovations, there's no excuse for a sandwich made from limp, tasteless bread. If you want your sandwich to stand out as a meal, using good, artisan bread or a specialty bread, such as pitas or tortillas, is the way to go. Keep reading for more on these great breads.

Finding flavor: Artisan breads

You may see displays for artisan breads in specialty bakeries or even your supermarket. *Artisan breads* are loaves produced in small batches, using little or no preservatives, colorings, or artificial flavorings (ask the baker or check the package for the specifics). The breads are coarse-textured and have a distinctive, chewy crust that comes from using brick ovens. Artisan bakers make their breads daily, which assures you of a fresh-tasting loaf.

You're likely to find a number of varieties, but the more common artisan breads are sourdough, French, Italian, and "country" styles — coarse white breads. Some supermarkets also feature flavored artisan breads, such as olive and rosemary bread or roasted garlic bread. These breads are even more tempting.

Because bread can go stale in a day or two, I suggest that you put aside enough for your sandwiches and then freeze the remainder. To freeze bread, wrap it in plastic wrap and then add a second layer of heavy-duty aluminum foil. Mark the date on the wrapping and freeze the bread up to 3 months. To use, thaw frozen bread in the refrigerator or on the counter. Then place the bread in a preheated 350-degree oven and heat it for 5 minutes to freshen the flavor and make the crust crisp again, or slice and toast the bread. Don't microwave artisan bread. Bread heated in a microwave oven is soft for about 10 minutes; then it gets hard and stale tasting.

However, if you should find yourself with a loaf or two of stale artisan bread, you can make use of it in five different ways:

✔ Tear the bread into chunks and dampen with water. Combine the bread pieces with chopped tomatoes, scallions, and basil. Add a vinaigrette dressing. Look in Chapter 10 for the recipe for Garlic Bread and Chicken Salad, using stale bread.

✔ Tear the bread into chunks and sprinkle on olive oil and a pinch of crushed, dried oregano. Toast the bread in a 350-degree oven for 5 minutes and use for salad croutons.

✔ Float a slice of bread on top of a bowl of chicken or onion soup. Add a tablespoon of grated Parmesan cheese to the bread if you like.

✔ Grind the bread in a food processor and use the crumbs to sprinkle over casseroles.

✔ Feed the birds. They deserve a great-tasting snack, too!

Don't clutch a bread loaf to your body to cut it. One slip of the knife and you can hurt yourself. Place the bread loaf on a bread board or nonslip cutting board and hold your hand around an end with one hand, curling your finger tips inward, so they don't accidentally get nipped. Using a serrated knife, make even bread slices, sawing down.

Wrapping up variety: Specialty breads

Pita bread, which is also called pocket bread, puffs up as it bakes. As a result, the bread forms a pocket when it's split open. How convenient! Filling the pocket with tuna or chicken salad or meat, vegetables, and cheese is mess-free and fun. Children love pita breads. As a parent, I share their enthusiasm, because I can sneak in vegetables and yogurt dressings that my family wouldn't eat in ordinary sandwiches. The combinations are endless! To assure you're getting pita breads that form pockets, read the package label. Some pita breads don't form pockets.

Flour tortillas are another way to wrap — literally — sandwich fillings. Using a flour tortilla, follow the four easy steps in Figure 11-1 to quickly wrap up dinner preparations.

Beef Wraps with Red Pepper Salad

Assemble these wraps and place them on a serving platter or offer wraps as a do-it-yourself dinner. Place the red pepper salad, beef, and flour tortillas on separate plates and let your family help themselves. You're getting vegetables, protein, and starch in a hand-held meal, but for more nourishment, serve homemade or deli coleslaw on the side.

Preparation time: *15 minutes*

Yield: *4 servings*

1 red bell pepper, cored, seeded, and diced

1 jalapeno chile, cored, seeded, and minced

½ cup finely chopped red onion

1 tablespoon capers

1 tablespoon olive oil

1 tablespoon white wine vinegar

¼ teaspoon pepper

12 ounces cooked, thinly sliced roast beef

4 flour tortillas, 8 inches in diameter

1 Combine the red pepper, chile, onion, capers, olive oil, wine vinegar, and pepper in a bowl and set aside for 5 minutes for flavors to blend.

2 Arrange 3 ounces of meat in the center of each flour tortilla. Spoon the red pepper salad in a strip down the center of each sandwich. Fold the sandwiches as shown in Figure 11-1. Serve with napkins; the wraps are juicy.

Vary It! *Substitute 12 ounces of smoked chicken for the roast beef. If desired, use leftover steak in these wraps. Also, try pita breads instead of flour tortillas or use flavored tortillas.*

Per serving: *Calories 251 (From Fat 82); Fat 9g (Saturated 3g); Cholesterol 41mg; Sodium 959mg; Carbohydrate 21g (Dietary Fiber 3g); Protein 23g.*

Add a couple of new wrinkles to a flour tortilla and turn it into a quesadilla (*kay*-suh-*dee*-uh) — a flour tortilla that's filled, folded, and fried. (See Figure 11-2.) Quesadillas serve as snacks or light brunch or dinner entrees. Cheese quesadillas are incredibly delicious. The cheese melts to a rich, chewy mass as it cooks.

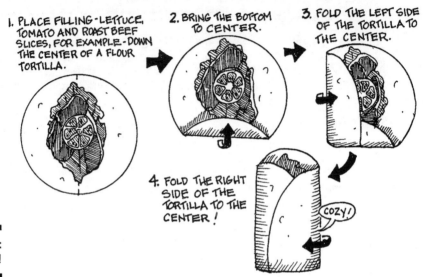

WRAPPING FILLINGS IN TORTILLAS

1. PLACE FILLING - LETTUCE, TOMATO AND ROAST BEEF SLICES, FOR EXAMPLE - DOWN THE CENTER OF A FLOUR TORTILLA.

2. BRING THE BOTTOM TO CENTER.

3. FOLD THE LEFT SIDE OF THE TORTILLA TO THE CENTER.

4. FOLD THE RIGHT SIDE OF THE TORTILLA TO THE CENTER !

COZY!

Figure 11-1:
It's a wrap!

☺ *Cheese Quesadillas with Maple-Flavored Sautéed Apples*

This luscious alternative to a grilled cheese sandwich makes a marvelous brunch entree. If you're serving a crowd, arrange the finished quesadillas on a cookie sheet and place in a 200-degree oven to keep warm. For a complete brunch menu, I'd add a platter of fried, thickly sliced, maple-cured bacon, and a salad of strawberries and spinach with bottled poppy seed dressing.

Preparation time: *5 minutes*

Cooking time: *15 minutes*

Yield: *4 servings*

3 tablespoons butter

4 flour tortillas, 8 inches each

4 slices fontina cheese

1 large apple, cored, peeled, and sliced into thin wedges, unpeeled

¼ cup maple syrup

¼ cup apple juice

⅛ teaspoon salt

¼ teaspoon grated nutmeg

1½ teaspoons fresh lemon juice

1 Melt 1 tablespoon of the butter over medium heat in a large nonstick skillet. Place the tortillas on a work surface. Arrange one cheese slice on one half of each tortilla. Fold the cheese in half if necessary to fit the tortilla half.

2 Fold each tortilla in half to form semicircles. Ease two tortillas into the skillet in one layer. Brown the tortillas over medium heat 3 minutes on each side or until the tortillas are lightly browned and the cheese is melted. Remove from the skillet and keep warm. Add 1 more tablespoon of the butter and repeat with 2 more folded tortillas and keep warm.

3 Add the remaining tablespoon of butter to the skillet. Add the apple slices and brown over medium-high heat for 1 minute. Add the maple syrup, apple juice, salt, and nutmeg. Cook over high heat until the apple slices are tender and the liquid is syrupy, about 2 minutes. Stir in the lemon juice.

4 To serve, cut each tortilla in half to form 2 quarters. Arrange 2 quarters on each of 4 plates and top with apple slices and syrup.

Vary It! *Add a slice of Canadian bacon with the cheese.*

Speed It Up! *Skip the apples and maple syrup, and instead, warm up a can of apple pie filling to serve over the quesadillas.*

Per serving: Calories 385 (From Fat 186); Fat 21g (Saturated 12g); Cholesterol 56mg; Sodium 336mg; Carbohydrate 40g (Dietary Fiber 4g); Protein 13g.

THE QUESADILLA FOLD

Figure 11-2: Follow these steps to encase and fold your favorite quesadilla filling.

1. PLACE A FILLING SUCH AS GRATED CHEDDAR CHEESE ON ONE HALF OF A QUESADILLA

2. FOLD THE TORTILLA IN HALF ENCLOSING THE FILLING.

3. FRY THE FILLED TORTILLA AS THE RECIPE DIRECTS....

THEN...

CUT THE TORTILLA INTO 2 QUARTERS TO SERVE.

Matching Breads to Fillings

With so many breads to choose from, deciding which loaf will complement your sandwiches is difficult. Taste has to be the first consideration. The better tasting the bread, the better your sandwich is going to be. And don't forget individual preferences.

For years, I fought a battle to introduce my children to whole wheat bread. The taste and texture were a little too strong for them when they were young. Now my children love the nutty flavor and coarse grains of whole wheat bread, but it's been an educational process. Give your children a taste of whole grains and let them get used to these breads before you insist on them.

If you hated whole-wheat bread as a child, give it another chance. You're probably going to discover it's a satisfying addition to your adult sandwiches.

While the world of bread and fillings is vast and varied, here are a few bread and filling combinations that are tried and true. (And for the whole scoop on fillings, check out the "Fillings Make the Feast" section, later in this chapter.) The flavors, colors, and textures blend together into delicious sandwich meals.

- **Brioche:** This specialty bread has a high proportion of eggs and butter in the batter. The bread's consistency is dense like a pound cake. Brioche (*bree*-oush) is sold in bakeries and better supermarkets. Try brioche in a Monte Cristo sandwich for a sumptuous dish.

- **Challah:** This bread is eggy, like brioche, but not as sweet or as rich. Challah (*hah*-lah) is a ceremonial bread served at the beginning of the Jewish Sabbath on Friday nights. Some stores sell it throughout the week, but you're more likely to find it on the shelf on a Friday. Challah is the perfect match for egg salad sandwiches. I recommend it for cream cheese and jelly as well.

- **Country:** This name usually refers to a rustic-looking loaf with a round or oval shape, crisp crust, and coarse, chewy interior. Top a thick slice of country bread with robust meats, cheeses, and a grainy mustard. Sprinkle country bread with a little olive oil and vinegar before you layer on the filling, and you have a real treat.

- **French bread:** French bread is typically formed into long, thin loaves. You get almost as much crisp crust as tender filling in every bite. Thinly sliced ham or melt-in-the-mouth French cheeses, such as Brie or Camembert, are wonderful in French bread.

- **Hawaiian bread:** Hawaii is known for its pineapples, which make their way into this sweet bread. The fruity taste is delicious when spread with cream cheese and jelly or peanut butter and jelly.

- **Italian bread:** This long bread has a slightly crisp crust and mild flavor. Italian bread is a great all-purpose bread. If you slice it in sections about 4- to 6-inches long, you can use it instead of hard rolls for submarines or hero sandwiches.

- **Pumpernickel bread:** Serve this dark bread with deli meats, such as corned beef, ham, and roast beef. Stronger cheeses, such as Swiss cheese and Munster cheese, also taste delicious served on pumpernickel.

- **Rye bread:** If you're making sandwiches for children, buy rye bread without caraway seeds. Young children don't like seeds in their breads. Rye bread and corned beef are a natural twosome. Rye bread, which is slightly tangy, makes a tasty Swiss cheese sandwich, too.

- **Sourdough:** Sourdough bread has a distinctive tangy taste and thick chewy crust. Sourdough stands up to bold-tasting cheeses.

Fillings Make the Feast

Packing sandwiches with your favorite fillings whets your appetite for that first bite. You crave the taste of rare roast beef or smoked chicken. Even if you don't have time to make fillings from scratch, and who's going to roast a chicken or piece of beef just to have sandwich meat — you can have the ingredients you need. Take a quick trip to the market, and stock your pantry and fridge. A few choice ingredients are all you need.

Deli meat to the rescue

Shopping your local deli gives you plenty of food for fillings. Buy enough sliced lunch meats to use within 5 days and keep the meats refrigerated until you use them. Allow 3 ounces of meat or poultry for each sandwich. If you're adding cheese as well, use one ounce of cheese and 2 ounces of meat.

Looking at sandwich photos in food magazines or advertisements, you see that fillings really stand out. To get that fullness without serving too much meat, ask the deli person to thin shave the slices. Layers of paper-thin meat add volume to your sandwich. Folding is another trick. Instead of placing flat slices of meat on a bread slice, fold the meat in half or in quarters to bulk up the filling.

Deli meats contain preservatives to keep the meat from spoiling. The U.S. government allows these ingredients in meats and poultry, but if you'd rather avoid them, shop for organic meat products. Several good brands are available in stores. Be sure to keep organic meats refrigerated and use them within a couple of days once you open the packages. Meats that are processed without preservatives are highly susceptible to bacterial spoilage.

Ham's rich flavor belies its low-calorie, low-fat profile. A 3-ounce serving of sliced ham has about 120 calories and less than 5 grams of fat. Starting with ham makes sense when you're looking for a diet sandwich.

Egging on the sandwich

Salads made with canned salmon or tuna are also delicious possibilities for sandwich fillings. For investing a couple of minutes to open a can of tuna or salmon and add mayonnaise, you have a flavor-packed filling. (In Chapter 3, I talk about the various types of canned tuna or salmon to stock for quick sandwich meals.)

When I'm too busy to grocery shop on Saturday mornings, egg salad sandwiches are my rescue food. Everyone in my household loves my egg salad sandwiches, studded with chives and sweet pickle relish. I heap the salad on thick slices of challah and add lettuce and tomatoes.

To hard-cook eggs, place them in a single layer in a pot and add cold water to cover. Put the lid on and quickly bring just to boiling. Turn off the heat and remove the pot from the burner if it retains heat. Set the eggs aside in the pot for 15 minutes for large-size eggs. Overcooking gives eggs the green color of a moon rock. Drain the eggs as soon as the 15 minutes are up and hold under cold, running water to chill.

Egg Salad Sandwiches

Making the egg salad filling for sandwiches in advance saves last-minute preparation time. Keep the egg mixture in a covered container in the refrigerator up to 4 days and stir before using. Even though lettuce and tomatoes turn this sandwich into a meal, I like to add a side dish of sliced cucumbers in vinaigrette dressing.

Preparation time: *10 minutes*

Yield: *4 servings*

8 hard-cooked eggs, peeled	*1 tablespoon minced chives*
2 tablespoons sweet pickle relish	*8 slices of challah, sliced ½-inch thick*
¼ cup light mayonnaise	*8 leaves romaine, or iceberg lettuce*
⅛ teaspoon paprika	*2 tomatoes, cored and thinly sliced*

1 Place the eggs in a medium bowl and dice with a sharp knife. Add the relish, mayonnaise, paprika, and chives and stir well to blend.

2 Place 4 slices of bread on a work surface. Divide the egg salad among the bread slices. Add 2 lettuce leaves to each sandwich. Add tomato slices over the lettuce and close with a top slice of bread. Cut the sandwiches diagonally in half to serve.

Vary It! *Substitute 2 tablespoons of minced celery or red bell pepper for the pickle relish. Or try substituting a can of drained tuna for half the eggs, making a hearty tuna and egg salad.*

Per serving: Calories 461 (From Fat 186); Fat 21g (Saturated 6g); Cholesterol 470mg; Sodium 707mg; Carbohydrate 46g (Dietary Fiber 3g); Protein 21g.

Filling up on veggies

Turning a sandwich into a wholesome one-handed meal is easy. Tucking a few vegetables between the bread slices adds vitamins, minerals, and flavor to sandwiches. Lettuce and tomatoes are perennial favorites. A BLT (bacon, lettuce, and tomato) sandwich would be pretty spare without the *L* for lettuce or *T* for tomato.

Many vegetables that you already have on hand are excellent in sandwiches. Choose vegetables that give a sandwich flavor and color as well as nutrients. Keep vegetable slices thin for easier eating. My top-ten list of sandwich vegetables is as follows:

- ✔ **Thinly sliced cucumbers:** Peeled or unpeeled, they're sensational.

- ✔ **Thin sliced yellow bell pepper rings:** Yellow peppers are the sweetest variety. Cut the peppers crosswise into ¼-inch thick slices, discarding the seeds.

- ✔ **Roasted red peppers:** Choose a jar of commercially roasted peppers to save time.

- ✔ **Raw spinach leaves:** Spinach is an excellent source of vitamin A, and you can buy pre-washed baby spinach leaves.

- ✔ **Broccoli slaw:** I talk about this shredded broccoli product in Chapter 5. It's a delicious alternative to shredded cabbage.

- ✔ **Avocado slices:** Peel and slice an avocado just before you use it, so the avocado flesh doesn't turn an unappealing dark color. Although avocados are high in fat, it's the kind of fat that health officials recommend that you eat. Adding ¼ of an avocado to a sandwich is a healthy choice.

- ✔ **Sliced mushrooms:** Select white, cultivated mushrooms for sandwiches.

- ✔ **Radishes:** The French eat butter and radish sandwiches as a snack or light meal. I'm guessing that you're not going to convince your kids to trade in their PB&J for radishes, but the strong-tasting vegetable makes a great garnish when thinly sliced over roast beef.

- ✔ **Onions:** I love the sweet taste and the tender texture of sautéed onions on a sandwich.

- ✔ **Shredded red cabbage:** Add a handful for instant color and crunch.

And while I'm on the subject of veggies, don't forget:

- ✔ **A dollop of coleslaw** is delicious on corned beef sandwiches.

- ✔ **Salsas** are flavor-enhancing toppings for low-fat chicken sandwiches.

Alfalfa sprouts, which were an essential accent in healthful sandwiches a decade ago, now carry cautions. The sprouts could be carrying harmful bacteria. If you or a loved one has a disease that compromises your immune system, avoid alfalfa sprouts for now. Don't serve alfalfa spouts to children or the elderly. Meanwhile, stay tuned. Researchers and growers are working to develop ways to bring safer sprouts to market.

Spreading Flavor

Mustard, ketchup (or do you say catsup?), and mayonnaise are the sandwich triumvirate — the big three. And no wonder; there's scarcely a filling that doesn't taste better when accented with one of these long-time favorites.

Turning to new tastes

But even your favorite mustard can get boring after a while. As for mayonnaise, at 100 calories and 11 or 12 grams of fat per tablespoon, you could be getting as many calories from the spread as you are from the filling.

Discover exciting new spreads you can buy or make. You can blend together a couple of condiments and get a hot new flavor in seconds, or you can explore the various ethnic condiments in supermarkets. Either way, you're adding more taste to sandwiches.

Some of my favorite spreads that you can make or buy are

- ✔ **Mustard-mayonnaise:** Buy a mustard-mayonnaise combination in the supermarket or mix equal parts of both condiments. If you enjoy a slightly sweet-tasting spread, substitute honey mustard for a Dijon-style mustard. You're getting a luscious spread with about half the calories of plain mayonnaise.

- ✔ **Horseradish mayonnaise:** For every tablespoon of mayonnaise you use, add 1 teaspoon drained white horseradish.

- ✔ **Chutney-mayonnaise:** Mix 1 part chutney to 2 parts mayonnaise.

- ✔ **Chutney-mustard:** Mix equal parts chutney and honey mustard.

- ✔ **Hot, sweet jam:** Mix ¼ teaspoon hot red pepper sauce into 1 tablespoon of orange marmalade. As an aside, this makes an outstanding spread for a ham sandwich.

Jam on a sandwich, you may ask in a dubious tone and rightly so. Before I ate a Monte Cristo sandwich, which I describe earlier in this chapter, the idea of a sweet jam with a savory sandwich would have struck me as being odd. But I'm hooked now that I know how pleasurable the mixture of savory and sweet can be. Think about sweet potatoes, cranberry sauce, and roast turkey, and you get the idea of how different tastes mingle together in an appealing way. Spreading jam on a sandwich provides the same taste delight.

Savory and Sweet Chicken Sandwiches

Thinly slice leftover rotisserie chicken or roast turkey to use in these sandwiches. Add a green salad and iced tea for a wonderful lunch.

Preparation time: *5 minutes*

Cooking time: *6 minutes*

Yield: *2 servings*

1 tablespoon butter	4 ounces sliced chicken breast meat
2 tablespoons cherry jam	2 slices Asiago cheese
4 small slices sourdough bread, cut ½-inch thick	

1 Melt the butter in a large nonstick skillet. Spread the jam on 2 slices of bread. Add half the chicken and half the cheese to each slice of the jam-covered bread. Top the sandwiches with the remaining bread.

2 Gently arrange the sandwiches in the skillet and brown over medium heat for 3 minutes per side or until the sandwiches are golden brown and the cheese melts. Remove from the heat. Cut the sandwiches diagonally in half to serve.

Vary It! *Using the same salty-sweet concept, substitute ham for the chicken and spread the bread with peach jam or orange marmalade.*

Per serving: *Calories 474 (From Fat 160); Fat 18g (Saturated 10g); Cholesterol 89mg; Sodium 779mg; Carbohydrate 48g (Dietary Fiber 2g); Protein 30g.*

Relishing the opportunity

Olive spreads for subs or heroes are available at supermarkets and Italian specialty food stores. But you can make a delicious, tangy olive spread in minutes using your food processor or a chef's knife and cutting board to chop the vegetables. Homemade relishes keep in the refrigerator about a week, so don't make more than you're going to serve in that time period.

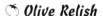 **Olive Relish**

Kalamata olives are dark, meaty Greek olives. You can find them in bulk in some supermarkets or in jars in stores' ethnic food sections. Using a food processor to chop the vegetables and olives takes less time than doing it by hand. Notice that this recipe doesn't call for salt. The olives and capers are salty enough for my taste, but you can add a pinch of salt if you like.

Preparation time: *10 minutes*

Cooking time: *5 minutes*

Yield: *about 1½ cups; 6 servings*

3 tablespoons olive oil	*1 tablespoon capers*
1 shallot, minced	*¼ teaspoon crushed, dried oregano*
1 garlic clove, minced	*⅛ teaspoon pepper*
1 celery stalk, trimmed and finely chopped	*1 tablespoon white wine vinegar*
1 cup pitted kalamata olives, coarsely chopped	

1 Heat 1 tablespoon of the oil in a small skillet. Add the shallot, garlic, and celery and cook over low-medium heat until the vegetables are limp but not browned, about 3 minutes.

2 Remove the vegetables from the skillet and spoon into a bowl. Stir in the olives, capers, oregano, pepper, the remaining 2 tablespoons of oil, and the vinegar. Let sit at least 5 minutes for flavors to blend.

Per serving: Calories 128 (From Fat 114); Fat 13g (Saturated 2g); Cholesterol 0mg; Sodium 418mg; Carbohydrate 3g (Dietary Fiber 1g); Protein 1g.

Finding the whole wheat in wheat bread

Sliced whole wheat bread is nutritious and convenient for sandwiches. Don't assume, however, that tan-colored bread is made from whole wheat, which has more vitamins and minerals than refined all-purpose flour. Some bakeries use caramel color to tint bread to a wholesome-looking shade. Read the ingredient list and look for the words *whole-wheat flour.*

The King of Sandwiches

Consuming 14 billion burgers a year — yes, *14 billion* — makes Americans the world's greatest hamburger lovers. Telling you something new about hamburger cooking is challenging, but I'm going to give it a shot.

Hamburger preparation is changing. Health experts recommend that you avoid rare hamburgers because of the risk of disease-causing bacteria. For safety sake, you should also take the temperature of a burger before you finish cooking it. Ground meat should cook to 160 degrees for medium doneness. Making a burger thick enough to insert a thermometer takes some getting used to as well. (Check out Figure 11-3 for a guide to taking a burger's temperature.) Okay, that's it for the negativity.

On to the positives: my tips for making hamburgers along with a recipe that fits my definition of the best burger.

- ✔ Use ground chuck for a good balance of fat and lean meat.

- ✔ Allow a pound of ground chuck for 4 moderate servings. Increase the weight to 1½ pounds for hearty appetites.

- ✔ Shape the beef patties using a light touch. Kneading meat toughens it.

- ✔ Preheat a heavy-bottomed cast-iron skillet before adding the beef.

- ✔ Check for external cues of doneness. The outside of the burgers should be a rich, dark brown. Any juices that naturally run from the meat should be clear. When you see these signs, use a meat thermometer to take the temperature of the beef patty.

And, if you're used to doing something to a burger to assure that it cooks, resist. Don't pierce, prod, poke, press, or pat the hamburgers as they cook — doing so only dries the meat out. Leaving meat alone is a battle in my household where old habits die hard, so I can understand if you want to hide the spatula from your cooking mate. If your partner is impatient, let him take the burger's temperature; the only exception to the do-not-pierce rule.

The Best Burger

I may have the nerve to suggest a great way to make a burger, but I can't decide the best condiment for you. That's a matter of individual choice. I even see quite a few variations at my table. My spouse mixes half ketchup and half mustard, my daughter uses steak sauce, and my son and I slather on the Olive Relish that I provide the recipe for elsewhere in this chapter. And we all agree on potato salad as the perfect side dish. Choose a mayonnaise or oil and vinegar version from the deli or make your own.

Preparation time: *5 minutes*

Cooking time: *12 minutes*

Yield: *4 servings*

1 pound ground chuck	*2 teaspoons vegetable oil*
¼ teaspoon salt	*4 hamburger buns, toasted*
¼ teaspoon pepper	*4 iceberg lettuce leaves*
2 teaspoons butter	*1 large tomato, cored and sliced*

1 Place the ground chuck in a bowl with the salt and pepper. Gently mix the seasonings into the beef with your hands. Divide the meat into 4 portions and flatten into patties about ¾ inch thick and 3 inches in diameter.

2 Place the butter and oil in a heavy-bottomed skillet and heat over medium-high heat. When the butter starts to foam, gently ease the patties into the skillet. Cook on the first side about 5 minutes, or until the meat is dark brown. Using a spatula, flip the patties over and cook the second side 3 to 5 minutes or until a meat thermometer inserted into the patty registers 160 degrees.

3 When the patties are cooked, remove and place on toasted hamburger buns. Top with the Olive Relish if you like. Add lettuce and tomato slices and close with the tops of buns. Serve immediately.

Per serving: Calories 417 (From Fat 218); Fat 24g (Saturated 9g); Cholesterol 82mg; Sodium 462mg; Carbohydrate 24g (Dietary Fiber 2g); Protein 25g.

CHECKING FOR BURGER DONENESS

I FEEL GREAT! CAN I GO OUT AND PLAY NOW?

160°!

INSERT A MEAT THERMOMETER AT A HORIZONTAL ANGLE INTO A HAMBURGER PATTY SO THE THERMOMETER DOESN'T TOUCH THE PAN! WHEN THE THERMOMETER REGISTERS 160° THE BURGER IS DONE!

Figure 11-3: Always check the hamburger's temperature.

Chapter 12

Skillet Meals

Skillet entrees combine old-style hearty one-dish meals with the modern need for convenience, speed, and exciting flavors. In days gone by, folks put their skillets to use for simple dishes, such as corned beef hash. But the recipes in this chapter take skillet meals to another level: You can cook these robust and flavorful dishes with ease.

In this chapter, you find out how to combine all the elements of a meal in one cooking vessel, so you have tempting, wholesome, and nutritious meals in half an hour or less.

I start off with some general tips and tricks you can keep in mind as you prepare one of the recipes in this chapter or strike out on your own and come up with a new skillet meal. Then I cover each of the three main players — veggies, meat, and starches. And I round things out with some international skillet flavor.

Skillet Savvy

Cooking skillet meals is a fast way to get a hearty dinner to the table. And you don't have to sacrifice nutrition in the name of convenience. Health experts recommend you fill one-third of your plate with food from animal sources, such as beef, pork, or cheese and two-thirds with foods from the vegetables and whole grains categories, which are plant foods.

Towing the line and obeying these rules could mean cooking three separate dishes — meat, vegetables, and a starch — but that's taxing on your schedule. Combining all the elements of a dinner into one or two dishes saves you time, reduces your stress levels, and makes the family dishwasher happy.

But the health argument doesn't carry weight in my home — and probably not in yours either — if the foods don't taste good. And that's the great thing about skillet dinners. You get the delicious combination of vegetables, grains, and meat, chicken, or fish in 30 minutes or less.

As the cook, you'll love the flexibility a skillet recipe gives you. You can switch one vegetable for another — say corn for peas — and not ruin a dish. There's very little you can do that won't be a hit with your family or dinner guests.

Getting your timing down

I'd say skillet dinners are goof-proof, but I've had flops when the ingredients took different amounts of time to cook. You don't want to bite into an unpalatable mess like hard rice and mushy asparagus. Getting a handle on timing is key, and checking out the recipe is a good place to start.

Read the entire recipe through before you do anything, keeping these guidelines in mind:

✔ Estimate how long it takes to complete each step before you start. Figure in the preparation times listed with the recipe to eliminate guesswork.

✔ Consider the cooking times of each ingredient before you begin preparing a dish. In this book, I deliberately avoid any ingredient that takes more than 25 minutes to cook because I'm dedicated to making a delicious meal in less than half an hour. For example, I skip wild rice and substitute long-grain rice or a fast-cooking version of brown rice.

Consider the following ingredient-related issues as you try to keep cooking times to a minimum:

✔ Cut long-cooking ingredients to a small, uniform size. If you're cooking carrots or potatoes, for example, cut them into small pieces. (See the "Picking Your Vegetables" section, later in this chapter, for more veggie tips.)

✔ Substitute frozen vegetables for their longer-cooking fresh counterparts. Lima beans is a good example.

✔ Start cooking a skillet dinner by sautéing any vegetable or meat that the recipe calls for. Lightly browned veggies and meats appeal to the eye, and sautéing brings out the sweetness in vegetables.

✔ Cooking the starch is usually the most time-consuming part of a skillet recipe. Rice takes about 20 minutes to cook. If you're running out of time, substitute a faster-cooking starch. For example, cook orzo (a rice-shaped pasta) or prepare couscous in a separate pan and serve with your skillet dish. (See the "Introducing the Star Starches" section, later in this chapter, for other ideas.)

Skillet dinners usually have a built-in starch like rice, pasta, or a grain. But sometimes you're making a nice saucy dish that you cook without the starch. In that case, you'll want a side to serve under your main course. Orzo is one of my favorites. The rice-shaped pasta cooks quickly and soaks up sauce. Don't make more orzo than you need for one dish. Leftover orzo doesn't taste good reheated.

☉ Lemon-Scented Orzo

Some supermarkets carry orzo that's the size of rice grains; other stores offer a smaller size as well. I prefer the larger pasta, which has a nice chewy texture.

Preparation time: *5 minutes*

Cooking time: *10 minutes*

Yield: *4 servings*

¾ teaspoon salt	1 teaspoon grated lemon rind
1 cup orzo	1 tablespoon minced Italian parsley
2 teaspoons olive oil	¼ teaspoon pepper

1 Fill a medium-sized pan with water and add ½ teaspoon of the salt. Bring to a boil. Add the orzo and cook over high heat for 10 minutes or until tender.

2 Drain the orzo well and return to the pan. Add the olive oil, lemon rind, parsley, pepper, and the remaining ¼ teaspoon salt. Stir and heat through 1 minute.

Per serving: *Calories 176 (From Fat 26); Fat 3g (Saturated 1g); Cholesterol 0mg; Sodium 439mg; Carbohydrate 32g (Dietary Fiber 2g); Protein 6g.*

Compatibility is key

As I mention in the "Skillet Savvy" section, earlier in this chapter, skillet meals usually feature three main players on the ingredient marquee — vegetables, protein from meat or fish, and a starch. Matching ingredients is key to pulling off a great skillet dinner, but the process isn't impossible. In fact, it's much easier than matching your best friend with a date, with a few caveats. You wouldn't think of a boring fix-up for a pal, and likewise, you wouldn't toss shrimp into a skillet of rice and cauliflower. You'd end up with a white meal, and monochromatic meals don't stimulate appetites.

As you pair vegetables, grains, and proteins, notice how certain matches work together. For example, chicken sausage, tomatoes, onions, garlic, and rice belong together. But the spicy seasonings in a chicken sausage over-whelm bland-tasting cauliflower.

The recipes in this chapter are balanced, so no one vegetable or grain is dominant. Prepare these recipes and discover how well the flavorings taste together. Then, if you like, experiment and find mixtures that you enjoy.

Picking Your Vegetables

Vegetables, like people, gravitate toward each other. In Louisiana, a typical gumbo recipe starts with onions, garlic, and bell peppers. In Italy, recipes often start with celery, onions, garlic, green peppers, and seasonings sautéed together. When you find vegetable combinations that taste good together, you instinctively reach for them. Keep reading to find out more about selecting the right vegetables for your skillet dinners. And I devote a bit of extra space to that family of vegetables — onions — that more often than not lays the flavor foundation for these one-pan wonders.

Colorful and quick

Red bell peppers, green broccoli, and orange carrots are lovely to look at, but Mother Nature designs vegetable colors with something more in mind. The deep hues are a signal that the vegetables are packed with nutrients and *phytochemicals,* another name for plant chemicals that may prove to have disease-preventive powers. When you consider what vegetables are going into your skillet dinner, be sure to include at least one that's brightly colored.

Time constraints mean that some vegetables are better options for quick skillet meals. The vegetables in the list that follows belong in the quick-cooking hall of fame:

- ✔ Asparagus
- ✔ Bell peppers
- ✔ Broccoli
- ✔ Cabbage
- ✔ Green beans
- ✔ Kale
- ✔ Peas
- ✔ Spinach
- ✔ Tomatoes

In general, the smaller the pieces of vegetables, the less time that they take to cook. If you don't want to dice and chop vegetables, look for products with some built-in convenience. (Chapter 5 describes some additional fresh vegetables that you can include in skillet dinners.)

Selecting frozen (or canned) vegetables offers even more options. Skillet meals can't get much faster than when you can skip one or more of the peeling, dicing, chopping, and cooking steps. Here are a few ways to take advantage of frozen vegetables:

- ✔ **Overlooked gems:** Frozen carrots, Brussels sprouts, and hardshell squash are all excellent sources of vitamins, but you may overlook them due to prep and cooking time constraints. Use the frozen versions to serve these vegetables within your time limits. (For more on the convenience that canned and frozen vegetables offer, see Chapter 3.)

- ✔ **Mixed veggies:** As I mention earlier in this section, some vegetables just have a natural affinity for each other. Your supermarket freezer case offers combinations of frozen mixed vegetables — another bonanza for the busy cook — that are already in perfect harmony for skillet dinners. My two favorites mixes are onions and red bell peppers and an Italian vegetable blend that includes onions and zucchini. I use this product for the Shrimp Stir-Fry over Couscous in Chapter 17, but you can add frozen stir-fry veggies to a skillet dinner, too.

Avoid using lettuce in a skillet recipe. Because of its delicacy and high water content, lettuce disintegrates when you cook it.

Tearful but tasty

All rules are meant to be broken, so my rule about varying the colors in skillet meals has two exceptions: onion and garlic. Although onion and garlic are white, don't overlook them. When it comes to cooking tasty meals quickly, onion and garlic are your ace in the hole. Many of my skillet dinners begin with *sauté an onion* or end with *stir in chives or scallions.* Onions, shallots, leeks, chives, and scallions deliver pungent taste that brings a tear to my eye. No other vegetables burst with so much flavor and so little effort.

In a pinch, you can substitute onions for scallions or shallots. But the more you cook with these pungent ingredients, the more you prize each vegetable for its distinctive flavor and texture. Cooking times differ for each of these vegetables and even different varieties of onions. Don't limit yourself to one kind of onion. Add different varieties (see Figure 12-1) and bring a range of flavors to your skillet dinners.

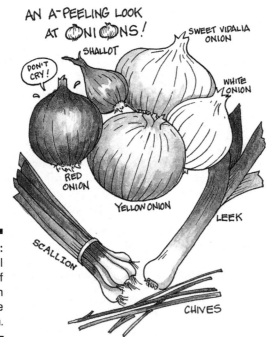

Figure 12-1:
The flavorful members of the allium family, the onion clan.

Green onions

Green onions all have long, green leaves and slender bulbs or stem ends. Refrigerate green onions and use within a few days.

- ✓ **Leeks** have long, thick white bulbs leading to green leaves. Chop and sauté the bulb as you would onions at the beginning of a skillet-dinner recipe. If you're a thrifty cook, use the green tops when making a broth from scratch. You can chop leeks in seconds, but take time to rinse them off. The layers trap sand and dirt. Leeks are really yummy in skillet dinners that feature chicken or veal and a touch of cream.

- ✓ **Chives'** long, thin leaves provide a spicy-hot taste with a hint of tartness to the foods that you cook. The flavor and aroma fade soon after you chop the herb; so prepare chives just before you use them. Sprinkle chives on a skillet dinner just when you pull it from the heat. Chives are great for adding color to a skillet dinner that's a little drab or flat tasting.

- ✓ **Scallions** have a hint of a white bulb but are used for their long, green leaves. Trim off the root end and then chop the bulb and the leaves for dishes. Treat scallions like herbs: Sprinkle them on a skillet dish during the last couple of minutes of cooking. Scallions are great when you want that wonderful onion taste but don't have the time to sauté an onion.

Dry onions

Dry onions are mature, which means they're covered with a thin papery skin. You don't have to refrigerate dry onions; they stay fresh for weeks if stored in a cool, dry place. You can choose savory, firm varieties, but supermarkets also carry several kinds of sweet onions that are mild and juicy.

- ✓ **Red onions** have thin red to purple skins and lovely red and white interiors. These onions have a mild taste that makes them suitable for salads and sandwiches. Don't waste these pretty onions in dishes that you're cooking for a long time, because the color fades with heat.

- ✓ **Shallots** may look like miniature onions, with their tan skins and pale brown to mauve flesh, but the resemblance is superficial. The flavor of shallots is milder and more refined than that of onions. Use shallots in risotto or with veal dishes in which you want a light onion taste.

- ✓ **White onions'** flavor can be mild to strong depending on the season, the region in which they're grown, and even the weather. Unfortunately, you can't tell what you're getting from the outside, so get ready for an eating adventure. Cook white onions for soups, stews, and skillet dinners.

- ✓ **Yellow onions,** with a light brown skin, are the workhorses of the allium family. Use yellow onions for almost any cooked dish.

Sweet onions

Sweet onions are slightly flattened globes with thin outer skins. Sweet onions more perishable than dry onions, so don't buy them for long-term storage. Wait 'til you taste what a sweet onion does for a skillet meal. When sautéed these onions make all the other skillet ingredients taste mellower.

Garlic

While I'm having this stinky conversation, I don't want to forget garlic — a cousin to leeks, chives, onions, and shallots. The garlic bulb is covered with parchment-like skin. Pull off the skin to get to the individual cloves. Garlic has a remarkable ability to change according to its culinary environment. Add raw garlic to a recipe, and it's pungent. Cook it in a skillet dinner and it's nutty, buttery, and even a little sweet. When cooking, be careful that you don't burn garlic. Burnt garlic has a bitter taste. Shop for firm bulbs with dry skin. Avoid garlic that's withered or sprouting green stalks, two signs of age.

Perch with Martini Sauce

Serve this piquant fish dish over cooked rice or orzo, or pass sourdough bread for dipping into the sauce.

Preparation time: *10 minutes*

Cooking time: *10 minutes*

Yield: *2 servings*

1 tablespoon olive oil	*2 tablespoons gin*
1 onion, chopped	*¼ teaspoon salt*
1 garlic clove, minced	*⅛ teaspoon pepper*
1 can (14½ ounces) diced tomatoes, undrained	*4 large perch fillets*
½ cup pimiento-stuffed olives, sliced	*1 tablespoon minced chives*

1 Heat the olive oil in a large sauté pan. Add the onion and garlic and sauté over medium heat for 2 minutes, until limp. Add the tomatoes, olives, gin, salt, and pepper and bring to a simmer.

2 Gently arrange the perch in the tomato sauce. Using a spoon, generously baste the fish with the sauce. Cover and simmer for10 minutes or until cooked through. Sprinkle with chives.

Per serving: Calories 383 (From Fat 156); Fat 16g (Saturated 2g); Cholesterol 218mg; Sodium 1,441mg; Carbohydrate 18g (Dietary Fiber 6g); Protein 48g.

Meeting the Protein Providers

Fast-cooking and low-fat proteins — fish, seafood, and chicken breast — are excellent selections for skillet dinners. Check your supermarket's deli or meat counter for low-fat poultry sausage. These chicken or turkey products are so well seasoned that you don't have to add much else to flavor a skillet dinner. Beef or pork is great too, but buy tender cuts. Diced pork tenderloin is low in fat and cooks in minutes.

Colorful, flavorful, and healthful pork

Lean, low-fat pork tenderloin also has the virtue of being quick cooking. What more could you want in a meat cut? Oh, did I also mention that pork tenderloin tastes so delicious that you can serve it for company or for family dinners. Look for packages of diced pork tenderloin if your meat counter stocks it. Otherwise buy one or two tenderloins; the average tenderloin weighs between 8 ounces and a pound. Remove the thin white cover of the pork with a sharp paring knife and then cut the pork into cubes.

Giving in to chicken's dark side

Use the force, Luke. Take advantage of dark chicken meat in the form of chicken thighs for your quick dinners. And if preparation times are still holding you back, try boneless, skinless chicken thigh meat, which cooks twice as fast as bone-in chicken thighs. Flattening chicken thighs by pounding them between two sheets of waxed paper speeds up the cooking time even more. Check the pounding details in Chapter 13. Cutting the thigh meat into chunks makes them a convenient addition to skillet dinners.

Pork and Olive Skillet Dinner

This Mediterranean-inspired pork dish doesn't include a starch, but I recommend instant mashed potatoes in plain or garlic flavor, instant rice, or the garlic bread in Chapter 4 as a side dish.

Preparation time: *5 minutes*

Cooking time: *20 minutes*

Servings: *4*

1 tablespoon olive oil

1 small onion, peeled and finely chopped

1 small red bell pepper, cored, seeded, and chopped

2 tablespoons flour

Salt and pepper to taste

1 pound boneless, diced pork tenderloin

⅓ cup dry vermouth

⅛ teaspoon hot paprika

¼ teaspoon crushed, dried oregano

¾ cup chicken broth

¼ cup sliced pimiento-stuffed olives

1 Heat the oil in a large nonstick sauté pan. Add the onion and pepper and sauté 2 minutes over high heat.

2 Combine flour, salt, and pepper on a plate. Dust the pork cubes with the flour mixture.

3 Add the pork to the skillet and brown over medium heat, about 3 to 5 minutes. Add the vermouth and scrape up browned bits in skillet. Reduce the vermouth by half. Add the paprika and oregano and cook 30 seconds. Stir in the chicken broth and olives. Cover and simmer 10 minutes or until pork is tender.

Vary It! *If you have the time, make the Lemon-Scented Orzo in this chapter to serve with the pork.*

Per serving: *Calories 221 (From Fat 93); Fat 10g (Saturated 3g); Cholesterol 76mg; Sodium 572mg; Carbohydrate 5g (Dietary Fiber 1g); Protein 25g.*

Braised Chicken Thighs Mediterranean Style

Chicken thighs have a sweet meaty taste that goes well with a variety of herbs and spices. The combination of tomatoes and olives reminds me of the South of France.

Preparation time: *10 minutes*

Cooking time: *15 minutes*

Yield: *4 servings*

2 tablespoons olive oil	*¼ teaspoon salt*
1 small onion, chopped	*⅛ teaspoon pepper*
1 garlic clove, minced	*4 plum tomatoes, chopped*
8 boneless, skinless chicken thighs	*⅔ cup pitted green or black olives*
¼ teaspoon crushed, dried oregano	*1 cup chicken broth*
¼ teaspoon paprika	*1 can (15 ounces) chickpeas, drained and rinsed*
¼ teaspoon ground cumin	

1 Heat 1 tablespoon olive oil in a large sauté pan. Add the onion and garlic and sauté over high heat for 2 minutes, until limp. Add the remaining oil and heat. Add the chicken thighs and brown 2 minutes per side on high heat. Do this in two batches if necessary. Remove the chicken and set aside.

2 Add the oregano, paprika, cumin, salt, and pepper. Stir in the tomatoes, olives, chicken broth, and chickpeas. Cook over medium heat 1 minute for flavors to blend. Add the chicken thighs and spoon the pan juices over the chicken.

3 Cover the pan and simmer the chicken for 5 minutes. Again, spoon the pan juices over the chicken. Cover and cook 5 more minutes or until the chicken is cooked through.

Vary It! *If you prefer, skip the peas and serve the dish over cooked rice or couscous.*

Per serving: *Calories 425 (From Fat 231); Fat 26g (Saturated 4g); Cholesterol 100mg; Sodium 1,274mg; Carbohydrate 17g (Dietary Fiber 4g); Protein 32g.*

Introducing the Star Starches

Putting the starch into skillet dinners gives your meal substance so each portion looks and tastes more filling. Just as you wouldn't serve a pot roast without a side of mashed potatoes — you do serve mashed potatoes, don't you? — you wouldn't serve a skillet dinner without some starch.

The best starches are those that soak up the skillet sauces, cook quickly, and taste good to you. Your options include

- ✔ **Grains:** In Chapter 3, I talk about the grains that make up the 30-minute cook's pantry. Couscous, in particular, is great for skillet dinners.

- ✔ **Pasta:** Cooking pasta in a skillet dinner is difficult because pasta cooks best in a large pot of water, but you can certainly serve a skillet dinner over pasta.

- ✔ **Potatoes:** In Chapter 5, I talk about the convenience of refrigerated cooked potatoes. Try these in skillet dinners and see what I mean. Cooked hash browned potatoes, for example, are great in a vegetarian or meat-based hash.

Rice, however, is my favorite because it's so readily available. Everyone has a box of rice in the cupboard.

Riding the rice-o-rama

Rice is an integral part of many skillet dinners. I prefer rice to other starches, because it often takes about the same time to cook as the vegetables and protein. I don't have to worry about one part of the meal cooking, while the remainder is ready and getting cold. Because the standard long-grain rice takes about 18 to 20 minutes to cook, you can have a 30-minute rice-based skillet dinner if you're organized. You can arrange your tasks so that you can prepare a delicious skillet dinner with rice on your timetable.

For a run-down on the basic types of rice (such as long-grain, parboiled, and instant) take a look at Chapter 3. If I'm cooking rice in a separate pan to serve under a stew, in a soup, or fill out a skillet dinner, I use parboiled rice simply because it's indestructible. The rice has distinctive grains and never gets mushy, even if I cook it too long or at too high a heat. But you'll probably find it takes too long to cook to use in a 30-minute skillet dinner.

Rice absorbs the seasonings that you add to a dish, so don't be shy with the flavorings. If you mistakenly add too much spice to a dish, just cook a little extra rice on the side and mix it into the skillet dinner just before serving.

Rice grains are short, medium, or long-grained. Keep in mind that short-grain rice becomes sticky when done (like sushi rice). Therefore, I don't recommend it for skillet dishes in which you want the rice grains to remain distinctive.

Risotto: A stirring story

Risotto (rih-*zaw*-toe) is one of Italy's culinary masterpieces. Fat grains of arborio rice simmer in stock in an open skillet. As the rice cooks, it becomes tender and creamy and nutty-sweet tasting. How something as simple as cooked rice could taste so incredibly good is no mystery. The only secret is paying undivided attention to what you're doing. Risotto can be flavored with saffron (see the "Piling on the paella" section, later in this chapter) and often includes vegetables, cheese, or meat or a combination of these ingredients.

To make risotto:

1. Start by sautéing onion or shallots. (For more on onions and shallots, check out the "Tearful but tasty" section, earlier in this chapter.)
2. Add arborio rice and sauté it for a minute.
3. This is where you have to avoid distractions. You add hot broth a little at a time and allow each measure to be absorbed by the rice before adding more. The process takes about 20 to 25 minutes.

The starch of arborio rice when cooked in a risotto creates a luscious sauce that you must savor immediately. Ordinarily, I'm not so insistent, but risotto doesn't taste good after it's been standing.

Be sure to keep the broth hot as you add it to the rice. Cold broth cools the rice, so it takes longer to cook.

Smoked Salmon Risotto

Think of how good smoked salmon and bagels taste. Smoked Salmon Risotto is an elegant dish that captures those flavors and more. Serve Smoked Salmon Risotto for Sunday brunch. Serve the same white wine that you use when preparing the risotto. I recommend a Chablis or Chardonnay.

Preparation time: *1 minute*

Cooking time: *25 minutes*

Yield: *2 servings*

1 tablespoon olive oil	*2 tablespoons minced chives*
1 shallot, peeled and minced	*¼ teaspoon salt*
¼ cup dry white wine	*¼ teaspoon pepper*
1 cup arborio rice	*4 ounces smoked salmon, diced or in strips*
4½ cups chicken broth, heated	*2 lemon wedges*
¼ cup half-and-half	

1 Heat the oil in a large skillet. Add the shallot and sauté over low heat for 1 minute. Stir in the wine and cook 1 minute or until the liquid is reduced by half. Add the rice and cook, stirring 1 minute.

2 Add ½ cup chicken broth. Stir and allow the rice to simmer until almost all the liquid is absorbed, about 5 minutes. Repeat, adding ½ cup broth at a time until rice has a creamy consistency and is almost tender. Stir in the half-and-half and chives. Simmer 1 minute and then remove from heat. Stir in the salt and pepper.

3 Stir the diced smoked salmon into the risotto or spoon the risotto onto 2 plates and arrange the smoked salmon in strips over the rice. Garnish the plates with lemon wedges.

Per serving: Calories 671 (From Fat 216); Fat 24g (Saturated 7g); Cholesterol 35mg; Sodium 3,692mg; Carbohydrate 90g (Dietary Fiber 2g); Protein 25g.

Universal Skillet Dinners

Masters of the skillet dinner, international cooks know that combining vegetables, grains, and proteins in one dish is economical yet robust. In all likelihood, some of your favorite restaurant meals have their origins as simple skillet dinners, such as those that follow:

✔ **Arroz con Pollo:** Rice with chicken is the translation for this Cuban specialty. Arroz con Pollo (ah-*rose* con *paw*-yoh) is also flavored with onions and tomatoes.

✔ **Country Captain:** This specialty of South Carolina may date as far back to the colonies when Americans traded with India for spices. Country Captain is chicken, simmered with onion, tomatoes, green pepper, raisins, and curry powder. Most cooks serve Country Captain over rice, but you can cook rice with the dish.

✔ **Ratatouille:** One of France's fabulous vegetable courses, ratatouille (rah-tuh-*too-e*) also makes a great vegetarian entree. If you don't mind adapting a classic, serve the vegetables over couscous for a more filling dish.

Now that your stomach juices are flowing, and your mental wheels are turning, keep reading to find out about my versions of some internationally inspired classics.

Tasting America's heritage: Jambalaya

Louisiana claims Spanish, French, African, and Native American ancestry, and all these influences are present in jambalaya (jum-buh-*lye*-uh). Some say the dish is named for *jambon,* which is French for *ham.*

Jambalaya is especially welcome during the cold weather months when you crave a stick-to-the-ribs dish. This Louisiana favorite starts with a spicy blend of cooked rice, tomatoes, onions, green pepper, and garlic. Depending on the cook, jambalaya also features sausage, chicken, seafood, or a combination of the three. Today, you can find as many versions of jambalaya as cooks who make it.

Authentic jambalaya contains *andouille sausage,* a smoked sausage that hails from Louisiana. Specialty butcher shops and gourmet food stores sell andouille. You can substitute Mexican *chorizo* (a very spicy raw pork sausage) or even diced Italian pepperoni.

However, you may choose to vary your jambalaya and include a spicy meat product. Its seasonings infuse the rice with the flavor that you don't get from jars of seasonings.

When cooking with fresh herbs, add the herbs at the end of cooking so their delicate flavors don't fade.

Chicken and Sausage Jambalaya

If you like your jambalaya hot, add ⅛ teaspoon of cayenne pepper with the seasonings. Jambalaya doesn't taste as good if the dish has to stand, so serve it as soon as it's ready.

Preparation time: *10 minutes*

Cooking time: *20 minutes*

Yield: *4 servings*

1 tablespoon olive oil	*1 cup long-grain rice*
1 red or green bell pepper, cored, seeded and diced	*1 can (14½ ounces) diced tomatoes with liquid*
1 celery stalk, trimmed and diced	*1 ½ cups chicken broth*
1 garlic clove, minced	*1 bay leaf*
1 onion, chopped	*¼ teaspoon crushed, dried thyme*
2 boneless, skinless chicken thighs, cut into 1-inch pieces	*½ teaspoon crushed, dried oregano*
4 ounces andouille or pepperoni sausage, cut into ½-inch thick slices	*½ teaspoon salt*
	¼ teaspoon pepper
	⅛ teaspoon crushed red pepper flakes

1 Heat the oil in a large nonstick sauté pan. Add the bell pepper, celery, garlic, and onion and sauté 3 minutes over high heat, or until the vegetables are limp. Add the chicken and sausage and sauté for 2 minutes over medium-high heat.

2 Stir in the rice, diced tomatoes, chicken broth, bay leaf, thyme, oregano, salt, pepper, and crushed red pepper flakes. Mix well. Bring the mixture to a boil. Reduce the heat to low, cover the pan and simmer 18 to 20 minutes or until the rice is tender and the liquid is absorbed. Remove the bay leaf and serve.

Per serving: Calories 370 (From Fat 183); Fat 20g (Saturated 6g); Cholesterol 49mg; Sodium 1,412mg; Carbohydrate 30g (Dietary Fiber 4g); Protein 17g.

Piling on the paella

Paella is a Spanish dish of rice, seasoned with saffron, shellfish, chicken, peas, and onions. Paella (pi-*ay*-yuh) is also the name of the shallow, two-handled cooking utensil that the recipe is prepared in.

Saffron (saf-run) is crucial to creating a great paella. Selling for around $50 an ounce, it's one of the more, if not the most, expensive spices that you can buy. Fortunately, you only need a pinch — about a dollar's worth — for a dish. Figure 12-2 shows you what saffron looks like. To use, crush saffron threads between your fingers and crumble it into very hot broth or other liquid, so the spice releases its flavor and color. A quick variation of paella serves as a great introduction to the charms of saffron. (For more info on saffron, check out the "Exclusive saffron" sidebar in this chapter.)

SEASONING WITH SAFFRON

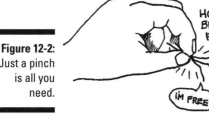

HOLDING 3 OR 4 THREADS BETWEEN YOUR THUMB AND FOREFINGER, CRUSH THE SAFFRON TO BREAK INTO SMALLER PIECES AND RELEASE THE FLAVOR!

IM FREE!

Figure 12-2: Just a pinch is all you need.

Spanish cooks use local ingredients for their paella recipes. Coastal cooks, for example, create dishes that are chock full of lobster and mussels; inland cooks substitute chicken and sausages. Use the same flexibility when you make your paella recipe. The first time, follow the directions that I provide. Then improvise. If your family isn't crazy about asparagus or the vegetable isn't in season, switch to peas.

Exclusive saffron

Saffron comes from the dried stamen of the crocus flower, but not your garden-variety crocus. The mauve-colored crocus yields the finest quality saffron, and Spain, Greece, Iran, India, and Morocco are the major producers. It takes about 50,000 to 75,000 flowers to yield a pound of saffron, which sells for about $50 an ounce. Is it any wonder that some supermarkets keep the spice behind the counter making it available by special request only?

Try saffron; you'll prize it for more than its rarity. The spice has a pungent and honey-like taste and an aroma that's exotic yet inviting. Saffron dyes the foods that it's cooked with to a golden yellow.

Considering its price, you want to buy the best saffron that you can find. I recommend buying saffron in *thread* rather than the powder form. The quality of some powdered saffron is excellent, but some is inferior. Telling the difference in quality is easier if you buy threads.

The ideal color is deep orange red; the texture should be firm, not wilted, or so brittle that it's old. Don't buy more than you need. Saffron's color and flavor fade over time. Store the spice in an airtight container away from heat and direct light. Paella, some risotto dishes, and Scandinavian breads use saffron.

Although authentic paella, using plump, short grains of rice, doesn't fit a 30-minute cook's schedule, this marvelous American version does.

Skillet Dinner Paella

If you can't find saffron for this dish, look for a package of saffron rice in the ethnic food department in your supermarket. Substitute the same amount of saffron rice for long-grain rice.

Preparation time: *5 minutes*

Cooking time: *25 minutes*

Yield: *4 servings*

¼ teaspoon crumbled saffron threads

2 cups boiling chicken broth

1 tablespoon olive oil

1 small onion, diced

1 garlic clove, minced

6 ounces chorizo, removed from casing and crumbled

1 boneless, skinless chicken breast, cut into 1-inch pieces

1 cup long-grain rice

2 cups fresh asparagus, cut into 1-inch lengths

8 ounces raw peeled shrimp

¼ teaspoon salt

⅛ teaspoon pepper

1 Stir the saffron into the chicken broth in a heatproof bowl. Set aside 2 minutes for the saffron to soften.

2 Meanwhile, heat the olive oil in a large nonstick sauté pan. Add the onion and garlic and sauté 2 minutes over high heat. Add the chorizo and chicken and sauté over high heat for 2 minutes, stirring frequently or until the chicken turns opaque and the chorizo no longer looks raw.

3 Add the rice and stir. Add the asparagus, shrimp, salt, and pepper. Pour in the saffron and chicken broth, getting all the crumbled saffron into the pan. Bring the mixture to a boil. Reduce the heat to low, cover the pan, and simmer the dish for 18 minutes or until the rice is tender, and the liquid is absorbed.

Per serving: Calories 527 (From Fat 212); Fat 24g (Saturated 8g); Cholesterol 142mg; Sodium 1,291mg; Carbohydrate 45g (Dietary Fiber 2g); Protein 32g.

If that's not quick enough, Even Faster Paella is a variation that cooks in about 15 minutes. You have no excuse for not making this mouthwatering recipe. Starting with leftover cooked chicken, cooked shrimp, and instant rice, you can make delicious paella. Use leftover chicken and shrimp or buy the ingredients at the deli department of your supermarket.

Even Faster Paella

Shop for fresh chopped onions and minced garlic in your supermarket produce counter. For extra color, top the paella with ½ cup of diced roasted red pepper just before you serve it.

Preparation time: *5 minutes*

Cooking time: *15 minutes*

Yield: *4 servings*

1 tablespoon olive oil	1¼ cups chicken broth
1 cup diced onion	1 cup frozen, thawed peas
1 tablespoon minced garlic	¼ teaspoon salt
¼ pound diced pepperoni	⅛ teaspoon pepper
1 cup cooked, diced chicken breast meat	1¼ cups instant rice
8 ounces cooked, peeled shrimp	

1 Heat the olive oil in a large nonstick sauté pan. Add the onion and garlic and sauté 2 minutes over medium heat. Add the pepperoni, chicken, and shrimp and sauté 1 minute to flavor the ingredients.

2 Add the chicken broth, peas, salt, and pepper and bring to a boil. Stir in the rice. Cover the pan and remove from heat. Set aside 5 minutes or until the rice is tender, and the liquid is absorbed.

Per serving: *Calories 460 (From Fat 173); Fat 19g (Saturated 6g); Cholesterol 165mg; Sodium 1,227mg; Carbohydrate 36g (Dietary Fiber 4g); Protein 34g.*

Chapter 13

Don't Forget the Beef, Lamb, Pork, Chicken, and Fish

*B*ring out the knives and forks. Sometimes, you just want to dig into a plain, simple entree. In this chapter, you find recipes that satisfy your cravings for hearty center-of-the-plate foods that aren't "stretched" with starches and vegetables. I tell you how to choose and prepare the quick-cooking cuts of beef, lamb, pork, chicken, and fish. (It's up to you to round out each meal according to your preferences. You can improvise, but I can't help myself: I supply some ideas along the way.)

Eating out whets your appetite for succulent meat dishes. And you can duplicate the marvelous flavors you savor in restaurants in your home meals as well. Tender cuts of beef, lamb, pork, and chicken that cook in less than 30 minutes are proof you can serve a family-pleasing meal without investing much time. These mouthwatering visions to a carnivore's heart are also ideal entrees for busy cooks. In this chapter, I tell you which cuts are best suited for quick meals.

Chops, steaks, and chicken breasts are center-of-the-plate entrees. But dressing a hunk of meat or fish with a simple sauce makes your meal even more appetizing. The recipes in this chapter, though quick and easy, include the sauces and seasonings that make for mouthwatering dinners.

A firm, flavorful fish steak is just as satisfying as a T-bone. Tuna steaks bring variety and good nutrition to your meals. Because you probably don't cook as much fish as you do beef or pork, you may have more questions about cooking fish than anything else. If you fear fish failure, relax. I tell you how to buy and cook fish steaks, so they're flavorful and tender.

Techniques, Again?

Knowing how to broil, pan broil, and sauté, will get you through any center-of-the-plate entree. Although you don't have to do much (or take much time) to produce a delicious steak or chop, you can produce a tough piece of meat, fish, or poultry if you choose the wrong cooking style. That's why I stress techniques for each entree in this chapter. See Table 13-1 to find out what method is appropriate for each kind of meat. And for an in-depth look at these and other 30-minute meal cooking techniques, check out Chapter 6.

Table 13-1	Quick-Cooking Meat, Fish, and Poultry
Food	*Technique*
Beef steaks	Broiling, pan-broiling
Lamb chops	Broiling, pan-broiling
Pork chops	Broiling, pan-broiling, sautéing
Chicken breasts, boneless, skinless	Sautéing
Fish steaks	Broiling, pan-broiling

What's at Steak?

Steak is often the food of choice when you want to splurge. In my home, the family member celebrating a birthday or achievement gets to choose his or her menu, and 9 times out of 10, the request is for a steak dinner. No one in my home can resist the aroma of meat sizzling in the pan. What I don't tell my family is that steak is so quick cooking that granting everyone's favorite birthday menu wish is a pleasure for me.

You don't have to reserve steak for some rare occasion. Work steak into your menus whenever you want a super-fast knife-and-fork entree that makes your family feel special.

Shopping for steak

Steaks are more expensive than tougher, slower-cooking cuts of beef so you want to make sure you get the best value and eating pleasure. You want to look for certain details when you shop for steak.

✔ **Grade:** Steaks don't come with report cards, but they do come with a grade. Grades rate the amount of fat in an animal's muscles, called the *marbling,* which you also read about in this list. Here are three grades you're going to see in stores.

- **Prime:** High proportion of fat and is the most tender and juicy of the grades. Most prime steaks are sold in restaurants. You can find them in butcher shops and some gourmet food stores, but they're a rare find in supermarkets. Prime steaks are also the most costly ones.

- **Choice:** Has some marbling which makes the beef tender and juicy.

- **Select:** One grade below choice and is a lean meat. If you buy select steaks cook them to medium-rare or use pan braising as your cooking technique.

✔ **Marbling:** The fat that runs through the muscle of a steak cut, not the fat that is on the outside of the steak. Looking at a steak you should see small flecks of fat evenly distributed throughout the meat. The more marbling a piece of beef has, the more tender and juicy it is. A well-marbled steak is easier to cut into than a lean one. On a nutritional note, those specks of fat contribute calories as Table 13-2 indicates. The higher the grade the more fat and calories the beef has.

✔ **Color and texture:** Lean edible portions of a steak should be bright, cherry red. Look for white or cream-white colored fat around the edges of the meat. Feel the fat with your finger. It should be firm to the touch.

Table 13-2	Steak Facts 101 (3.5 Ounce Broiled Beef Tenderloin)	
Grade	*Calories*	*Fat*
Prime	232	12.4 grams
Choice	222	11.2 grams
Select	199	8.7 grams

Love me tender

Asking a meat lover which is the best tasting steak is like asking a parent which child is the best one. There's no answer. Every steak is excellent. Making a selection will depend on your personal preference and your budget.

Although I wouldn't want the job of singling out selective steaks for praise, the experts (cattlemen) say that when you want to stake a claim to the most-tender steaks, the cuts on the following list are the ones to choose. (Please note that the most-tender steak isn't necessarily going to be the most flavorful.) The descriptions below, courtesy of the National Cattlemen's Beef Association and Cattlemen's Beef Board, are designed to make you a savvy and hungry shopper. You can also check out Figure 13-1 to see what some of these steaks and others look like.

- **Chuck eye steak:** This boneless and flavorful steak is also tender because it shares the same muscle of the very tender ribeye.

- **Chuck top blade steak:** Also sold as a *flat iron,* this oval-shaped boneless steak with a thick layer of connective tissue running through the center is very flavorful and tender. Remove the tissue before eating.

- **Rib/ribeye steak:** These steaks are similar, but the rib steaks have bones; ribeyes don't. These premium steaks are juicy and flavorful with generous marbling.

- **Chuck shoulder steak:** This steak, also sold as *London broil,* is a favorite for grilling or broiling. Although it ranks in the tenderness hit parade, shoulder center steak should be marinated, like the flank steak in the "Reviewing the other contestants" section, later in the chapter.

- **T-bone/Porterhouse:** These close relatives in the steak family contain both loin and tenderloin steaks. The difference is that a Porterhouse, by definition, must have more tenderloin muscle.

- **Tenderloin steak:** Ranking numero uno in tenderness, this steak is also a lean cut of beef with less than 10 grams of total fat for a 3-ounce serving. You may know this cut by its popular name — filet mignon.

- **Top loin (strip) steak:** Tender, lean, and full-flavored, this premium steak is available bone-in or boneless.

- **Top sirloin steak:** This is a boneless steak that's usually big enough to serve a family. Ask a butcher to cut this into strips for stir-fry for a quick and tasty beef dinner.

Reviewing the other contestants

Sirloin and Porterhouse aren't your only choices for meaty dinners. Flank steak and skirt steak (see Figure 13-1) are less pricey, though no less flavorful alternatives. *Flank steak* is a chewy and intensely flavored beef cut. Flank steak is also called *London broil.* I know; I know. I just told you that this name also belongs to chuck shoulder steak, but flank is the original baby. Most cooks soak flank steak in a mixture of wine, vinegar, and seasonings to tenderize it before cooking. Marinating a flank steak can take up to 24 hours, so I'm not including a recipe in this chapter.

But I can't resist passing along a tip for all you cooks who are more efficient than I am. First thing in the morning, put a flank steak in a shallow glass bowl and pour in enough bottled balsamic or Italian salad dressing to cover. Refrigerate the meat until dinnertime. Broil flank steak about 3 to 5 minutes a side and slice thinly to serve.

Skirt steak, which is cut from the rib cage of the steer, has a stringy texture and a good amount of fat on the outside of the meat. Its rich, beefy taste is most often enjoyed in the Tex-Mex dish, fajitas. The skirt steak's name comes from *fajita,* which is Spanish for *belt.* A long strip of skirt steak resembles a fashionable belt. Skirt steak is in and out of the broiler in 10 minutes tops making it ideal for busy cooks.

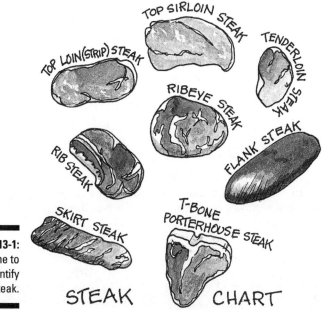

Figure 13-1:
It's time to play Identify that Steak.

How are things in guacamole?

Avocados come in two distinct styles, from different parts of the country. The California avocado is smaller than the palm of your hand. It has a pebbly skin texture. The flesh is dense, and the taste is sweet and buttery. When it's ripe, the skin of the California avocado turns dark green; almost black. The Florida avocado can grow to the size of a football but is usually the size of your hand. The flesh is more watery and the flavor milder. The skin is bright green and darkens only slightly as the avocado ripens. Squeezing avocados, you can tell the ripe ones, because they give in to gentle pressure. For guacamole, I prefer California avocados for their creamy, richer taste.

Skirt Steak with Guacamole

Arrange strips of skirt steak on a platter and pass warm flour tortillas, so everyone can wrap beef strips in tortillas. Serve the guacamole on the side or in the tortillas.

Preparation time: *15 minutes*

Cooking time: *9 minutes*

Yield: *4 servings*

1 ripe, medium avocado	¼ teaspoon pepper
2 teaspoons lemon juice	1 pound skirt steak, trimmed of excess fat
1 medium tomato, cored and finely diced	1 garlic clove
1 small jalapeno chile, cored, seeded, and minced	½ teaspoon ground cumin
1 tablespoon minced scallion	Juice of 1 lime
1 teaspoon salt	4 large flour tortillas

1 Preheat the broiler. Set the rack in the broiler 4 inches from the heat source.

2 Peel the avocado and discard the seed. Dice the avocado and place in a serving bowl. Coarsely mash the avocado with the back of a fork. Stir in the lemon juice, tomato, chile, scallion, ¼ teaspoon salt and ⅛ teaspoon pepper. Set aside.

3 Taking a sharp knife, score the steak. You do this by making shallow diagonal slashes in one direction on the steak, then across in the other direction. Smash the garlic clove with the flat of a knife. Rub the smashed garlic over the surface of the meat. Rub the ground cumin on both sides of the meat. Then drizzle on the lime juice. Sprinkle the meat with the remaining ¾ teaspoon salt and ⅛ teaspoon pepper.

4 Place the meat on an oiled rack over a broiler pan 4 inches from heat and broil 3 to 5 minutes on the first side and 3 to 4 minutes on the second side. Remove from the broiler and let stand 1 minute. Cut the meat into thin strips crosswise and arrange on a serving plate. Pass the guacamole separately or serve it in the tortillas.

Speed It Up! *Buy a half-pint of prepared guacamole from a deli or supermarket.*

Per serving: *Calories 255 (From Fat 135); Fat 15g (Saturated 5g); Cholesterol 50mg; Sodium 557mg; Carbohydrate 7g (Dietary Fiber 4g); Protein 24g.*

Use tongs to turn a steak over as you cook it. Piercing a steak with a fork allows flavorful juices to escape.

Applying some heat

Okay, now I finally get to the subject that makes a carnivore's mouth water — the steak dinner. This is the place to find out how easy it is to prepare the type of entree you usually eat in restaurants. Start the process off by choosing the steak you prefer, using the info I outline in the "What's at Steak?" section earlier in this chapter.

I think broiling, hands down, is the best technique for a fabulous center-of-the-plate, 30-minute-meal steak. (For more broiling info, check out Chapter 6.) Check out the following steak-cooking tips:

- ✔ Bring the beef to room temperature before you broil it. Cold meat doesn't cook as evenly or quickly as room temperature meat.

- ✔ Have everything else ready before you broil the meat. Set the table, sharpen the steak knives, and read the recipe. Also prepare any sauce or accompaniment before you broil. The seasonings in the sauce have a chance to blend while you broil the beef.

You also need to know when a steak is done. Overcooking ruins a steak's flavor and texture. Check out the "Is it done yet?" sidebar in this chapter for the scoop.

Some steak lovers insist the sweetest meat is next to the bone. A T-bone steak, which you can ID by the T-shaped bone, has that next-to-the-bone flavor. Grill a T-bone to a medium stage of doneness and serve the meat with a garlicky herb sauce. Now that your appetite is whetted, move on to the broiler.

Is it done yet?

Checking a steak for doneness is an essential step. Using an instant-read meat thermometer provides an accurate gauge. Insert the thermometer at an angle, so the thermometer penetrates the center of the meat without touching the grill pan or any bone.

The temperatures for the various states of doneness:

- ✔ 145 degrees is medium-rare.

- ✔ 160 degrees is medium.

- ✔ 170 is well-done.

You can also do a visual test. Make a small incision in the center of the steak and take a peek inside. The interior should be red, not bloody. Steak should be a tad less cooked than you want it to be, because the meat continues to cook off the heat for another few minutes. Pulling steak from the broiler when it's completely done can result in overcooked meat.

Argentinean-Style T-Bone Steak

Argentineans are so enamored of grilled meat, they set up barbecue grills outside of even mom and pop restaurants. Walking down a busy street, a tourist can't help but be tempted by the aroma of steaks on the grill. Chimichurri (chee-*mee*-choor-ee), an uncooked sauce of herbs, garlic, oil, and vinegar, is the classic accompaniment to grilled meat in that South American country. Make a gutsy salad using a bag of baby spinach, a fistful of garlic croutons and a bottled Caesar salad dressing to go with this main dish.

Preparation time: *10 minutes*

Cooking time: *15 minutes*

Yield: *4 servings*

2 garlic cloves, chopped

⅔ cup packed cilantro leaves

2 tablespoons Italian parsley

1 scallion, trimmed and coarsely chopped

¾ cup olive oil

1½ teaspoons salt

¼ teaspoon pepper

¼ cup white wine vinegar

2 T-bone steaks, each about 1 pound in weight and 1 inch thick

1 teaspoon coarsely ground or cracked black pepper

1 Set the rack in the broiler 4 inches from heat source. Preheat the broiler.

2 Make the chimichurri sauce: Place the garlic cloves in a food processor or mini chopper fitted with a steel blade. Mince the garlic using on/off turns of the machine. Add the cilantro, parsley, scallion, and ¼ cup of the olive oil. Turn the machine on and process until the herbs are finely minced. Remove the herbs and oil from the food processor. Place in a bowl with the remaining oil, ½ teaspoon of salt, and ¼ teaspoon of pepper. Stir in the vinegar and set the mixture aside.

3 Place the steaks on an oiled rack over a broiler pan. Season the steaks on both sides with the remaining 1 teaspoon of salt and coarsely ground black pepper. Position the steaks under the broiler and broil for 7 minutes on the first side. Remove the steaks, turn over and broil 7 minutes on the second side or until the beef tests done.

4 Remove the steaks from the broiler, cover loosely with foil and let stand for 5 minutes. Cut the steaks into ½-inch slices and serve with the chimichurri sauce on the side.

Vary It! *Chopping the garlic, cilantro, Italian parsley, and scallion by hand results in a mixture that isn't as pulpy. You can prepare the chimichurri sauce using a chef's knife if you prefer.*

Per serving: Calories 580 (From Fat 457); Fat 51g (Saturated 9g); Cholesterol 61mg; Sodium 957mg; Carbohydrate 1g (Dietary Fiber 0g); Protein 29g.

Lamb for Dinner

Lamb chops are a natural for 30-minute meals. Lamb comes from young sheep that are usually less than a year old, so you're pretty much assured a tender cut of meat.

Like beef, lamb is graded. The three most common retail grades are

- **Prime:** Usually reserved for restaurants.
- **Choice:** The grade you're most likely to see in supermarkets.
- **Good:** Often used for processed meat products.

Unfortunately, lamb isn't as popular in the United States as it is in Europe and the Middle East. Americans probably eat less than a couple of pounds of lamb a year on average. For that reason, lamb is expensive. To get the best quality for your money, look for the following when you shop:

- **Color:** Lamb meat should be light to berry red. Avoid lamb that's a deep wine shade of red. That's a sign of older, tougher, gamy-tasting lamb. The fat should be smooth, firm, and white.
- **Odor:** Avoid strong-smelling meat or fat — a sign that the meat is too old.
- **Texture:** Look for moist, plump lamb. Stay away from shriveled or dried-out looking meat.

Quick lamb cuts

Butchers cut lamb chops from various parts of the carcass. Depending on your budget and taste preferences, you can select from several lamb chops.

- **Rib chops:** have a distinctive rib bone with an "eye" of lamb meat attached. Rib chops, which have a high proportion of fat, are tender and measly (if you believe the grumbles that come from my lamb-loving family). Each rib contains a nugget of meat. Ask your butcher to cut lamb rib chops an inch thick and allow 2 to 3 per serving.

  Fancy caterers scrape the bits of meat off the rib bone of a rib chop and serve the chops as "lollipop" appetizers. And you tell your children not to play with their food!

- **Loin chops:** Meatier than rib chops, loin chops resemble a miniature T-bone steak. Loin chops are often the most expensive lamb cut your butcher offers. Buy loin chops that are at least an inch thick and allow 2 per serving.

- ✔ **Sirloin chops:** Carved from the hip of the lamb, these are larger than rib or loin chops. Although they have less fat than other chops and are less tender, sirloin chops can still be grilled. Their flavor is robust, which makes the slightly tougher texture acceptable to diners. Sirloin chops should be at least ½ inch thick. These are heftier chops, so figure on a 6- to 8-ounce chop per serving.

- ✔ **Shoulder chops:** These flavorful and most economical cuts are also called *arm chops* or *blade chops*. Braising is usually the best way to cook shoulder chops. I'm mentioning them, because I sometimes successfully grill them. If your butcher cut the meat near the rib, it's going to be tenderer, so you can grill it. Ask your butcher for shoulder chops cut near the rib if you want to grill the meat. Shoulder chops are usually cut about ½ to ¾ inch thick, which is fine for grilling. Take a look at the chops to determine servings. Blade chops have bones, and the more bones you have, the less meat. Allow one 6-ounce chop per person; select larger chops if the chop has more bones.

Pan-broiling lamb chops

These days, I don't use my well-seasoned cast-iron skillet very often. But I always make an exception when I'm cooking lamb chops. I love pan-broiled lamb chops. The meat hits the hot skillet and the sizzling sound vibrates through the house. In less time than it takes for me to call the family to dinner, the lamb turns crusty brown. (For a full-scale pan-broiling discussion, see Chapter 6.)

Keep these few suggestions in mind when pan-broiling lamb:

- ✔ Bring the meat to room temperature first, so it cooks quickly and evenly.

- ✔ I suggest seasoning the lamb with salt and pepper if you want a crustier exterior. If you're not sure whether to salt, read what I have to say about salted meat in the "Salting savvy" sidebar in this chapter.

- ✔ Make sure the skillet or sauté pan is hot before you add the lamb. Add a couple of drops of water to the skillet. If they dance and evaporate in less than 30 seconds, you're ready to cook.

Spring like a lamb

You may see the term *spring lamb* in older cookbooks or food books. Spring is lamb-birthing time. Buying spring lamb was an assurance of getting young and tender meat. Thanks to modern breeding techniques, lambs are bred and born the year round now, assuring you of juicy, fresh meat cuts in any season.

Pan-broiling is exacting cooking. Stand by ready to turn the lamb chops over after the recommended time. Well-done lamb is dry and tough.

Rosemary-Scented Lamb Chops

Woodsy smelling rosemary tastes marvelous with lamb. But use even fresh rosemary in small amounts or it will overpower the subtle meat. Make sure you chop the rosemary before you start the recipe, so the lamb doesn't get cold while you're making the sauce.

Preparation time: 10 minutes

Cooking time: 6 to 8 minutes, if cooking lamb in one batch

Yield: 4 servings

8 (1 inch thick) lamb loin chops or rib chops

1 tablespoon olive oil

1 teaspoon salt

½ teaspoon pepper

1 garlic clove, peeled and minced

½ teaspoon fresh chopped rosemary, or ¼ teaspoon crumbled, dried rosemary

½ cup dry red wine

¼ cup beef broth

1 tablespoon butter

1 Brush all the lamb chops with the tablespoon of olive oil and season the lamb with salt and pepper. Heat a large, heavy-bottomed skillet. Arrange the lamb in a single layer in the skillet. If necessary, do this in 2 batches.

2 Cook the lamb over high heat for 3 to 4 minutes on each side for rare or 4 minutes per side for medium-rare. As soon as the lamb is done, remove it from the skillet. Place the cooked lamb on a platter and arrange a loose sheet of aluminum foil over the dish so the lamb stays hot. Cook the remaining chops and then add to the platter and cover.

3 Add the garlic clove and rosemary to the skillet and lightly sauté in the skillet fat for 30 seconds. Add the red wine and scrape up any browned bits in the skillet. Cook the wine over high heat for 1 to 2 minutes or until reduced by half. Add the broth and bring just to a boil. Remove the skillet from heat and add the butter. Tilt the skillet so the butter melts into the sauce.

4 Arrange the lamb chops on 4 plates and spoon the wine sauce over each serving.

Per serving: Calories 259 (From Fat 137); Fat 15g (Saturated 5g); Cholesterol 95mg; Sodium 722mg; Carbohydrate 1g (Dietary Fiber 0g); Protein 28g.

Reducing your sauce time

My Rosemary-Scented Lamb Chops recipe in this chapter uses a red-wine reduction to make a tasty sauce. Reducing wine or broth in a skillet or pan is a quick way to make a sauce.

Reducing is cooking a liquid over high heat until some of the volume evaporates. The remaining liquid is slightly thick and has a concentrated flavor.

New-Fangled Pork Chops

Pork chops come from the loin or from the ribs. Take a look at a pork chop recipe in a cookbook from the '40s or '50s, and you see directions to braise the meat for an hour or more. Pork used to be a tougher meat that needed long, slow cooking. Pork was also more likely to contain parasites and lengthy cooking was the remedy.

Things have changed. Pork you buy in supermarkets today doesn't have parasites. You don't have to cook pork forever to kill the bugs. However, you still need to follow the safety guidelines you'd use for any meat. Cook pork to an internal temperature of 160 degrees.

The good news is that you can enjoy succulent pork chops in half the time it took your parent's generation to cook the meat.

This little piggy went to market

Like beef and lamb, pork gets a grade. But the grade is a number, not a word, and only food-industry insiders use it. You won't see it on a package.

When you're in the market for some pork, inspect the meat to make sure you're getting the quality you pay for:

- Rosy pink describes a healthy piece of pork.
- Just as with other meats, pork fat should be white and firm.
- Fresh pork has a very mild odor, not a strong smell of meat.

The taste and texture of pork chops will vary according to the cut you select. The pork chops that you can choose from in your supermarket are

- ✔ **Blade chops** or pork loin blade chops are cut from the loin. Loin chops are usually cut ¾- to 1½ inches thick. Choose the thicker chops for pan- or oven-broiling. Thin chops dry out too easily. You can also braise blade chops to doneness in less than 30 minutes, which means this cut has a place on your menu if you're doing a simple recipe. One blade chop, about 6 to 8 ounces, makes 1 serving.

- ✔ **Loin chops** come from the back of the pig. This cut contains the pork tenderloin, which is lean and tender. Its shape resembles a beef Porterhouse steak, and it's comparably good eating. Loin chops can easily dry out, so choose pieces that are an inch thick. A loin chop, about 8 ounces, serves 1 and cooks in less than 20 minutes

- ✔ **Rib chops** are the Miss America of the pork case, beautiful to behold. The thick eye of meat anchored by the rib bone is tender, delicate tasting, and so easy to overcook, but you'll like the short cooking time. Cut rib chops 1½ inches thick and sauté or broil the meat. A good-size rib chop weighs 8 to 12 ounces and serves 1 generously.

- ✔ **Sirloin chops** have more bones than some cuts, but compensate with good flavor and tenderness and can fit into your time budget. Ask a butcher to cut sirloin chops about 1 inch thick and braise the meat briefly. One sirloin chop, about 8 ounces, serves 1.

Hoofing it to the kitchen

Pork chops deliver a substantial serving of meat. No one in my household grouses about not having enough to eat when pork chops are on the menu. I like the chops because they're ready to cook. I don't have to trim fat or mess with the meat in any way. Although there are many ways to cook pork chops, I prefer a method that keeps the meat tender and enhances the subtle pork flavor.

Today's lean pork loin chop — which is more successful at weight loss than I am — keeps its moisture and flavor if you prepare it using my favorite two-step process.

1. Brown the pork chops in a little oil to get a wonderfully tasty crust on the meat.

2. Add a few sauce and flavoring ingredients, cover the pan or skillet, and simmer briefly.

I share my technique for cooking loin chops with peaches in my Peach-Glazed Pork Chops recipe in this chapter. Make sure you get pork chops that are an inch thick.

Salting savvy

Salting meat before you cook it, especially when you broil it, draws out moisture and inhibits browning, say some meat experts. But chefs and other professional meat cooks argue that meat tastes better after broiling if you salt it beforehand.

I salt meat before I broil it. Salt melts and saturates the meat flavoring while it cooks. Meat that's salted after cooking never tastes quite as good. Salting a skillet or sauté pan before you pan-broil also improves the taste of meat in my opinion. Try it and see if you agree. Salt a skillet and then add a steak. The salt quickly draws the moisture to the surface of the steak, creating an appealing crust.

Peach-Glazed Pork Chops

Fruit and pork are a delightful duet. Add a little vinegar or lemon juice to fruit to prevent the sauce from tasting too sweet. When fresh peaches are in season, peel and slice two large fresh peaches for this recipe. Other times of the year, use frozen peach slices.

Preparation time: *5 minutes*

Cooking time: *20 minutes*

Yield: *4 servings*

1 tablespoon vegetable oil	½ cup peach jam
4 boneless pork chops, 1 inch thick	2 cups peeled, sliced peaches
¾ teaspoon salt	¼ teaspoon ground ginger
½ teaspoon pepper	1 tablespoon honey mustard
½ cup chicken broth	1 tablespoon cider vinegar

1 Heat the oil in a large sauté pan over medium heat. Season the pork chops with ½ teaspoon salt and ¼ teaspoon pepper. Add the pork chops in a single layer to the sauté pan and brown for 2 minutes per side. Remove the pork chops from the pan and set aside. Add the broth and cook over high heat scraping up browned bits from the pan. Reduce the heat to low.

2 Stir together the peach jam, peaches, ginger, honey mustard, vinegar, remaining ¼ teaspoon salt, and ¼ teaspoon pepper in a bowl. Stir the peach mixture into the pan. Return the pork to the pan and baste with the jam mixture. Cover the pan and simmer for 15 minutes.

Vary It! *Oranges and pork are also a delicious combination. Use a cup of orange marmalade and one navel orange, peeled and divided into segments. Taste the dish before adding the vinegar. Oranges may add just enough tartness. Also, try serving the pork and sauce over cooked egg noodles.*

Per serving: Calories 348 (From Fat 99); Fat 11g (Saturated 3g); Cholesterol 64mg; Sodium 629mg; Carbohydrate 39g (Dietary Fiber 2g); Protein 23g.

Chicken Convenience

Boneless, skinless chicken breasts have practically revolutionized the dinner hour, showing that a low-fat and delicious meal in short order really is possible. Chicken breast weights vary greatly, but as a rough estimate, expect to get about 5 to 7 ounces of chicken, which makes boneless, skinless chicken breast meat as filling as it is fast.

Boneless, skinless chicken breast is a whole or half breast of a chicken, with the skin, bone, and some of the surface fat trimmed off. Cooking a boneless, skinless chicken breast takes about ⅓ to ½ the time of a bone-in breast. No wonder this is the most popular choice among American shoppers when they purchase chicken. Bone-in chicken breast by the way, is number two.

Serving boneless, skinless chicken breast not only assures you of quick meals, but varied ones, too. You can cook your way through every ethnic cuisine's chicken repertoire and never repeat a recipe for a year. I haven't tried that. But just thinking about the possibilities gets my creative juices going.

Speaking of juices, boneless, skinless chicken breast comes from the young broiler, brought to market at 6 to 8 weeks of age. Although you're getting tender chicken, it can dry out easily. But you won't have that problem when you follow my suggestions in this section on how to buy boneless, skinless chicken breast meat and how to prepare it so you get both a flavorful and a fast entree.

Breast or breasts

A chicken breast, which is the raw meat of a chicken's chest, includes both lobes. But when cooks refer to a chicken breast, it's usually half the breast. Supermarkets carry both whole and half breasts. To separate a whole breast, use a chef's knife and split the breast in half. If parts of the center breastbone are still attached to the meat, remove them with a paring knife.

Pounding it down to size

As chicken breasts are growing in popularity, they're also getting heftier. The chicken breasts you pick up in the supermarket are a couple of ounces heavier than those of a decade ago, according to chicken producers.

Although that means more chicken meat for you and me, it also means boneless, skinless chicken can take longer to cook. But the cooking time doesn't only depend on the weight of the chicken. The shape is also a factor. Take a look at a boneless, skinless chicken breast: It's plump in the center, and it tapers off at the ends. When the ends are done, the center may still be pink.

Pounding chicken breasts to an even thickness ensures quicker and more even cooking. You can use a large wooden hammer to pound the chicken or do what I do: flatten chicken using the heaviest skillet you own. For the step-by-step guide, check out Figure 13-2. But keep these items in mind as well:

- ✔ Clear your counter space. The vibrations can start your kitchenware jumping.

- ✔ Brush the chicken breasts with a damp paper towel to remove any bone chips that are a natural part of chicken processing. You want to avoid pounding bone fragments into the chicken.

- ✔ Do extra chicken breasts at the same time. After you're set up, pounding a few more breasts just takes minutes. Wrap and freeze the extras.

FLATTENING A CHICKEN BREAST

HERE'S HOW TO POUND A BONELESS, SKINLESS CHICKEN BREAST HALF TO AN EVEN THICKNESS.

Figure 13-2: Give it a good whack!

1. PLACE THE CHICKEN BREAST ON A SHEET OF WAX PAPER OVER A CUTTING BOARD SO YOU DON'T DENT THE COUNTER!

2. PLACE A SECOND SHEET OF WAX PAPER OVER THE CHICKEN, COVERING IT.

3. USING A HEAVY SKILLET OR MALLET, POUND THE CHICKEN BREAST TO AN EVEN THICKNESS.

HEY!

You can freeze raw chicken parts, such as pounded boneless, skinless chicken breasts, up to 12 months in a freezer set at zero degrees.

Kids and hammers

In this chapter, I recommend that you pound chicken breasts flat to ensure quicker and more even cooking. If you have children who love to bang and make plenty of noise (what child doesn't like to make noise?), bring them into the kitchen to help with the chore. I don't recommend asking children younger than age 7 or 8 to do chicken pounding. Younger children might get distracted and accidentally whack themselves. In addition, keep an eye on your helpful assistants.

Cooking juicy chicken breasts

You can cook tender chicken breasts outdoors on the grill or in your oven broiler. However, because chicken breasts are so lean, which means so low in fat, preventing the chicken from drying out is more of a concern than cooking it fast. Keeping the skin on during cooking is the best way to keep the moisture in a chicken breast. But if you're buying boneless, skinless chicken breasts, you can compensate in other ways.

✔ Marinate boneless, skinless chicken breasts for 10 to 15 minutes in salad dressing before cooking. (See Chapter 7 for more on marinating in salad dressing.)

✔ Start chicken breasts at a high temperature to seal in the juices and then turn the heat down, so the chicken doesn't dry out.

✔ Cook chicken in a sauce.

✔ Set boneless skinless chicken breasts aside for 5 minutes before serving. That way the juices are re-absorbed into the chicken.

My favorite way to cook chicken in less than 30 minutes — while keeping it moist and tasty — is to sauté the chicken to brown it and then simmer it in a flavorful sauce. Even if I cook chicken a couple minutes more than I intend, the sauce will hide my goof.

Spirits, such as wine and brandy, are wonderful flavoring agents for chicken breast meat. Cooking destroys most, but not absolutely all of the alcohol in liquor, according to university studies. If you have children or adults who should not be imbibing, substitute chicken broth for the alcohol.

Chicken Breasts with Brandy and Mustard Sauce

This heady brandy sauce that flavors the chicken demands rice or noodles to catch every luscious drop. If you prefer, simply serve the chicken with a crusty French bread for dipping into the sauce. If chicken breasts are very thick, however, pound them to an even thickness as shown in Figure 13-2.

Preparation time: *5 minutes*

Cooking time: *20 minutes*

Yield: *4 servings*

1 tablespoon olive oil	*1 garlic clove, peeled and minced*
4 chicken boneless, skinless breast halves	*¼ cup brandy*
½ teaspoon salt	*1 cup chicken broth*
¼ teaspoon pepper	*1½ tablespoons Dijon-style mustard*

1 Heat the oil over high heat in a large sauté pan. Season the chicken breasts with salt and pepper. Add the chicken to the hot oil and brown 2 minutes per side. Remove the chicken to a plate. Add the garlic and sauté 30 seconds.

2 Add the brandy and scrape up the browned bits in the sauté pan. Stir in the broth and mustard and whisk until the mustard is well mixed. Return the chicken to sauté pan.

3 Cover the pan, reduce the heat to low and simmer until chicken is completely cooked, about 10 minutes. Remove the chicken and keep warm. Bring the liquid to a boil and cook 1 minute, or until the volume is reduced by ¼. Arrange the chicken on plates and top with pan juices.

Per serving: Calories 173 (From Fat 68); Fat 8g (Saturated 2g); Cholesterol 64mg; Sodium 737mg; Carbohydrate 1g (Dietary Fiber 0g); Protein 24g.

Fish Steaks

Fish steaks are thick, firm cuts that satisfy big appetites. People who tell me they never eat fish, hunker down for a fish steak. Fish steaks have a chewy texture and robust taste that satisfies meat lovers. A *fish steak* is fish that's cut down at a perpendicular angle.

Salmon, tuna, and halibut are the big three to net for your 30-minute meals. Salmon and tuna are prized for their fat content. Having a high amount of fat means you can grill or broil the fish without worrying that it will dry out.

Halibut has less fat. You can still grill or broil it, but be sure to baste halibut with oil to keep it moist.

Visiting your fishmonger

Fishmongers, the old-fashioned term for people professionally trained to dress fish, are your best friends when it comes to fish shopping, but first do a little scouting:

- ✔ Look at the display. The fish should be arranged in bowls over ice so it stays cold but doesn't get too chilled.
- ✔ The fish should look glossy and firm, not shriveled.
- ✔ The fish display shouldn't have a strong odor.
- ✔ The fish should turnover frequently. I don't expect the fish to flip itself, but I do expect it to sell and be replaced by other fresh fish daily or at least every other day.

After you decide this is the fish counter for you, tell the fishmonger how you intend to cook the fish and ask for help. For example, if you're broiling fish, ask that the fish steak be sliced at least ½ inch thick. Fish cooks so fast that thinner pieces are likely to dry out. If you see a piece of fish that catches your eye and you're unfamiliar with it, ask the fishmonger what it tastes like and how to cook it.

I can't think of a single piece of fish cut as a steak or *fillet* (fish cut along the length so you get long thin slices) that won't be ready in less than 30 minutes. The fish counter is made for 30-minute meals.

Broiling fish steaks

Although you can cook fish steaks many ways, I prefer to broil them. That way I get the same meaty texture I do from beef. The even thickness of a steak, such as tuna or salmon, means that the fish surface cooks evenly with no underdone spots. And the blast of heat means you spend mere minutes cooking.

Using a little math and your senses, you can cook fish to perfection. The general fish-cooking rule comes from Canada, where fishermen haul in quite a catch each year. Canadians say allow 10 minutes of cooking time for every inch of fish thickness. A ½-inch fish cooks in 5 minutes; an inch-thick cut in 10 minutes. Because this is a guesstimate and every cut is slightly different, keep these points in mind:

✔ Start checking one or two minutes before the recipe indicates the fish is done, so you don't overcook fish.

✔ Look at the fish. As it cooks, the flesh goes from translucent to opaque and firms up. As soon as you see that happening, insert a thin-blade knife and gently pull a part of the flesh aside, so you can peek at the interior. If it's just turning opaque, remove the fish from the heat. It will continue to cook for a minute or two as it rests.

✔ Use an instant-read thermometer. Insert the thermometer in the center of the fish, not touching a bone or the pan. The temperature for safely cooked fish is 145 degrees.

Following the inch rule, you can see how important it is to have all the other components of your meal ready before you start cooking fish. Serving overcooked or cold fish is so annoying that I insist everyone sit down at the dinner table before I run a fish steak under the broiler. I'm sure you're not as tyrannical in your kitchen.

Preparing a sauce or relish in advance is the best way to assure a fish dish is ready to serve the instant the fish is pulled from the broiler.

Broiled Tuna with Red Pepper Tapenade

Tapenade is a Mediterranean relish of olives, olive oil, and herbs. Many versions of this recipe call for roasting a red pepper. I substitute roasted peppers from a jar for convenience sake. Serve with a crusty French bread.

Preparation time: *10 minutes*

Cooking time: *16 to 18 minutes*

Yield: *4 servings*

2½ tablespoons olive oil	½ teaspoon crushed, dried oregano
2 large shallots, peeled and minced	2 teaspoons fresh lemon juice
1 clove garlic, minced	4 tuna steaks (4 to 6 ounces each), cut ¾ inch thick
2 roasted red peppers, drained and chopped	
2 tablespoons capers	1 teaspoon coarsely ground black pepper
¼ cup minced, pitted ripe olives	1 lemon, cut into wedges

1 Set the rack of the broiler 4 inches from the heat source. Preheat the broiler.

2 Heat 1½ tablespoons of the olive oil in a medium-sized skillet. Add the shallots and garlic and cook over medium heat for 1 to 2 minutes. Remove the vegetables and any remaining oil and spoon into a bowl. Add the roasted peppers, capers, olives, oregano, and lemon juice to the shallot mixture. Set aside for the flavors to blend while making the tuna.

3 Place the tuna steaks on the greased rack of a broiler pan. Brush the tuna steaks with the remaining 1 tablespoon of olive oil and sprinkle with the pepper. Broil the tuna 3 to 4 minutes per side or until the fish is cooked through. Remove from the broiler and set aside for 1 to 2 minutes to finish cooking. To serve, arrange the fish on plates and add lemon wedges to each serving. Pass the tapenade on the side.

Per serving: Calories 221 (From Fat 94); Fat 11g (Saturated 2g); Cholesterol 49mg; Sodium 257mg; Carbohydrate 5g (Dietary Fiber 1g); Protein 26g.

Chapter 14

Sweet Nothings

"*W*hat's for dessert?" is the favorite dinner-time question in my household and probably in yours as well. And it's not an idle question. Everyone assumes you have a sweet treat that you're hiding away until the end of the meal. And the question isn't just about food; it's an abbreviated way to tell you that everyone's having a good time at the table, so no one is ready to leave yet. If you're enjoying a meal by yourself, adding a dessert lets you stretch the pleasures of the table a little longer. Of course, you're not about to disappoint your family, yourself, or your guests even though you don't have time to bake a cake or a batch of cookies.

Supermarkets are bulging with packaged cookies and bags of candy, but a dessert that includes your personal touch still wins out. Homemade desserts don't have to mean intricate multi-layered cakes with piped frosting that you see in some lifestyle magazines. You don't have to be on a first-name basis with a certain queen of the kitchen to satisfy your family's sweet tooth.

As you'll discover in this chapter, you can quickly turn ready-to-eat foods, such as ice cream, cakes, biscuits, or that ultimate ready-to-eat food — fruit, into a signature dessert that's worth asking for. I provide my time-tested tips for whipping up a dessert in minutes. I cover fabulous sauces that you can use to enhance dessert staples. I take my fondue pot out of the attic to relay the fondue facts. And I show you how to add a bit of variety — and fun — to tried-and-true ice cream. With the luscious, tempting, and quick-preparation desserts in this chapter, you can answer the what's-for-dessert question with ease and pleasure.

Satisfying and Simple Ideas

In the Bennett theory of anatomy, your eyes are connected directly to your stomach. Beautiful-looking food puts your tummy into a state of eager anticipation. And because dessert is often the most anticipated part of the meal, every cook facing time constraints needs to have a collection of stunningly attractive but easy dessert ideas that you can assemble in minutes. Don't worry about whipping egg whites for a soufflé or poaching fresh fruit. I won't demand a degree in pastry making before you get to the delicious part of this section — eating mouthwatering desserts.

Skipping any elaborate steps, you can make a treat using mostly food staples that you have in the refrigerator, freezer, or cupboard. Five of my sweetest ideas are as follows:

- ✔ **Strawberry thrill:** Buy lush, picture-perfect strawberries with the caps on. Dip each berry in a small bowl of Grand Marnier or brandy and eat. Or, taking this to another level, dip each strawberry in the liqueur, then roll the berries in a mixture of 3 tablespoons unsweetened cocoa and 1 tablespoon sugar and eat.

- ✔ **Peach delish:** Arrange 2 canned or frozen peach halves in a bowl. Mix together ⅓ cup ricotta cheese, 1 tablespoon sugar, and ½ teaspoon vanilla extract and spoon the mixture into the peach cavities. Sprinkle on chocolate chips.

- ✔ **Ice-cream sandwich deluxe:** Take a scoop of butter pecan ice cream and sandwich it between two store-bought chocolate chip or oatmeal cookies. The ice cream should come to the edges of the cookies. Spread chopped pecans on a plate; then roll the ice cream edges of the sandwich in the nuts to coat. Eat this instantly — as if that's a problem — or place the ice cream sandwich in the freezer for a couple of hours.

- ✔ **Parfait perfection:** Place a ¼ cup of fresh or frozen thawed raspberries in a parfait glass. Stir together ¼ cup of sour cream or reduced-fat sour cream, 1 tablespoon sugar, and ½ teaspoon vanilla extract in a small bowl. Top the raspberries with half the sour cream mixture. Add another ¼ cup of raspberries and finish with the remaining sour cream.

- ✔ **Elvis would'a loved this:** Take one sheet of a chocolate graham cracker and spread with peanut butter. Sprinkle with chocolate chips and peanuts. Serve the cracker open-face or top it with a second graham cracker.

Getting Saucy

Put away that revealing outfit. In this case, *saucy* covers all the desserts you can enhance. Add dazzling flavor and color to frozen pound cake or eliminate the word *plain* from vanilla ice cream with a sauce topping. In this section, I review some of my favorite picks for fruit, fruit and spirits, caramel, and chocolate sauces. Keep reading for mouthwatering and almost instant dessert recipes that start with sauces.

Picking fruit

Spooning a fruit sauce onto a scoop of ice cream or a piece of packaged cake or folding it into sweetened whipped cream is a quick and refreshing way to end any meal. I used to wait until summer when fresh berries are in season to make fruit sauces. But I discovered that frozen berries packed without added sugar, are equally tasty.

Dividing blocks of frozen fruit into the portions that you want is difficult. Instead, select frozen fruit by the bag. Bagged fruit is individually quick frozen (IQF), so you can pour out what you need and keep the remainder in the freezer. You don't have to thaw the frozen fruit that you're going to use to make a cooked sauce.

Check out the following words of wisdom (if I do say so myself) for making your fruit sauce shine:

- ✔ Taste fruit before you use it in a sauce. That way, you can add a little sugar if the fruit is sour or add a dash of lemon juice if the fruit is bland.

- ✔ Although sauces are a great way to use up scraps of fruit, don't include any fruit that you wouldn't want to eat. Shriveled fruit doesn't have the juicy texture that makes sauces, well, saucy.

- ✔ Fresh fruit sauces don't keep well. The fruit flavor deteriorates quickly, so make a fruit sauce within a couple of hours of serving.

If you're watching your weight but don't want a meager dessert, spoon raspberry sauce over angel food cake or frozen vanilla yogurt. Top frozen, thawed peach slices with raspberry sauce and you have a delicious, low-cal variation on the classic dessert of peaches Melba — a dessert of raspberry sauce over peaches named for the opera singer Nellie Melba.

For a knockout dessert, split store-bought baking powder biscuits in half. Add a scoop of fresh raspberries to the bottom of each biscuit and close with the top half. Top each biscuit with a large dollop of whipped cream and drizzle on my Raspberry Sauce.

🍅 Raspberry Sauce

Raspberry sauce, the color of garnets, can brighten any ho-hum dessert. In our household, we like raspberry sauce over pound cake.

Preparation time: *2 minutes*

Cooking time: *About 6 minutes*

Yield: *4 servings*

2 cups fresh or frozen raspberries	*1 tablespoon water*
3 tablespoons sugar	*Grated zest of 1 lemon*

Combine the raspberries, sugar, and water in a small pot. Bring to a low boil. Cook the raspberries for 5 minutes. Add the lemon zest and cook at medium heat 1 to 2 minutes or until the mixture has a sauce-like consistency.

Vary It! *If you prefer a thicker consistency, stir 1 teaspoon of cornstarch into 1 tablespoon of cold water and add the mixture to the pot along with the lemon zest. Try substituting strawberries for the raspberries. Cut any large berries in half before cooking. You can also place the raspberry sauce in an ice cream machine and process it according to your manufacturer's directions for raspberry sorbet.*

Per serving: *Calories 67 (From Fat 0); Fat 0g (Saturated 0g); Cholesterol 0mg; Sodium 0mg; Carbohydrate 17g (Dietary Fiber 4g); Protein 1g.*

Getting into the spirit

Nothing says summer like tropical fruit and rum. They make a delightful dessert combination. One taste of a spirited and saucy dessert and you forget that your life is in overdrive. It's like having an after-dinner vacation break in the Caribbean.

Select golden to dark rum for dessert. The more color that a rum has, the more flavor it has. Golden rum has a light fruity and caramel taste. Dark rum is rich and buttery. Light rum's flavor isn't distinctive enough to partner with fruit in a dessert. Save it for cocktails.

🍑 *Mango-Rum Sauce*

A luscious, ripe mango doesn't need much adornment. Cook a little rum and sugar with diced mango and serve over frozen vanilla yogurt for a festive yet simple dessert. Because the fruit varies so much in sweetness, you may want to add sugar, but taste the sauce first.

Preparation time: *5 minutes*

Cooking time: *5 minutes*

Yield: *4 servings*

1 tablespoon butter	*¼ cup dark rum*
2 cups diced fresh mango (1 large or 2 medium mangos)	*1 to 2 tablespoons sugar (optional)*

1 Melt the butter in a medium-size skillet over medium heat. Add the mangos and sauté over medium heat for 3 to 5 minutes or until the fruit is pulpy. Add the rum and cook over high heat for 1 minute or until the rum becomes syrupy.

2 Taste the mixture. If it isn't sweet enough, add 1 to 2 tablespoons sugar and simmer 1 minute or until the sugar dissolves.

Vary It! *You can also double this recipe and store the leftovers in the refrigerator up to three days. Mix the remaining mango-rum sauce with a little pineapple juice in a blender, add ice, and you have a tropical cocktail.*

Per serving: *Calories 82 (From Fat 28); Fat 3g (Saturated 2g); Cholesterol 8mg; Sodium 2mg; Carbohydrate 14g (Dietary Fiber 2g); Protein 1g.*

Buttering up

My husband loves a buttery, rich caramel sauce, and I make the sauce from scratch when I have time. But, like sap trickling from a tree, the process is long and tedious, but with sweet results. When my husband recently hinted for caramel sauce — right in the middle of a busy evening — I experimented with a shortcut. Instead of melting sugar, I mixed brown sugar, butter, and cream. The result doesn't taste like caramel sauce, but it's just as delicious.

"It tastes just like those praline candies," says my hubby. And, being a fan of very buttery, sweet New Orleans praline candies, he couldn't resist. Neither can I. Try the Praline Sauce recipe in this section to see what all the fuss is about. It's great with ice cream and pecan pound cake or as a dipping sauce for banana chunks.

⟳ Praline Sauce

Ladle pools of praline sauce over your favorite ice cream or cake. Store any leftover sauce in a covered container in the refrigerator up to one week. Stir the sauce well before serving it.

Preparation time: *2 minutes*

Cooking time: *5 minutes*

Yield: *6 servings*

⅔ *cup brown sugar*	½ *cup heavy cream*
¼ *cup butter*	¼ *teaspoon salt*

Combine the brown sugar, butter, cream, and salt in a small, heavy-bottomed pot. Cook the mixture over low heat 5 minutes or until the brown sugar dissolves and the butter melts. Do not let the mixture come to a boil, which causes the sauce to separate. Serve warm.

Vary It! *Add a tablespoon of whiskey or scotch to the pot and simmer with the other ingredients.*

Per serving: *Calories 228 (From Fat 134); Fat 15g (Saturated 9g); Cholesterol 48mg; Sodium 115mg; Carbohydrate 25g (Dietary Fiber 0g); Protein 1g.*

Chocolate — enough said

Prepare a dense and intense chocolate sauce, and dessert takes care of itself. Although gourmet food shelves are stacked high with chocolate sauce — plain chocolate, chocolate with mint, hazelnuts, and coffee, or any number of versions — you don't need to stock up on commercial products. You can make a thick and velvety smooth chocolate sauce in no time.

Diving into the ingredients

Chocolate defines the sauce. The better quality the chocolate, the better tasting your sauce is.

Take a bite of chocolate and close your eyes. Let the chocolate melt in your mouth. Do you taste chocolate or some other flavor, such as coffee, orange, or a sharp burnt taste. You should just taste chocolate, slightly bitter, a hint of wine, sweet, but not like candy and very complicated. If you have trouble describing the chocolate, but can't wait to take another bite, you've got a good brand.

Tasting is the best way to choose chocolate for sauce, but labels provide plenty of information as well. Chocolate makers are in competition to see which one can make a product with the highest amount of cocoa "liquor." Cocoa liquor isn't alcoholic, unless chocolate makes you intoxicated. The liquor is the cocoa essence after the *cocoa butter* (fat) is removed.

The more liquor a chocolate contains, the more intense the chocolate taste. Good-quality chocolate brands, such as Lindt (which is pronounced like the not-too-tasty *lint*), Valrhona (*va*-rona), and Scharffen Berger (*shar*-fen berger) are high in chocolate liquor. Find these brands in supermarkets, better food stores, gourmet food stores, and even some upscale coffee shops.

Supermarkets usually sell high-quality chocolate bars in the candy section, not the baking section.

Along with the best-quality chocolate, I always insist on these ingredients to make a marvelous chocolate sauce:

- **Unsalted butter:** I recommend unsalted butter, so you can control how much salt to add.

- **Salt:** Salt is a surprising, though necessary ingredient in a sweet sauce; it brings out the sweetness. Without a pinch of salt, a sweet dish tastes flat.

- **Heavy cream:** Cream's high fat content gives sauce a smooth, silky feel in your mouth.

- **Corn syrup:** Many chocolate sauce recipes call for sugar. I prefer light corn syrup, because it gives chocolate sauce a chewy consistency.

Preparing a melted masterpiece

Right now, I hope you're digging around your kitchen drawer for an ice cream scoop. In this section, I share one of my best recipes for chocolate sauce along with the absolutely most indulgent sundae to be topped with chocolate. This recipe can be a guilt-free treat — but only if you black out the nutritional analysis that follows the recipe.

Selling kids on fruit for dessert

Fruit can be your secret weapon for creating simple yet satisfying desserts. But convincing children that fresh fruit counts as a dessert is a hard sell. You're more likely to make a case for a fruit-and-dip combination in which fruit is flavored with a sweet or rich coating. Check out how simple it can be: Arrange apple, pear, or banana chunks on a plate with honey, peanut butter, whipped light cream cheese, or sweetened sour cream for dipping.

Ice cream is the obvious match for chocolate sauce. However, you can discover how versatile chocolate sauce is after you make your first batch. See about using chocolate sauce as the base for a fondue in the "Spearing Dessert" section, later in this chapter.

Always melt chocolate over low heat, so it doesn't burn. If your chocolate develops a scorched aroma, it's burned, and you can't revive it. It's time to wash out the pan and start again.

Excellent quality chocolate bars are usually sold in 3-ounce sizes. To make chocolate bits, take a small hammer and break the chocolate into bite-size pieces. Each 3-ounce bar yields ½ cup of chocolate bits. Hint: If you get the job of breaking up the chocolate, then you get to eat the crumbs.

♻ Intense Chocolate Sauce

This chocolate sauce is thick, rich, and sweet. It's the flavor combination that adults and children can agree on. If you prefer a more sophisticated taste that isn't as sweet, cut the corn syrup by one tablespoon. Also, the espresso cuts the sweetness of the recipe but doesn't give the sauce a coffee flavor.

Refrigerate any leftovers (am I kidding?) in a plastic container with a tight-fitting lid for up to one week. The sauce will thicken as it chills. Heat the leftover sauce on low in a microwave oven or place the sauce in a heatproof bowl set over a pot or larger bowl that's filled with hot water. Stir the sauce occasionally and let it set until it softens enough to pour.

Preparation time: *About 5 minutes*

Cooking time: *About 5 minutes*

Yield: *6 servings*

1 cup bittersweet chocolate bits	*1 tablespoon butter*
½ cup light corn syrup	*½ teaspoon vanilla extract*
½ cup heavy cream	*1 teaspoon instant espresso powder (optional)*
Pinch of salt	

Combine the chocolate bits, light corn syrup, heavy cream, salt, butter, vanilla extract, and espresso (if desired) in a small heavy-bottomed pot. Cook over low heat, stirring frequently until the chocolate and butter just melt.

Per serving: Calories 298 (From Fat 150); Fat 17g (Saturated 10g); Cholesterol 32mg; Sodium 72mg; Carbohydrate 41g (Dietary Fiber 0g); Protein 2g.

✎ *Mocha-Walnut Sundae*

If you like the taste of coffee in dessert dishes, you'll love the combination of espresso beans, fudge sauce, and coffee ice cream. And you don't have to wait in line in your local latté joint to enjoy this luscious treat.

Preparation time: *10 minutes*

Yield: *6 servings*

Intense Chocolate Sauce (see recipe earlier in this chapter)

3 cups coffee ice cream

2 tablespoons ground espresso beans, or 3 tablespoons coarsely chopped chocolate-covered espresso beans

6 tablespoons coarsely chopped walnuts

1 Keep the chocolate sauce warm in a heatproof bowl set over a pot or larger bowl containing very hot water.

2 To assemble the sundae, spoon ½ cup of the ice cream into each of 6 bowls or sundae glasses. Top each serving with some of the chocolate sauce. Sprinkle on 1 teaspoon espresso beans and 1 tablespoon walnuts. Serve immediately.

Per serving: Calories 515 (From Fat 292); Fat 32g (Saturated 17g); Cholesterol 58mg; Sodium 107mg; Carbohydrate 59g (Dietary Fiber 1g); Protein 5g.

Spearing Dessert

Having a fondue pot from the first go-round of this food fad, which reached its peak in the '70s, puts me in a certain age range. How embarrassing! But how else can I convince you to fondue if I can't vouch for having had years of dipping fun.

Fondue delivers the greatest pleasure for the least amount of work. Fondue is death-by-dessert in two parts: You have dippers, such as chunks of cake or cookies, pieces of fruit, marshmallows or nuts, and a warm dipping sauce that could come in chocolate, praline, caramel, or marshmallow flavors. With long forks or some other long, pointed object, you dip the cake, fruit, and so on into the warmed sauce. It doesn't get much simpler than that.

Acquiring the hardware

The dipping sauce should remain warm while you're eating a fondue. Warm sauce does a better job of coating the dippers. Besides, the contrast of a warm sauce and cold dippers (such as fruit chunks) is amazingly good. You have a few options for serving the warm sauce:

✔ **An electric fondue pot** does a great job of keeping sauce at an even warm temperature. My pot — invented just after the wheel — has a control attachment for adjusting the heat. The bowl of the appliance has a nonstick coating for easy clean up. You can find similar models in better cookware stores.

✔ **Nonelectric fondue pots** that use butane burners or candles are very popular as well. Depending on how hot your fondue heating unit gets, you may have to make your sauce on the stove and then transfer the warm mixture to the fondue pot for serving. If you're planning a fondue party, figure out the temperature issue before the big day with a trial run. The glow of the candle or even the butane flame makes fondue a romantic as well as a delicious dessert.

✔ **Ceramic serving bowls** are practical if your family breathes in dessert. You won't even need a fondue pot; the fondue will vanish before it cools. Just heat the sauce and pour it into a ceramic serving bowl.

Avoid overheating the sauce or dippers, like marshmallows, that can melt into the sauce.

Everyone also needs a plate and two forks. One is the usual dessert fork. The second is a fondue fork (a thin fork with a very long stem, so you can dip the food without burning your fingers). If you don't have a fondue fork, substitute long bamboo skewers that are used for kabobs. You can find skewers in the housewares or cooking departments of many stores.

Sharpening your skills

To get your fondue session underway, prepare a dessert sauce, such as the Praline Sauce from the "Buttering up" section, earlier in this chapter. Following the recipe directions, you can make the sauce at the table using an electric fondue pot with a low heat setting. If you have a nonelectric fondue pot, make the sauce on the stovetop and pour it into a fondue pot to warm it. If you're pouring the sauce into a bowl and not a fondue pot with a heat source, prepare the sauce at the last minute.

Adding an additional ¼ cup of heavy cream to the Intense Chocolate Sauce in the "Chocolate — enough said" section, earlier in this chapter, turns it into a satisfying dipping sauce.

For Praline Sauce, use the following proportions of dippers with the sauce recipe for 4 servings:

✔ 1 cup of pound cake cut into 1-inch cubes

✔ 1 cup of banana in 1-inch chunks

✔ 1 cup of apple wedges

✔ ½ cup of large pecan halves

For Intense Chocolate sauce, use

- ✔ 1 cup of pound cake in 1-inch cubes
- ✔ 2 cups of large, whole strawberries
- ✔ ½ cup of large pecan halves

In Figure 14-1, I provide you with a dip-by-dip account of the fondue process. Just be sure to limit your use of the fondue fork to dipping the food and bringing it back to your plate; then use your own dessert fork to actually eat the tasty morsel. Eating from the fondue fork that you're dipping into the sauce can spread germs.

When fondues first became popular, people who lost their dippers in the sauce had to give a kiss to someone sitting at the table as a forfeit. If that's not still the case, it should be!

HAVING FONDUE FUN!

Figure 14-1: Dipping into fondue is easy.

1. POUR CHOCOLATE OR OTHER DIPPING SAUCE INTO A POT WITH A HEAT SOURCE AND WARM THE SAUCE.

2. ARRANGE COMMUNAL DIPPERS ON PLATES THAT EVERYONE CAN REACH. GIVE EVERYONE A FONDUE FORK AND A REGULAR FORK.

3. DIP THE CAKE, FRUIT OR WHATEVER YOU WANT TO COAT IN THE SAUCE.

Mixing in the Fun

An ice cream parlor in my neighborhood does standing-room-only business because of this simple concept: You order the ice cream and then specify the flavoring bits, such as nuts, candied fruit, chocolate bars, or jelly beans that you want to add. The server sprinkles the flavoring chunks on a chilled marble slab and then adds scoops of ice cream. With the dexterity of a sushi chef and a knife twice as big, the behind-the-counter wizard chops the ice cream together with the flavorings. Doing this in seconds on chilled marble keeps the ice cream cold and the line quiet. Why so quiet? No one wants to be responsible for a server losing a finger.

Discover how easy and fun it is to create this kind of ice-cream-parlor drama in your home for weeknight desserts or for a casual dinner gathering with friends. Getting everyone focused on the task at hand is easy when they see what delightful ice cream treats are in store. You can come up with a ton of combinations, but check out the following ideas to get your wheels spinning:

- ✔ Strawberry ice cream with marshmallows, walnuts, and dried strawberries.
- ✔ Chocolate ice cream with coffee beans, caramels, and peanuts.
- ✔ Butter pecan ice cream with chunks of Snickers bars.

You need to do just a bit of additional prep work before the mix-in magic can begin. The work surface gets very scratched, so don't use your good marble serving board or cookie sheet. Find inexpensive marble slabs at kitchen supply stores or substitute an old heavy-gauge cookie sheet. Place the marble or cookie sheet in the freezer for up to 12 hours before using it.

Just before the dessert drama, set out bowls of everyone's favorite mix-ins, including plenty of chopped candy bars, nuts, and marshmallows. To prevent the marble from slipping or scarring your table, place the slab over a towel on the table. Bring out the ice creams and follow the steps in Figure 14-2.

MAKING ICE CREAM MIX-INS

1. brr!.... PLACE A MARBLE SLAB OR COOKIE SHEET IN THE FREEZER UNTIL IT FROSTS. USE MITTS WHEN YOU REMOVE IT SO YOU DON'T FREEZE YOUR FINGERS!

2. SPRINKLE CANDIES AND NUTS ON THE MARBLE.

3. DROP LARGE SCOOPS OF ICE CREAM ON THE CANDIES.

4. USING A CLEAVER OR CHEF'S KNIFE QUICKLY CHOP THE ICE CREAM INTO THE CANDY AND NUT MIX-INS.

5. YUM! SCOOP THE CHOPPED ICE CREAM INTO A BOWL AND ENJOY!

Figure 14-2: So you say you wanna turn your kitchen into an ice cream parlor, eh?

Part IV
Even Quicker Meals without the Hassle

The 5th Wave   By Rich Tennant

"It's a microwave slow cooker. It'll cook a stew all day in just 7 minutes."

In this part . . .

Getting to the heart of fast cooking, this part shows you how to make a pot roast dinner on a hamburger deadline. You get the lowdown on how to turn precooked meats that you can find in your supermarket's meat department into meals that look and taste like you've spent all afternoon in the kitchen. You can discover how to turn odds and ends of restaurant doggie bags into dinners for the family. And I also know that sometimes your busy schedule doesn't even give you 30 minutes to prepare a meal, so I include recipes and tips that allow you to *really* kick your meal prep into high gear and get food on the table in 20 minutes or less. Get ready to hit the warp-speed button!

Chapter 15

Making Every Minute Count: Precooked Meats

Meat loaf, pot roast, and pork loin are such delicious, and infrequent, entrees in busy households that you delight in bringing the satisfaction of these dishes to the table. Quick stir-fries, skillet dinners, soups, and salads are probably your typical weeknight choices, so you know how pleasing an old-fashioned main course can be.

Complaining about meat dishes taking too long to prepare is paying off for consumers. Meat and poultry manufacturers are listening. Their response is to offer fully cooked meat dishes that look just like the entrees you make when you have the time. Checking your supermarket refrigerated meat case, you're going to find such products as pork tenderloin, pork roast, braised pork, meatballs, seasoned ground beef, barbecued pork, beef tips with gravy, and barbecued chicken.

Cooking, or to be more precise, *warming* these products cuts your dinner preparation time by at least half. Using these new foods and new dinner strategies means that you can enjoy an old-fashioned meal no matter how hectic your schedule.

In this chapter, I tell you how to take advantage of innovations in the meat and poultry industries that allow you to dine on traditional dishes that cook in only minutes. I provide a flavorful range of quick recipes that start with convenience meat and chicken products.

Introducing Precooked Meat and Poultry

Telling you how to cook fully cooked meat is like telling you how to heat hot water. You're not cooking fully cooked meats; you're heating them to an appropriate and appealing temperature.

Although you may want to experiment and find better ways to heat precooked meats, I urge you to follow the directions on the package the first time. Manufacturers spend a fortune developing their products, so prepare them the way the manufacturer thinks they taste best. After that, you can try new ways to heat and serve fully cooked meat and poultry.

If you or a loved one has serious food allergies, read the labels of fully cooked meats carefully before making your purchase. Some manufacturers use unexpected ingredients such as *whey,* a milk by-product, or *soy,* which is made from soybeans.

Buying fully cooked meat or poultry can change your mealtime for the better. They can save you precious time when you incorporate them into your meal schedule, but they're unbeatable for saving dinner on the fly. Having a fully cooked meat product in my refrigerator is my insurance against having to order out for dinner when I unexpectedly find myself pressed for time. In less than 5 minutes, I can have pot roast on the table. That's no small feat.

See the following examples of how precooked meat and chicken save the dinner hour:

- ✔ When you forget to thaw frozen meat for dinner, open a package of precooked meat instead.

- ✔ When unexpected guests arrive, prepare one of this chapter's delicious entrees along with what you're already planning to serve and be assured that you have enough food for company.

- ✔ If you're trying to cut back on the amount of meat you eat, but your family isn't ready to go along with your diet change, serve them a fully cooked meat product while you have a vegetarian entree.

- ✔ When hunger just won't allow time for the meal you've planned, microwave precooked meat and put a stop to gnarling stomachs fast.

Meating Your Limitations

Fully cooked meat products shouldn't replace from-scratch cooking, despite the many attractions of the foods. I outline the positives in the preceding "Introducing Precooked Meat and Poultry" section, but the products have drawbacks as well. I can't discuss fully cooked meat products without pointing out some disadvantages.

Comparing costs

Fully cooked meat and poultry items are more expensive than raw foods. You're paying for the convenience of having a food company make your entree. Foods can cost as much as double what you pay if you're doing the cooking. A pound of cooked pot roast costs twice as much as what I pay for an uncooked roast.

Developing a salt solution

Fully cooked meat and poultry foods often contain high sodium levels. If you're supposed to be on a low-sodium diet, you're going to have to read labels carefully to find a precooked meat product that meets your dietary needs. Checking packages, I see products that deliver 30 to 45 percent of the maximum amount of sodium that you should have in an entire day, in just one serving of meat or chicken.

Using a number of strategies, you may be able to serve convenience meat products if you're on a restricted sodium diet. But I'm not a dietitian or a doctor, so check with a health professional first. To be safe, take a Nutrition Facts food panel to your healthcare provider and see whether the food you're interested in is appropriate for you.

Check out the following ways in which you can reduce your day's sodium intake even when you're eating a high-sodium, fully cooked meat:

✔ Don't add any more salt to the meal.

✔ Season vegetable side dishes with lemon juice, herbs, and spices, not salt.

✔ Add rice and vegetables to a fully cooked meat or poultry dish. Serve smaller portions of the meat or poultry and fill up on low-sodium rice and veggies instead.

✔ Find balance in your meal plan. If you know you're serving a high-sodium dinner, eat plenty of low-sodium fresh fruits and vegetables the rest of the day.

✔ Read labels carefully. The range of sodium differs greatly according to the brand.

It's a Fowl Call

Fully cooked chicken comes in two basic forms — whole rotisserie-cooked chicken and chicken breast strips. You won't find fully cooked whole chicken in the supermarket refrigerated meat case, because many supermarkets sell rotisserie-cooked chicken hot off the spit. And who wants a whole cold chicken when you can get a warm tasty one for just a few bucks?

Rotisserie-cooked chicken with its crisp skin and moist flesh is a marvelous entree, and one that needs no touching up. Take a look at Chapter 16 for tips on using leftover chicken. And check Chapter 10 for some almost-instant side-salad ideas to go with that bird. If you can't make a side, pick up some coleslaw or a potato salad along with the chicken.

Fully cooked chicken breast strips, on the other hand, are most useful as a building block. Chicken breast strips, unlike chicken delicatessen meat, aren't pressed, rolled, and robbed of their natural texture. You get the natural taste and look of chicken cut right from the breast. Manufacturers offer a choice:

- **Plain chicken:** This route gives you more options for adding the chicken to soups, salads, sandwiches, or skillet dinners.

- **Pre-seasoned chicken:** With these flavorful strips, you can skip the spices that many recipes demand.

I keep both kinds of chicken in my refrigerator. The following suggestions are my favorite ways to use cooked chicken breast strips:

- Topping a salad of romaine lettuce, blue cheese, tomatoes and Thousand Island dressing. (See the dressing recipe in Chapter 10.)

- In a club sandwich layered with bacon, lettuce, and tomatoes.

- In canned cream of chicken soup. Somehow, a can of soup never has enough chicken.

- On a pizza. Starting with a frozen cheese pizza, sprinkle on a package of cooked chicken breast strips and drizzle with a little barbecue sauce. Then bake the pizza according to the package directions. Outstanding!

- In a skillet dinner that combines odds and ends of the foods that I have in the cupboard or refrigerator.

Spanish Rice with Chicken

Using seasoned convenience products, such as spicy chicken and canned tomatoes with chiles, means that you don't have to measure out as many seasonings when you cook. If you prefer to tame the heat, choose plain cooked chicken breast meat.

Preparation time: *5 minutes*

Cooking time: *22 minutes*

Yield: *4 servings*

1 cup long-grain rice

1 can (14½ ounces) diced tomatoes with chiles and lime juice or diced tomatoes with chiles

1¼ cups chicken broth

2 packages (6 ounces each) cooked chicken breast with Southwestern seasonings

1 cup frozen peas

1 tablespoon minced cilantro

2 tablespoons minced chives

¼ teaspoon salt (optional)

¼ teaspoon pepper

1 Place the rice, tomatoes, chicken broth, and chicken in a large sauté pan and stir to mix. Bring the liquid to a boil. Cover the pan and reduce the heat to low.

2 Simmer the mixture 12 minutes. Stir in the frozen peas and cook another 6 minutes or until the rice is tender and the mixture is moist. Stir in the cilantro, chives, salt (if desired), and pepper.

Speed It Up! *Use instant rice in place of long-grain rice. Follow the recipe, but omit the rice. Bring the vegetables, liquid, and chicken to a boil. Stir in 1½ cups instant rice. Cover the pan. Remove from the heat and let stand for 2 minutes.*

Per serving: *Calories 367 (From Fat 43); Fat 5g (Saturated 2g); Cholesterol 73mg; Sodium 1,371mg; Carbohydrate 51g (Dietary Fiber 3g); Protein 28g.*

No More Stewing over Beef

Manufacturers design their beef and pork dinners for good, plain eating. Looking at a box of pot roast, for example, you see beef front and center on the plate. Don't be limited by the producer's intent. You have plenty of options, but they fall into two general categories:

✔ You can use fully cooked beef and pork just as you would raw ingredients, which allows you to prepare mouthwatering recipes in far less time than if you use raw meats. Using fully cooked meat as an ingredient in other dishes means that you can flavor foods according to *your* taste, rather than the food company's preferences.

✔ You can serve straight-from-the package beef and pork with glazes, seasonings, and vegetables that you add to enhance the eye-appeal as well as the flavor of these foods. You're making these foods taste more homemade, but in a fraction of the time.

I do recommend that you prepare precooked meats plain from the package when you use a product for the first time. Different brands of beef and pork use different flavorings. So you want to get an idea of what the product tastes like before you add additional seasoning as you experiment.

Perish the thought

When you talk about packaged, boxed, bagged, canned, and bottled convenience foods, *fresh* may not be what pops into your mind. But these products do have their own particular brand of freshness that you have to consider. To get the most from your prepared purchases, look for an easy to understand date on the package. Some packages have *sell-by dates* that tell the supermarket when to get the product off the shelf. However, I (and most food manufacturers) prefer the use-by date that's stamped on many perishable food products. The *use-by date* tells you the last date that the manufacturer recommends you keep the product on hand to eat. Perishable foods, such as precooked meats, are most likely to include use-by dates.

Choose packages that provide use-by dates. Supermarkets push their older products to the front of the display, so customers pick them first, but you don't have to. Dig to the back and get the package that fits your use-by timeframe.

Unfortunately, some use-by labels are as hard to decipher as a prescription from your physician. Shelf-stable products often use codes that are simply numbers indicating the day, month, and year that the food starts to decline in quality. If you can't make out what the use-by code on your product says, ask a supermarket manager. Don't buy a product if you don't know how long it stays fresh.

Note: After you open a package of precooked meat, you have to ignore the use-by label. Instead, treat the product like leftover food and finish it within a few days.

Pot Roast with Chili-Mustard Sauce

Serve this sauced-up, sliced pot roast over instant mashed potatoes.

Preparation time: *5 minutes*

Cooking time: *7 minutes*

Yield: *4 servings*

1 jar (12-ounces) chili sauce	2 tablespoons brown sugar
1 tablespoon Dijon-style mustard	1 package (1 pound) fully cooked boneless beef pot roast with gravy
1 tablespoon white wine vinegar	

1 Stir together chili sauce, mustard, white wine vinegar, and brown sugar in a large saucepan. Simmer over low heat for 2 minutes or until heated through.

2 Add the beef pot roast with gravy to the pan. Baste the meat with the chili-mustard sauce mixture. Cover the pan and simmer 4 to 5 minutes or until the meat is hot. Remove the pot roast to a serving platter and thinly slice. Top with about 1 cup of the chili-mustard sauce. Pour the remaining sauce into a gravy boat and pass separately.

Vary It! *Use any leftover beef and chili-mustard sauce for hot beef sandwiches.*

Per serving: *Calories 368 (From Fat 100); Fat 11g (Saturated 4g); Cholesterol 101mg; Sodium 2,811mg; Carbohydrate 33g (Dietary Fiber 0g); Protein 34g.*

 Check your supermarket's refrigerated meat case for fully cooked beef tips with gravy. This versatile product is excellent in beef stew, soup, or casseroles. Serving the beef in a recipe that calls for vegetables adds color and texture to the dish.

Speedy Beef Stew

Starting with fully cooked beef tips and cooked, diced potatoes, you can have a robust beef dinner on the table in less than 20 minutes. Look for cooked, diced potatoes in your supermarket's produce section.

Preparation time: *5 minutes*

Cooking time: *10 minutes*

Yield: *4 servings*

1 tablespoon vegetable oil	*1 package (about 1 pound) refrigerated, cooked, diced potatoes*
1 medium red bell pepper, cored, seeded and diced	*1 package (about 17 ounces) fully cooked beef tips with gravy*
1 medium onion, thinly sliced	*½ cup beef broth*
1 garlic clove, minced	*¼ teaspoon pepper*

1 Heat the oil over high heat in a large sauté pan. Add the bell pepper, onion, and garlic and sauté the vegetables 5 minutes or until tender.

2 Add the potatoes, beef tips with gravy, beef broth, and pepper. Cover and simmer 5 minutes or until the potatoes and beef are hot.

Vary It! *Skip the potatoes and serve the stew over cooked noodles. Add a cup of frozen sliced carrots along with the red bell pepper and onion. It's an effortless way to serve more vegetables.*

Per serving: *Calories 257 (From Fat 79); Fat 9g (Saturated 2g); Cholesterol 43mg; Sodium 943mg; Carbohydrate 25g (Dietary Fiber 1g); Protein 28g.*

Precooked ground beef is my favorite new meat product. Ground beef is such an important player in my dinners. Sloppy Joes, chili, tacos, lasagna, and more call for me to brown a pound of ground beef.

Although I don't mind actually cooking ground beef, I hate the cleanup. Wiping up the grease splatters from browning beef ranks with pot cleaning on my list of hated chores. And thanks to precooked ground beef, I crossed one thing off my list.

Several food companies sell precooked ground beef. Find it in plain or seasoned varieties. A 12-ounce package of cooked beef is the equivalent of one pound of raw ground beef. A 20-ounce tub of seasoned ground beef that's prepared with a sauce is about the same as 1½ pounds of raw beef.

Texas-Style Brunch

Messy, gooey, savory, and delicious . . . and that's not the best part. Starting with precooked ground beef, you can make this meal in minutes.

Preparation time: *5 minutes*

Cooking time: *12 minutes*

Yield: *6 servings*

1 tablespoon vegetable oil	*8 eggs*
1 small onion, diced	*1 cup crumbled tortilla chips*
1 tomato, cored and diced	*1 cup grated cheddar cheese*
1 package (12 ounces) Mexican-seasoned ground beef, or half a 20-ounce carton or tub of taco sauce with seasoned ground beef	*½ cup salsa*

1 Heat the oil in a large, nonstick sauté pan over high heat. Add the onion and sauté 2 minutes or until limp. Add the tomatoes and cook 2 more minutes. Stir in the ground beef and cook over medium heat 1 minute to warm.

2 Beat together the eggs in a bowl and pour into the sauté pan over the ground beef. Let the mixture set for 2 minutes or until the eggs are almost firm.

3 Stir in the tortilla chips and cook 1 more minute. Stir gently and briefly to break up the mixture into large chunks. Sprinkle on the cheese and heat 1 minute or until the cheese melts. Serve the salsa over the eggs or on the side.

Vary It! Substitute taco-seasoned grated cheese for the plain cheddar cheese. You can also serve warm flour tortillas on the side and allow everyone to spoon the egg and beef mixture into flour tortillas.

Per serving: *Calories 388 (From Fat 230); Fat 26g (Saturated 10g); Cholesterol 359mg; Sodium 506mg; Carbohydrate 8g (Dietary Fiber 1g); Protein 30g.*

Feeling Spicy with Succulent Pork

Cooking pork has always been a challenge for me, and it may be for you as well. Undercooked pork, like any undercooked meat, can be a food safety risk. Overcooked pork is dry and tough. Having fully cooked pork products available eliminates both concerns — along with any worries about your meal taking hours to prepare. One finger presses a button or two on the microwave oven and dinner is ready.

My favorite pork recipes replicate the long, slow cooking of Southern barbecues. Tangy sweet flavors enhance pork's delicate taste and are especially good when you start with precooked pork products. Whether it's with barbecue sauce, jam, and salsa or brown sugar and vinegar, you can make pork taste like a gift from the South in minutes.

Sweet-Hot Pork

Fully cooked pork roast is available in most supermarkets, but if you can find another more economical pork cut, substitute it. Look for a brand of pork that has *au jus* on the label. This is the fancy name for the delicious pork cooking liquids.

Preparation time: *5 minutes*

Cooking time: *5 minutes*

Yield: *4 servings*

1 package (16 to 17 ounces) pork roast au jus	*¼ cup apricot jam, or orange marmalade*
1 teaspoon medium-hot chili powder	*2 cups cooked rice*
1 jar (12 ounces) mild to medium salsa	

1 Drain the liquid off the pork, pouring the liquid into a skillet. Cut the meat into 1-inch chunks.

2 Add the chili powder, salsa, and jam to the skillet and stir well. Add the pork chunks. Simmer over low heat 5 minutes, or until hot, stirring occasionally. Serve over rice.

Per serving: Calories 290 (From Fat 38); Fat 4g (Saturated 1g); Cholesterol 53mg; Sodium 1,130mg; Carbohydrate 45g (Dietary Fiber 2g); Protein 20g.

Slaw-Topped Barbecued Pork Sandwiches

Backyard summer lunches and barbecued pork sandwiches are a natural match. Look for tubs of barbecued pork in supermarket meat cases. You can substitute barbecued chicken if you prefer. Serve with potato chips.

Preparation time: *10 minutes*

Cooking time: *5 minutes*

Yield: *4 servings*

4 Kaiser rolls, or buns

2 cups shredded cabbage

2 tablespoons mayonnaise

½ tablespoon cider vinegar

1 tablespoon chopped chives, scallion, or red onion

¼ teaspoon salt

¼ teaspoon pepper

1 container or tub (about 20 ounces) barbecue sauce with shredded pork, fully cooked

4 dill pickle slices

1 Preheat the oven to 325 degrees. Place the buns in the oven to warm for 5 minutes.

2 Meanwhile, place cabbage in a bowl and stir in mayonnaise, vinegar, chives, salt, and pepper. Set aside.

3 Heat the barbecued pork in a microwave oven according to the manufacturer's directions. Remove the buns from the oven. To serve, divide the barbecued pork on the bottom halves of 4 rolls. Top each portion with ½ cup of coleslaw and a pickle slice. Close the sandwiches with top halves of rolls.

Speed It Up! *If this isn't fast-cooking enough, you can shave off a couple of minutes if you use store-bought deli coleslaw.*

Per serving: *Calories 482 (From Fat 190); Fat 21g (Saturated 6g); Cholesterol 84mg; Sodium 1,641mg; Carbohydrate 37g (Dietary Fiber 3g); Protein 35g.*

Chapter 16

Two for One: Dining Once, Eating Twice

*L*eaving food on your plate is not only acceptable when you're an adult; it's the healthy thing to do, say nutrition experts. This advice is especially true when you go out to eat. Restaurant portions are too big, and the excess calories that you're getting when you dine out can make you fat.

In this chapter, you can find out how to turn the leftovers into a dish that's just as appetizing, though different from the original. After all, you don't want a re-run of the same steak.

I start with restaurant food by outlining the foods that work well the second time around, and the ones that don't. Restaurants have some pretty clever ways of packaging your unwanted food for you, such as aluminum foil-shaped swans, but that's not how you want to store your food. This chapter provides safe solutions for storing food and suggestions for preparing new meals with some common restaurant leftovers.

You create your own potential for second meals as you cook. You really can recycle foods, so they don't become UFOs — unidentifiable food objects in your refrigerator. Discarding food is a waste of your time as well as the food. After all, why not enjoy what you cooked twice, not just once? I relay my experiences with clean-out-the-fridge dinners and short-notice meal preparation, too.

Bagging It Up

Choosing food from a restaurant menu according to what you can serve a second time around isn't practical or desirable. Order the food that you want to eat in a restaurant. Then decide how to use whatever you put aside.

When a restaurant menu promises you a 32-ounce Porterhouse or jumbo serving of shrimp, tell your wait staff to package half the food into a carryout bag before it comes to the table. That way you're not tempted to clean your plate. At the end of the meal you feel satisfied, not stuffed. What's more, you're presented with the makings of a second meal.

Spoiled leftover restaurant food isn't a bargain. Ask the wait staff to store your food in the refrigerator until you're ready to go home. Don't ask for leftovers if you're heading out for a night on the town (unless you just happen to keep a frozen chill pack and insulated container in your car). Your food should go from the restaurant's refrigerator to yours as soon as possible. As a general rule, refrigerate food within two hours during cold weather and within an hour when the temperatures are high.

The simpler the dish, the more options you have. Half a steak gives you more recipe options than say, beef stew. A plain chicken breast is more versatile than chicken with dumplings. (Later in this chapter, two mouthwatering recipes start with a piece of beef — Steak and Mushroom Salad and Steak Sandwiches with Tomato Relish. Look in Chapter 17 for tips on using cooked chicken in your menus.)

Check out Table 16-1 for a list of foods that are the easiest to prepare as seconds and the best uses for each food. Note that Table 16-1 suggests putting leftover fish or shrimp in salads. Seafood doesn't reheat well.

Don't pass all those vegetables on to your doggie bag. Steak houses are famous for serving huge vegetable portions. Thick asparagus stalks, the pride of restaurants, are filling and nourishing. But I recommend that you eat half and package half. The same goes for baked potatoes, which often come in one-pound sizes. Have the restaurant kitchen divide the spud, with half on your plate and half in a bag. Like all leftovers, cooked vegetables should be refrigerated ASAP.

Table 16-1	What to Do with Doggie Bag Contents
Food	*Preparation*
Asparagus	Casserole, salad, soup, stir-fry
Baked potato	Casserole, soup
Chicken	Casserole, salad, sandwich or wrap, soup, stir-fry
Fish	Salad
Mashed potatoes	Soup
Pork chops	Stir-fry, sandwiches
Rice	Casserole, salad, soup, stir-fry
Shrimp	Salad
Steak	Salad, stir-fry, sandwich, or wrap

I also have a short list of menu items that you shouldn't bother to take home:

 ✔ **Breads:** Leftover bread goes stale fast and reheating it in a microwave dries the bread out even faster. However, you can find a great bread salad in Chapter 10 should you want to bring bread home.

 ✔ **Egg dishes:** Scrambled, poached, or fried eggs become easily contaminated with bacteria. Don't take a chance of suffering food poisoning by keeping egg dishes around.

 ✔ **Pudding or custard desserts:** These are highly perishable.

 ✔ **Sauces:** Luscious sauces are marvelous in a restaurant but spoil quickly. The delicate concoctions are also difficult to reheat without curdling.

Seconds on steak

Steak is still the most popular restaurant entree, and it's no wonder. Everyone loves steak's succulent flavor. Promising a huge steak is a great lure on a restaurant menu. However, many of these monster steaks are more meat than you should eat in a meal for health's sake. Save half the restaurant's portion for another meal.

Leftover steak is a great ingredient for almost instant meals. Because steak is a celebration dish in my household, I'm always trying new ways to stretch it and make the treat last longer. If your steak portion doesn't have much fat, you can serve it hot or cold. Steak that contains too much fat should be reheated to serve. Cold, congealed fat is unappetizing. Microwave the meat to thoroughly warm it.

Steak kabobs are easy to make and fun to eat. Threading steak and vegetables onto wooden skewers, you can divide what looks like one steak portion into several kabob entrees.

Slice the steak into ¼-inch strips and weave the strips on a wooden skewer, alternating the meat with cherry tomatoes, green pepper strips, and white mushrooms. Start with one end of a steak strip. Push the end of the beef onto a skewer. Add a vegetable and then add the opposite end of the beef, so the steak wraps around the vegetable. Serve the steak and vegetables cold with a blue cheese or ranch-style dressing. As another option, cut the steak into bite-size cubes and arrange on a skewer with the raw vegetables of your choice. (See Figure 16-1.)

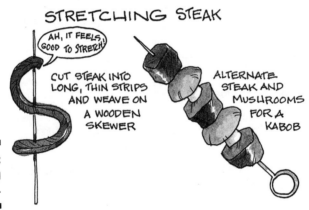

STRETCHING STEAK

AH, IT FEELS GOOD TO STRETCH!

CUT STEAK INTO LONG, THIN STRIPS AND WEAVE ON A WOODEN SKEWER

ALTERNATE STEAK AND MUSHROOMS FOR A KABOB

Figure 16-1:
Skewering
your steak.

Steak is also a great base for substantial salads or sandwiches. Steak cut into thin strips is easier to eat and looks more elegant. Use a serrated steak knife for easy slicing.

Steak and Mushroom Salad

Toothsome strip steak, mushrooms, and capers are delicious tossed with a balsamic vinaigrette dressing. Add a crusty bread, and you have a filling meal.

Preparation time: *8 minutes*

Yield: *4 servings*

1 pound cooked leftover strip, Kansas City or T-bone steak, cut into ¼-inch thick strips

1 cup sliced white mushrooms

1 cup grape or cherry tomatoes, halved

1 tablespoon capers

¼ cup chopped red onion or scallions

Balsamic Dressing (recipe follows)

Place the steak strips in a salad bowl. Add the mushrooms, tomatoes, capers, and red onion. Toss gently but well. Make the Balsamic Dressing (recipe follows) and pour over the steak salad. Toss gently but well.

Vary It! *Arrange the salad in cups of Bibb lettuce. You can also toss the salad with a cup of cooked rice. If necessary, add more dressing.*

Per serving: *Calories 480 (From Fat 336); Fat 37g (Saturated 12g); Cholesterol 90mg; Sodium 428mg; Carbohydrate 5g (Dietary Fiber 1g); Protein 30g.*

◌ Balsamic Dressing

Steak can stand up to a strong-tasting dressing. This vinaigrette uses balsamic vinegar, a barrel-aged Italian vinegar, for its full flavor.

Preparation time: *2 minutes*

Yield: *¼ cup; 4 servings*

1 tablespoon balsamic vinegar

½ teaspoon 5-spice powder

3 tablespoons extra-virgin olive oil

½ teaspoon salt

¼ teaspoon pepper

Place the vinegar, 5-spice powder, olive oil, salt, and pepper in a bowl. Whisk to blend. Pour over your favorite salad.

Per serving: *Calories 93 (From Fat 92); Fat 10g (Saturated 1g); Cholesterol 0mg; Sodium 291mg; Carbohydrate 1g (Dietary Fiber 0g); Protein 0g.*

Steak Sandwiches with Tomato Relish

Use leftover tenderloin or filet mignon for this robust steak and tomato open-face sandwich. Buy the meaty and briny Greek kalamata olives at better supermarkets.

Preparation time: *10 minutes*

Yield: *4 servings*

1 medium shallot, minced	¼ teaspoon salt
¼ cup finely chopped kalamata olives	¼ teaspoon pepper
½ teaspoon crushed dried oregano	4 large slices Italian bread
2 small-medium tomatoes, cored and chopped	1 cup arugula leaves
2 teaspoons olive oil	12 ounces rare, cooked beef tenderloin, sliced ¼ inch thick
1 teaspoon white wine vinegar	

1 To prepare the tomato relish, combine the shallot, olives, oregano, tomatoes, olive oil, vinegar, salt, and pepper in a bowl. Stir well.

2 To assemble the sandwiches, place the bread on a work surface. Arrange ¼ cup of arugula on each slice of bread. Place the beef strips over the arugula and top each sandwich with ¼ cup of the tomato relish. (Save any leftovers to serve as a spread over garlic bread.)

Vary It! *For a hand-held-sandwich, serve the tomato relish on the side and add a second slice of bread. You may want to add a spread to the sandwich for moisture. Mustard is the obvious choice, but you can make a luscious blue cheese spread that's divine, as follows:*

Combine ¼ cup blue cheese, 1 tablespoon mayonnaise and 1 to 2 tablespoons of milk to make the mixture a spreading consistency. Mash the ingredients together with the back of a fork until light and smooth.

Per serving: *Calories 435 (From Fat 256); Fat 29g (Saturated 10g); Cholesterol 75mg; Sodium 513mg; Carbohydrate 20g (Dietary Fiber 2g); Protein 24g.*

Fries again?

One of my cooking students recently told me that she always takes home French fries when she eats out. The fries, she says, make a great potato soup. What a great idea. Thick, oven-baked fries or steak fries are ideal in this recipe. Avoid extra-crisp fries, because they remain crunchy even when pureed. Keep your hand off the saltshaker when you cook with fries. Most spuds have plenty of salt added in the restaurant.

French Fry Soup

Who would've thought that there'd be a use for leftover fries? Admittedly, this soup is more of a novelty than a prize-winning recipe. But if you can't resist a few fries with a restaurant burger, this is the perfect alternative to eating the whole delicious-but-fattening order. French fries have an alluring aroma that comes through in this robust and satisfying soup. And don't tell the family what you're serving until you hear the compliments. French fry soup is quite a surprise.

Preparation time: *5 minutes*

Cooking time: *6 minutes*

Yield: *4 servings*

1 tablespoon butter	*½ cup cream*
1 garlic clove, minced	*¼ teaspoon pepper*
2 packed cups cooked French Fries	*1 teaspoon minced fresh dill weed*
2½ cups chicken broth	

1 Melt the butter in a large pot. Add the garlic and sauté 30 seconds over high heat.

2 Meanwhile, place the French Fries and ½ cup chicken broth in a blender. Blend the fries to a puree, scraping down the sides of the blender occasionally if necessary. Remove the fry puree and add to the pot.

3 Add the remaining 2 cups chicken broth, cream, pepper, and dill weed. Cook the soup over low heat 5 minutes or until thoroughly hot. Do not boil.

Vary It! *Season the soup with 1 teaspoon fresh minced thyme instead of dill weed. Sprinkle the soup with 4 strips of cooked bacon. You may also try adding leftover onion rings to this soup for delicious onion-potato chowder.*

Per serving: *Calories 349 (From Fat 224); Fat 25g (Saturated 11g); Cholesterol 52mg; Sodium 806mg; Carbohydrate 29g (Dietary Fiber 3g); Protein 3g.*

Storing the Goods

Doggie bags, cardboard, or Styrofoam containers are fine for carrying your food home from a restaurant. Do not, however, store food in these kinds of packages longer than you have to. Food picks up the taste of cardboard or paper. Restaurant packaging also allows the aroma of the food to travel throughout your refrigerator. Having all the food in your refrigerator smell like garlic-mashed potatoes isn't pleasant.

Transfer food to plastic or glass microwave-safe containers with tight-sealing lids. I suggest microwave containers, because you can heat the dish right from the refrigerator. Mark the container with the following:

- ✔ The name of the food. If you or your loved ones have food allergies, list the food ingredients as well.
- ✔ The date you put it in the refrigerator.
- ✔ The date by which you have to use the food or discard it.
- ✔ Any ideas you have for using the food. If you've ever looked at a carton of leftovers and asked yourself what you intended to do with the food, you know how important this is.

The following is a list of use-by dates for cooked restaurant foods stored in a refrigerator at 40 degrees or below:

- ✔ **Chicken with gravy:** 1 to 2 days
- ✔ **Fried chicken:** 3 to 4 days
- ✔ **Plain chicken:** 3 to 4 days
- ✔ **Rotisserie chicken:** 3 to 4 days
- ✔ **Fish:** 3 days
- ✔ **Meat:** 3 to 4 days
- ✔ **Shellfish:** 3 days

Raiding the Refrigerator

At times, your home-cooked meals probably yield an abundance of leftovers. Throwing out odds and ends of rice, handfuls of cooked vegetables or chopped onions used to be par for the course in my household. No longer. Putting together small amounts of various foods adds up to a delicious dinner. Some of the best-tasting meals in my home are what I dub *clean-the-refrigerator dinners.* Embark on an adventure: Root around and come up with some creative ways to use leftovers.

I recently put together a meal that my family raved about. Foraging through my fridge, I found a carton of rice cooked in chicken broth; a carton of cooked, toasted couscous; a bag of raw, limp but not moldy broccoli crowns; leftover rotisserie chicken; and a wedge of cheddar cheese with no blue or green spots — yet. These pieces added up to a comforting and delicious dish that I called Chicken, Cheddar, and Broccoli Casserole.

Chicken, Cheddar, and Broccoli Casserole

Using a combination of vegetables, starch, and chicken or meat, vary this recipe according to what's in your refrigerator. I call for half-and-half and milk because that's what I have in my refrigerator. You can use whatever combination works for you.

Preparation time: *5 minutes*

Cooking time: *15 minutes*

Yield: *4 servings*

1 package (10 ounces) frozen chopped broccoli, thawed and drained

1 cup cooked rice

1 cup cooked couscous, or another cup of rice if that's what you have

1 cup diced cooked chicken breast meat

2 tablespoons minced scallions

1 tablespoon butter

1 tablespoon flour

⅔ cup half-and-half

1⅓ cups milk

½ cup grated extra-sharp cheddar cheese

2 drops hot red pepper sauce

1 Preheat the oven to 325 degrees. Stir together the broccoli, rice, couscous, chicken, and scallions in a bowl. Spread onto a shallow casserole dish or deep 10-inch pie plate.

2 Melt the butter in a small pan. Stir in the flour and cook over medium heat to form a paste. Reduce the heat to low. Gradually pour in the half-and-half, stirring constantly, until the mixture is smooth and thick. Stir in the milk. Add the cheese stirring constantly, until the cheese melts and the sauce is thick. Add the hot red pepper sauce. Pour the sauce over the broccoli mixture.

3 Place the dish in the oven for 10 to 15 minutes or until the food is hot.

Per serving: Calories 327 (From Fat 130); Fat 15g (Saturated 9g); Cholesterol 70mg; Sodium 162mg; Carbohydrate 28g (Dietary Fiber 3g); Protein 21g.

Feeling confident about putting meals together on a moment's notice helps when emergencies arise. My grown son, who frequently comes home for a meal and announces his intentions 30 minutes before knocking at the door, often inspires me to root through the refrigerator.

A delicious and robust salad of baby carrots and artichoke hearts was the result of one recent effort. It takes minutes, although my son thought that I was cooking half the day.

Baby Carrots and Artichokes Vinaigrette

Tossing hot, cooked vegetables with the vinaigrette dressing lets the flavors permeate the vegetables. During the winter serve this side dish warm or at room temperature. During the summer, refrigerate the vegetables up to four hours if you like.

Preparation time: *5 minutes*

Cooking time: *15 minutes*

Yield: *4 servings*

1 bag (1 pound) baby carrots	*1 tablespoon white wine vinegar*
1 cup chicken broth or water	*1 teaspoon Dijon-style mustard*
1 package (9 ounces) frozen quartered artichoke hearts	*¼ teaspoon salt*
	¼ teaspoon pepper
3 tablespoons extra-virgin olive oil	

1 Place the carrots in a medium-size pot. Add the chicken broth and bring the liquid to a boil. Reduce the heat to low, cover the pot, and cook the carrots for 10 minutes. Add the artichoke hearts. Cover and cook on low heat for 5 more minutes or until the vegetables are tender and the liquid is almost absorbed. If any liquid remains in the pot, remove the lid, increase the heat to high and cook off the liquid.

2 While the vegetables are cooking, stir the oil, vinegar, mustard, salt, and pepper together in a cup.

3 Spoon the vegetables into a serving bowl. Pour the vinaigrette over the vegetables and toss gently, but well to coat.

Speed It Up! *Use 2 packages (9 ounces each) of sliced frozen carrots instead of the fresh baby carrots. Reduce the cooking time to 5 to 10 minutes.*

Per serving: *Calories 169 (From Fat 109); Fat 12g (Saturated 2g); Cholesterol 1mg; Sodium 497mg; Carbohydrate 14g (Dietary Fiber 5g); Protein 3g.*

Chapter 17

Cooking at Warp Speed

. . . .

In This Chapter

▶ Bringing homemade taste to packaged foods

▶ Assembling the parts

▶ Nutritional know-how

. . . .

*H*aving to get dinner on the table instantly — or quicker — causes mealtime mania. But panic is the last thing that you need when it's time to whip up a meal like a genie. In this chapter, I show you how you can easily avoid the stress. Although you can't snap your fingers and make dinner magically appear, it seems almost that easy.

Sitting down to a meal can be a well-needed transition from a busy day to your evening routine. You may have less than 30 minutes to prepare a meal, but that doesn't mean you have to give up this often-anticipated table time. Using a combination of fresh ingredients and prepared foods allows you to cook at warp speed — I'm talking less than 20 minutes, and in some cases, much less. And you can get mouthwatering results.

This chapter shows you how to take advantage of a wealth of convenience products available in supermarkets. Incorporating convenience-added foods can cut your meal preparation time by half — if not more. (If you haven't read about fast, fresh vegetable options in Chapter 5 or prepared meat and poultry products in Chapter 15, I recommend that you do so. They provide additional fuel for your warp-efforts.) Discover how manufacturers' food products can fit your lifestyle.

Assembling Convenient Meals with a Personal Touch

This chapter on cooking at warp speed should come with one of those "some assembly required" tags. In essence, warp speed cooking is taking convenience products such as precooked meats, fresh prepared vegetables, and frozen or canned foods and adding your personal touch to make a tasty meal in minutes. With warp speed cooking, you're heating foods someone else prepared, but making your unique flavor combinations. You get the best of both worlds — creativity and speed.

Canned, frozen, and precooked products provide several built in timesaving advantages.

- ✔ Foods are washed, trimmed, and cut into the appropriate shapes. You eliminate most of the preparation time.

- ✔ Food packages tell you how much you're getting. In most cases you don't have to measure food before adding it to a recipe.

- ✔ You're warming, not cooking, so you spend less time doing so.

Marketers toss around the phrase "assembling meals," as if it's a revolutionary concept. But assembling meals is nothing new. If you ever stirred chopped up hot dogs into a macaroni and cheese mix or added a can of beans to a can of chili, you've assembled a meal. Although the ideas in this chapter go a bit beyond beans and wieners, the concept is the same: Putting boxes, cans, and a few fresh ingredients together results in a quick meal whenever you're pressed for time.

You may feel that you should only use fresh, raw ingredients to prepare your meals. Or perhaps you feel guilty using convenience products because you're not slaving over a hot stove. But rest assured that the quality of convenience food products is better than ever. And the shear number of products available almost guarantees choices for almost all dietary preferences and kitchen routines.

Your supermarket offers meal kits from manufacturers. In theory, meal kits are a great idea. Meal kits often package a starch and a sauce for flavor. Some include meat or poultry as well. However, saving time isn't guaranteed just because a food product is packaged as a kit. Before you buy a new product, read the directions on the package label, so you know how long the food has to cook. Some meal kits take as long as 25 minutes to prepare. In that stretch of time, you can prepare any of the recipes in this chapter.

Adding a little balance and flexibility to the warp-speed formula gives you foods with the same delicious appeal as just plain fast cooking. These kitchen-gymnastic terms are my way of saying that fruits, vegetables, and grains make convenience foods look and taste better. And you can make plenty of substitutions if you can't find (or want to change) some of the ingredients I suggest. You can't get bent out of shape when you're cooking at warp speed — unless you take a break for kitchen yoga.

Keeping your balance

A warp-speed meal that's well balanced for appeal and nutrition contains a starch, a protein, and a vegetable. You can get all three parts — the starch, protein, and vegetable — in canned, frozen, or packaged precooked versions.

But adding a fresh touch to packaged food perks up the flavor and color of assembled meals and keeps a nice balance between packaged and fresh. You can do this by one of the following means:

- Add a sprinkling of fresh herbs to a cooked dish just before you pull it from the heat. Chopped chives or scallions brighten up most meat dishes. Rice-based dishes and Southwestern foods, such as chili, taste better with a tablespoon of fresh, minced cilantro.

- Add a squeeze of fresh lemon juice or a teaspoon of grated fresh lemon rind and simmer the dish for 5 minutes, so the acid taste of the lemon blends into the food.

- Stir a pinch of crushed red pepper flakes into a skillet dish at the start of cooking.

- Add a salad of exotic greens on the side. Just open a bag and pour on your favorite dressing. Chapter 5 covers exotic greens.

- Place washed grape tomatoes and baby carrots in a bowl. Pour ranch, blue cheese, or buttermilk dressing into a second bowl for dipping and serve the veggies instead of the usual salad.

You also have to balance convenience and content. Packaged foods don't all come in the macaroni-and-powdered-cheese variety. You don't have to eat like a 7-year-old when you cook from a box.

For example, risotto — slowly stirred rice and flavorings — is often on fancy restaurant menus and in gourmet cookbooks. You can prepare packaged risotto mix in about 15 minutes, half the time it would take you to make the conventional recipe from scratch. (And for a few minutes more, you can have a complete meal, such as with the Bacon and Vegetable Risotto recipe in this chapter.)

Bacon and Vegetable Risotto

Look for precooked bacon strips in the deli meat case of your supermarket. Choose plain bacon for this recipe. (Maple-flavored bacon is too sweet.) Serve this risotto with a salad of bagged exotic greens and the vinaigrette dressing in Chapter 5.

Preparation time: *1 minute*

Cooking time: *15 minutes, depending on the brand of risotto mix*

Yield: *4 servings*

1 package (2 to 3 ounces) precooked bacon strips

1 package (5.4 ounces) chicken risotto mix

1 cup frozen peas

1 tablespoon minced fresh cilantro

1 Place the bacon strips in a hot skillet and heat 1 minute to crisp. Remove from skillet, cut into 1-inch squares, and set aside.

2 Prepare the risotto according to package directions, adding the peas with the risotto seasonings. Cook the risotto as the package directs, stirring occasionally. When the rice is tender, stir in the bacon and cilantro.

Vary It! *Sprinkle 2 tablespoons grated Parmesan cheese into the dish along with the bacon and cilantro. Also, replace the bacon with a cup of leftover cooked, diced chicken breast meat or a 6-ounce package of cooked, diced chicken breast if you prefer. A cup of cooked, diced chicken breast meat is the equivalent of 1 small, raw chicken breast half.*

Per serving: *Calories 240 (From Fat 65); Fat 7g (Saturated 2g); Cholesterol 17mg; Sodium 772mg; Carbohydrate 32g (Dietary Fiber 3g); Protein 11g.*

Staying flexible

Just as designers introduce new clothing styles every season, food manufacturers perpetually tinker with their products, marketing yet another new and improved version of the former version.

When you're shopping for ingredients in this chapter, don't be afraid to experiment if you don't find the exact flavor or product size. My recipes have room for variations. If you're wedded to cooking from a precise recipe, break the habit for the sake of warp-speed cooking. Replacing your usual products with new alternatives gives you more, not fewer.

Read over the Ham and Noodle Dinner recipe and check out my suggestions that demonstrate how easily you can introduce a little variety into any dish.

Ham and Noodle Dinner

Winter is when you crave foods that not only cook fast but also thaw you right through to your toes. This rich, one-pan dinner does both marvelously well.

Preparation time: *2 minutes*

Cooking time: *10 minutes*

Yield: *4 servings*

2 boxes (4 to 5 ounces each) Alfredo noodle mix	*1 package (9 ounces) frozen green beans*
1 cup milk	*1 pound cooked, diced ham*
2 tablespoons butter	*½ cup chopped scallions*
	½ cup sour cream

1 Pour both boxes of the noodle mix into a large pan. Add the amount of water that the package recommends. Add the milk and butter and stir. Add the frozen green beans and bring the mixture to a boil.

2 Remove the pan from the heat and let it stand for 2 to 3 minutes to thicken. Drain off any juices from the ham package. Add the ham, scallions, and sour cream to the noodle mixture. If necessary, reheat the noodles and ham.

Per serving: Calories 514 (From Fat 222); Fat 25g (Saturated 13g); Cholesterol 159mg; Sodium 2,393mg; Carbohydrate 45g (Dietary Fiber 3g); Protein 33g.

The following examples are a few quick ways that you can change up the Ham and Noodle Dinner recipe:

1. Start with the noodles. Alfredo noodle mix is widely available, but try Romanoff noodles, which are also a creamy style mix. Substituting a box of macaroni and cheese is another delicious possibility.

2. If you don't like green beans, replace the vegetable with the same-size package of frozen corn, frozen peas, or broccoli spears.

3. Say you can't find cooked, diced ham in your supermarket deli or prepared meat counter. Don't give up the recipe. Give up the ham and switch to cooked chicken breast meat or even canned tuna.

As long as you keep the same proportions of vegetable, starch mix, and meat or poultry in this recipe, you can use the alternatives. The payoff is enjoying at least three different recipes instead of just one.

Each recipe in this section includes tips for changing the ingredient list. You'll have more fun with less hassle if you're willing to change your recipe slightly. I promise.

Barbecued Chicken Pizza

Keeping a supermarket pizza in the freezer is fine for emergencies, but if your pizza choices are like those in my supermarket — thin-crusted and skimpy on the cheese and meat — you're getting more of a snack than a meal. Buy an inexpensive pizza for this recipe. Check the directions and choose the brand that bakes the fastest. Then heap the crust with barbecued chicken and cheese for a mouthwatering meal. Serve salad on the side.

Preparation time: *5 minutes*

Cooking time: *15 minutes*

Yield: *6 servings*

1 frozen, thin-crust cheese pizza, about 12 inches in diameter

1 container or tub (20 ounces) barbecue sauce with shredded chicken, fully cooked

1 large tomato, thinly sliced

1 cup shredded Mexican-style cheese

1 Preheat the oven to 400 degrees. Place the pizza on a cookie sheet. Spread the barbecue sauce with shredded chicken over the surface of the pizza. Arrange the tomato slices over the chicken. Sprinkle the cheese over the chicken.

2 Bake the pizza for 15 minutes or until the cheese is melted and lightly browned. Remove the pizza from the oven and let stand 1 minute. Cut into wedges to serve.

Vary It! *Substitute barbecue sauce with shredded pork, fully cooked, for the shredded chicken. Use shredded cheddar cheese over the pork.*

Per serving: *Calories 459 (From Fat 203); Fat 23g (Saturated 12g); Cholesterol 71mg; Sodium 1,311mg; Carbohydrate 37g (Dietary Fiber 2g); Protein 27g.*

Teriyaki Pork and Rice Skillet Dinner

The pork strips and teriyaki rice mix are so well seasoned that you don't have to add any condiments to get the sweet-smoky flavor of a Chinese teriyaki dinner. And don't worry about thawing the pork in advance; you can skip that step.

Preparation time: *2 minutes*

Cooking time: *12 minutes*

Yield: *4 servings*

1 tablespoon vegetable oil

1 red bell pepper, cored, seeded and diced

1 small, sweet onion, thinly sliced

12 ounces (half a 24-ounce bag) frozen, cooked teriyaki-seasoned pork strips

1 package (about 5 ounces) teriyaki rice

1 Heat the oil over high heat in a large wok or sauté pan. Add the bell pepper, onion, and pork strips and stir-fry 5 minutes or until the vegetables are limp. Add the rice mix and the amount of water that the package recommends.

2 Bring the liquid to a boil. Reduce the heat to low, cover the pan, and simmer 5 minutes. Stir the rice and set aside 1 or 2 minutes for the mixture to thicken.

Vary It! *Substitute 2 packages (6 ounces each) of cooked, diced oven-roasted chicken breast for the pork. Add a dash of bottled teriyaki sauce to the dish along with the chicken.*

Speed It Up! *Skip the fresh vegetables. Combine the pork strips, rice, and water and bring to a boil. Cook as the recipe directs. When the rice is tender, stir in 2 tablespoons minced scallions and 2 tablespoons minced cilantro. If desired, stir in a tablespoon of stir-fry sauce.*

Per serving: *Calories 281 (From Fat 61); Fat 7g (Saturated 1g); Cholesterol 41mg; Sodium 805mg; Carbohydrate 34g (Dietary Fiber 1g); Protein 19g.*

A 12-ounce package of cooked beef is the equivalent of one pound of raw ground beef. A 20-ounce tub of seasoned ground beef that's prepared with a sauce is about the same as 1½ pounds of raw beef.

8-Minute Chili

Who would think you could serve 8-minute chili? This may be the most revolutionary idea since adding beans to a bowl of red.

Preparation time: *2 minutes*

Cooking time: *6 minutes*

Yield: *4 servings*

1 carton or tub (20 ounces) taco sauce with seasoned ground beef, fully cooked

1 package (9 ounces) frozen corn

1 can (14½ ounces) diced tomatoes with chiles, undrained

1 can (15½ ounces) red kidney beans, undrained

2 tablespoons minced cilantro

2 tablespoons minced scallions

Place the sauce and seasoned ground beef, corn, tomatoes, and beans in a large pan. Cook over medium heat 5 minutes, stirring occasionally or until the mixture is hot. Sprinkle in the cilantro and scallions and simmer 1 minute.

Vary It! *Pass a bowl of grated taco cheese and let everyone help themselves to a cheese topping.*

Speed It Up! *For a healthy vegetarian alternative, cut out the taco sauce with seasoned ground beef. Add a second can of red kidney beans and a can of stewed zucchini in tomato sauce. Trim the cooking time by a minute or two. Season with a pinch of crushed red pepper flakes.*

Per serving: *Calories 541 (From Fat 219); Fat 24g (Saturated 9g); Cholesterol 115mg; Sodium 958mg; Carbohydrate 38g (Dietary Fiber 10g); Protein 44g.*

Stir-Fry Ramen Noodles with Pork and Snow Peas

My teenage daughter wants to live on ramen noodles, so I have to find ways to make the dish more healthful and filling. Using the seasoning packet from only one package of ramen noodles and the water for one package of noodles, I can create a luscious stew-like dish instead of ramen noodle soup.

Preparation time: *2 minutes*

Cooking time: *10 minutes*

Yield: *4 servings*

1 tablespoon vegetable oil

2 cups fresh snow peas

12 ounces (half a 24-ounce bag) frozen, cooked teriyaki-seasoned pork strips

2 packages (0.3 ounces each) ramen pork noodles

2 cups hot water

1 Heat the oil over high heat in a large wok or Dutch oven. Add the snow peas and stir-fry for 1 minute. Add the pork strips and stir-fry for 1 minute. Add the ramen noodles. Add the seasoning packet from one of the two noodle packages. Add the hot water.

2 Cook the noodles over medium heat for 2 to 5 minutes or until the noodles are tender and the liquid is mostly absorbed.

Vary It! *Use 2 packages (6-ounces each) of cooked, diced oven-roasted chicken breast and 2 packages ramen chicken noodles. For a shrimp stir-fry, substitute 1 package (12-ounces) cooked salad shrimp and shrimp-flavor noodles.*

Per serving: Calories 315 (From Fat 110); Fat 12g (Saturated 5g); Cholesterol 39mg; Sodium 778mg; Carbohydrate 32g (Dietary Fiber 2g); Protein 21g.

Turkey and Gravy
over Cornmeal Muffins

Preparation time: *5 minutes*

Cooking time: *8 minutes*

Yield: *2 servings*

If you have leftover turkey from a holiday feast, blend it into this savory turkey and gravy brunch entree. Otherwise, pick up 2 packages (6 ounces each) of cooked, diced oven-roasted chicken breast and substitute for the turkey.

2 tablespoons butter	*¼ teaspoon dried, crushed thyme*
2 cups coarsely chopped mushrooms	*2 cups cooked, diced turkey*
2 tablespoons flour	*¼ teaspoon salt*
1 cup chicken broth	*¼ teaspoon pepper*
½ cup milk	*2 baked corn muffins*

1 Melt the butter in a large skillet. Add the mushrooms and cook over high heat for 2 minutes or until tender. Stir in the flour to make a paste. Stir in the chicken broth and cook for 1 minute over medium heat, stirring until the mixture thickens slightly. Add the milk, thyme, and cooked turkey and simmer 1 to 3 minutes to heat through. Do not boil. Season with salt and pepper.

2 To serve, split the muffins in half, one on each of 2 plates. Spoon the turkey and gravy over the muffin halves.

Vary It! *Use smoked turkey from your deli counter in place of the usual cooked turkey or substitute baking powder biscuits for cornmeal muffins.*

Per serving: *Calories 617 (From Fat 247); Fat 28g (Saturated 12g); Cholesterol 163mg; Sodium 1,220mg; Carbohydrate 41g (Dietary Fiber 3g); Protein 50g.*

Comforting Creamed Chicken over Rice

Frozen mixed vegetables and chicken are as close as you'll get to almost instant "crustless" chicken potpie. If you're feeding a family or last-minute company, double the recipe.

Preparation time: *5 minutes*

Cooking time: *7 minutes*

Yield: *2 servings*

1 can (10¾ ounces) condensed cream of chicken soup

1 package (about 6 ounces) cooked, diced oven-roasted chicken breast

¼ cup cream, or half-and-half

2 teaspoons minced, canned hot chiles

1½ cups frozen mixed vegetables, such as peas, corn, and carrots

2 cups cooked instant rice

Place the chicken soup in a medium-size pan. Add the chicken, cream, chiles, and frozen, mixed vegetables. Simmer the mixture for 5 minutes or until hot. Spoon 1 cup of rice onto each of 2 dinner plates and top with the chicken stew.

Vary It! *Instead of serving the chicken over rice, spoon it over cornbread or baking powder biscuits.*

Per serving: *Calories 628 (From Fat 211); Fat 23g (Saturated 10g); Cholesterol 125mg; Sodium 1,358mg; Carbohydrate 65g (Dietary Fiber 7g); Protein 39g.*

Nutrition at Warp Speed

Looking at convenience food products, you may wonder what you're eating. I know I do. When I cook from scratch, I know what I'm eating, down to the last quarter teaspoon of salt.

Food manufacturers share their recipe and the nutritional value of the foods they sell. A product's recipe is the *ingredient list.* Each food or substance must be listed in the order of predominance. If you're concerned about eating healthy, take a look at the ingredient list and keep these things in mind:

✔ The first ingredient in a product's ingredient list should be the food that you're buying. A seasoned rice mix should list rice as the first ingredient. A container of barbecue sauce with shredded chicken probably contains more barbecue sauce than chicken, although food companies can be more generous with the chicken if they choose.

✔ Avoid products that list salt and sugar, which includes corn syrup and fructose, high up in the ingredient list.

✔ If you want to avoid foods that contain a high percentage of preservatives and additives, as a general rule, the less seasoned or flavored a food is, the fewer additives it has. For example, plain couscous doesn't list any four-syllable chemical compounds, but you may not be able to say the same for a box of couscous with Southwestern flavoring. You're more likely to find preservative- and additive-free foods in natural food stores.

✔ Mixes, meal kits, and precooked meat and poultry products are usually high in sodium. Read the tips in Chapter 15 if you're trying to limit your sodium intake.

If you're a nutrition sleuth, you'll want to look at the Nutrition Facts panel in addition to the ingredient list. The *Nutrition Facts panel* is a box on most food packages that tells you about the food's nutritional content. Simply put, you want to eat foods with less of what's towards the top of this panel — fat, cholesterol, and sodium — and more of the vitamins and minerals towards the bottom.

Shrimp Stir-Fry over Couscous

My nearby natural foods supermarket stocks bags of stir-fry vegetables that include baby corn, mushrooms, bamboo shoots, and green soybeans called *edamame* (eh-dah-ma-meh). The mixture is delicious cooked with shrimp and your favorite bottled stir-fry sauce. If you don't know which sauce to choose, select one that includes soy sauce and honey, for a sweet and smoky taste.

Preparation time: *5 minutes*

Cooking time: *5 minutes*

Yield: *4 servings*

¼ teaspoon salt

1 cup couscous

1 tablespoon canola oil

1 package (1 pound) frozen stir-fry vegetables

1 package (12 ounces) frozen cooked, peeled salad shrimp

½ cup Asian stir-fry sauce

1 Add 1¼ cups water and the salt to a small pot. Bring the water to boiling and stir in the couscous. Cover the pot and remove from heat. Set aside 5 minutes.

2 Meanwhile, heat the oil over high heat in a wok or large skillet. Add the vegetables and shrimp and stir-fry 5 minutes or until the vegetables are hot and any pan juices evaporate. Pour in the stir-fry sauce and mix well.

3 To serve, fluff up the couscous with a fork. Spoon the couscous into a serving bowl and top with the shrimp and vegetables.

Per serving: *Calories375 (From Fat 54); Fat 6g (Saturated 1g); Cholesterol 127mg; Sodium 1,944mg; Carbohydrate 53g (Dietary Fiber 3g); Protein 24g.*

While you're in a convenience food frame of mind, you can check out Chapter 15, which has information on those use-by dates that are often on packaged food.

Part V
The Part of Tens

The 5th Wave   By Rich Tennant

"...because I'm more comfortable using my own tools. Plus, the sander attachment is actually quite efficient."

In this part . . .

Every *For Dummies* book has a Part of Tens. This is where you get the tips and shortcuts that let you spend more time at the table and less time preparing food. Discover all the cheap, unsung kitchen gadgets that are far more useful than their price tags would indicate and ten ways to make your evening meals less stressful. Read and use these suggestions to make your dinners more enjoyable.

Chapter 18

Ten Great Timesaving Tools

Gadgets are the support team that help busy cooks speed up ordinary tasks. They aren't as glamorous as the shiny, stainless steel or trendy color-of-the-year appliances that fill the pages of food magazines, but these small items (which many folks toss into their kitchen junk drawer) can save you time and energy when you're trying to get dinner on the table. I'd be lost without the following economical and very practical products, and I'm guessing that each of these handy contraptions can benefit you as well. (For the straight scoop on the larger appliances that are essential for preparing meals quickly, check out Chapter 2.)

The list starts with my favorite item — the one to reach for if or when you don't have a strong-muscled jar-opener around — and goes down to my tenth favorite gadget.

Rubber Helpers: Opening Jars with Ease

You can find many versions of jar openers, but my favorite is the absolutely low-tech sheet of rubber with one textured side. Talk about *getting a grip,* this gadget, which is often called a *rubber helper,* is a great tool for opening screw-top jars. A rubber helper is a 3- to 4-inch piece of flexible rubber. Drape the rubber helper over a screw-top jar lid and twist to loosen the lid. The textured surface of the rubber helper prevents the lid from slipping from your grasp.

Hardware stores and other businesses sometimes give away rubber helpers as promotional items. But if you have to buy one, it will only set you back a couple of bucks. Look for a thick sheet of rubber and a well-defined, textured surface. Thin rubber sheets tear easily, and if the rubber's surface is relatively smooth, you don't get the gripping action that you need. For $7 to $8, you can buy the king-size version in cookware stores. These larger, 7-inch square silicone mats grip jars and double as potholders, because they withstand heat up to 600 degrees.

Scissors: Cutting Down on Chopping

Scissors take the place of knives for several of my cooking chores and save me time in the process. In a fraction of the time that it takes to mince fresh herbs using a chef's knife on a cutting board, I can snip herbs with a pair of scissors directly into a soup or stew. Set a bunch of washed and dried herbs over a pot with one hand. With the other hand holding a pair of sharp scissors, make close cuts into the herbs. The closer the cut is, the finer the mince. If you need an accurate measurement as to the quantity of the ingredient, snip the herbs into a measuring cup.

For herb chopping, look for scissors with a 5- to 6-inch stainless steel or nonstick blade. I prefer stainless, because stainless steel is easier to sharpen. You may prefer a nonstick surface, because herbs don't cling to nonstick materials, which is also a benefit. Expect to pay anywhere from $10 to $30 for a good pair of scissors. Check hardware and discount general merchandise stores for sales on kitchen scissors.

Poultry sheers make cutting up a cooked chicken a breeze. Taking a whole, cooked chicken, find the joints and separate the point where the joints meet with the sheers. Having thicker blades than conventional scissors, poultry sheers cut through chicken bones easily.

Select a pair of poultry sheers with comfortable handles. You're putting plenty of pressure on the handles to cut through chicken joints and small bones, and padded handles won't strain your fingers as you cut. Look for a notched blade that clips bones easily.

Whenever you use a pair of scissors or poultry sheers to cut food of any kind, thoroughly wash them before using and dry them completely. Don't use kitchen scissors for cutting cardboard, because this can dull the blades.

Parchment Paper: Less Mess

Greasing cookie sheets is messy and slow, but cleaning up cookie sheets stained with oozing butter or sticky toffee is worse yet. Using parchment paper eliminates both the preparation and clean-up steps. *Parchment paper* is available in rolls, just like aluminum foil, plastic wrap, and wax paper, but don't substitute any of these for parchment paper! Foil, plastic wrap, and wax paper aren't designed for baking. You can find parchment paper in cookware stores or cookware catalogues for about $9 for an 8-ounce roll.

A Cook's Wares is one supplier. Call 1-800-915-9788 or check the Web site at www.cookwares.com for more information. The Baker's Catalogue also carries parchment paper. Call 1-800-827-6836 or check the Web site at www.bakerscatalogue.com for more information.

Aluminum Foil: Don't Get Foiled Again

Covering food and cleaning up after meals is a snap when I use heavy-duty aluminum foil. Honest. I'm not on the payroll of an aluminum foil company either, although I'm sure that I contribute considerably to the aluminum industry's bottom line. I lay a sheet of foil over cooked foods, such as roasts, steaks, or chicken, which require a resting period before serving. When using cookware for sticky foods, such as barbecued beef, pizza, or garlic bread, I line the cookware with heavy-duty foil before baking in the oven to make cleaning up easier. Select 18-inch or wider rolls of aluminum foil to cover roasts or other large foods.

I don't suggest using foil to cover refrigerated foods however. First, if you're going to put the food in the microwave to reheat it, you have to switch to microwave-safe plastic or dishes. Second, highly acidic foods eat into the foil, making the food inedible. For that reason, don't let tomato sauce touch foil for any length of time.

Frothers for Your Coffee

A *frother* is a small, battery-operated whisk or beater that turns coffee into a deluxe latté. In the past, making lattés and cappuccinos required a large, expensive, industrial-type espresso machine that you could only find in restaurants. But today, almost half the gourmet coffee beverages that Americans drink are enjoyed at home. You can get just as good a head of foam using a handheld frother as you do with a serious Italian import espresso machine.

Just in case it's been awhile since you've had a latté or cappuccino, please allow me to refresh your memory:

- **Espresso:** Strong, steamed coffee, made from finely ground Italian-roast coffee
- **Latté:** Espresso combined with frothy steamed milk
- **Cappuccino:** Espresso topped with the froth from steamed milk

Using a frother, you can also whip fat-free milk to a higher foam than regular milk. You get all the foam with fewer calories. If you're not a coffee drinker, use a frother to make hot chocolate, whip salad dressing, or beat eggs for an omelet.

Look for frothers that are about the size of electric toothbrushes at cookware stores and some coffee shops. Battery-operated frothers cost less than $25. Make sure the frother runs on a common battery size. Most use double-A batteries. The Aerolatte frother from Aerolatte, Ltd., in the U.K., and the Turbo Latte frother from BonJour, Inc., in California, make two of the best small frothers.

Spatulas for Stirring and Folding

Spatulas are as essential as measuring spoons in the cook's drawer. Made from rubber or silicone, spatula heads are scoop, flat, or spoon shaped and sit on wooden or plastic handles. Each shape has a specific function.

- **Flat-shaped** spatula heads are excellent for cutting or folding one ingredient into a batter. You can slice down into a batter using a spatula. Bring the spatula to the bottom of the bowl and up, folding in ingredients as you move the spatula.
- **Scoop-shaped** spatula heads "scoop" ingredients, such as flour or shortening.
- **Spoon-shaped or bowl-shaped** spatula heads are great for the usual mixing and stirring functions.

Instead of using several spatulas, however, Hatch Housewares makes Nestlings, a set of three spatula heads that fit on one handle. The spatula heads are made from silicone materials and fit into a convenient container. This is my idea of convenience and function. Better cookware stores carry it. This item is so new that I don't know the price yet.

When you shop for any spatula, however, look for silicone materials, which are heat resistant to 500 degrees or more, so you can use them for stirring stovetop foods as you cook.

Saltshakers that Stay Put

"Where's the salt?" is a frequent refrain in our household. Because salt is one of my vital cooking ingredients and one of my family's greatest pleasures, I can't quite keep track of the saltshaker. One nifty solution is a salt grinder and holder on a magnet. The product, Salt Ball, resembles a rabbit's head. Press on the ears or handles to grind sea salt. When you're not using the salt ball, place it on the refrigerator or another convenient metal spot. Chef'n also makes a Pepper Ball. Discover both products in cookware and general merchandise stores. This item is just being introduced into stores, so I don't know the price yet.

Measuring Cups with a New Angle

Measuring liquids into a typical glass measuring cup means that you have to stand back or bend down to eye the glass to make sure that you're adding the correct amount. *Angled measuring cups* allow you to read the measure while looking straight down into the cup. The measurements are printed on an angle — not straight up and down along the side of the cup — so that you can easily read how full the cup is as you look down into it. No more filling, checking, and refilling. The Good Grips Angled Measuring Cup (Internet: www. oxo.com) is available in one-cup capacity for about $4.95 or a two-cup capacity for about $6.95. It has a rubber-grip handle and is dishwasher safe.

Timers: Avoiding Shoe Leather Meals

Accuracy is important when you're cooking. If you broil your fish for 2 minutes more per side than the recipe says, you'll have the food equivalent of shoe leather, and it'll be about as palatable. Using a timer is more precise than checking the clock, unless you want to watch the minutes tick by. If you don't want to be tied to the kitchen, buy a portable timer on a string to hang around your neck. If you're standing by your food, use a countertop timer. A big-dial timer is easier on the eyes. Being a technophobe, I go for the easiest timers. A 60-minute mechanical timer with a loud ring is more than sufficient for 30-minute meals. The less complicated timers sell for about $12.95 and the bells-and-whistles models cost about $18 to $25.

Swivel Peeler: Peeling Safely

Professional chefs use paring knives to peel carrots, potatoes, and other vegetables. I prefer a *swivel peeler,* because it's safe enough for all but the youngest children to use. In fact, if you have children helping you scrape vegetables, or if you get distracted peeling vegetables, you're going to find a swivel peeler is safer than the typical paring knife. The gadget has two vertical blades on a handle. The gadget is called a swivel peeler, because the blades turn slightly to pare curved vegetables, such as cucumbers. Rubber-handled peelers are easier on the hands. Expect to pay $4 to $6 for a good-quality vegetable peeler.

Chapter 19

Ten Tips for Eliminating Mealtime Hassles

· ·

· ·

Getting dinner on can be a challenge when you're faced with all the other tasks that you juggle during a typical day. Throughout this book, I cover my best tips, tricks, and recipes to help you bring some great meals to the table quickly. But you know that other factors figure into getting that meal on the table than just putting the ingredients together and cooking.

Scheduling a little relaxation toward the end of the day is essential, too. If you're frazzled by the time that you're ready to serve dinner, you may drop your 30-minute meal on the floor somewhere between the stove and the table. Thus, your 30-minute meal has turned into a 60-minute meal with a 25-minute cleanup to boot. Besides, you won't enjoy your culinary efforts nor will anyone else. So, in this chapter, I lay out battle-tested tips to help you avoid those outside stresses and hassles that can interfere with your meal-time efforts.

Planning Ahead

The art of planning is a valuable tool for many aspects in life, but if you're like most folks, you may not always apply the same forethought to your meals. You should, because planning is one of the easiest ways to reduce dinner tension. Think of what you do in advance, such as deciding what you're wearing to work or getting your children to pack their homework for school. Those steps eliminate the aggravation of rushing around at the last minute. Now, apply that same philosophy to dinner.

Planning can take simple forms: Set out the package of spaghetti the night before, saving yourself a few valuable moments; transfer a package of ground beef from the freezer to the refrigerator before you go to bed, so it thaws before the next evening's dinner (depending on the temp in your fridge); take inventory of the vegetable compartment to make sure that you have the right fresh produce for a salad.

After you get the hang of planning the small things, you can be a bit more daring: Post a week's worth of menus on the refrigerator door, so you're not asking yourself what's for dinner as you rush in the door in the evening. Chapter 8 shows you how to get several meals from one starter recipe. If you have some extra time, you can use these recipes during a weekend cooking marathon. Invite a couple of friends to spend the afternoon in the kitchen with you. If you usually cook for one or two, divide the foods you prepare among your friends, so you're all rewarded for planning ahead.

Making Relaxation a Priority

Immediately after I arrive home around dinnertime, I put a pot of salted water on the fire and bring it to boiling. After the water is going, I look for ways to unwind. Changing to casual clothes helps to put your workday behind you. Having a glass of wine and listening to some music as you stretch out on the sofa for ten minutes is another. Puttering in the garden alleviates tension for me. Meditating while seated on a mat works for some people. Even if you face the demands of young children, I recommend that you take time out. Reading a story with your children or taking a late afternoon stroll through the back yard with your spouse or significant other to look at the flowers can put you in a calmer frame of mind.

Keeping Everything Handy

It's no use scattering the tools that you need to cook thither and yon. You need to store what you need to cook right where you use it. Accessibility is key. If you have to get out a stepladder to grab a salad bowl that you use at least once a week or you don your winter jacket, scarf, and gloves to plunder the sometimes below-zero-temperature-during-winter pantry for canned goods that you cook with every other day, then you need to do some reorganization before attempting your 30-minute meal.

If you find that you use a spatula every day, then keep a few of them in a decorative pitcher or crock pot right on your counter where you can grab one. Or keep them in a special drawer that's right underneath the countertop that you use most. If you find that you have 3 or 4 pots and pans that you use at least four times a week, don't store them in a cupboard that's about a quarter of a mile from the stovetop. Hang them behind the stove on a pegboard with hooks.

In other words, organize your cooking tools in such a way that they're accessible.

Communicating while Cooking

If you have young children, your return home in the evening ignites an explosion. Your children are primed for both a celebration and retribution. They're delighted to see you and ready to air every grievance they experience during the day. You're the audience for triumphs or the judge of who wins in petty squabbles.

If you try to discuss a term paper while stirring a pot of soup on the stove, or if you and your spouse try to negotiate a summer cottage rental while browning the ground beef, you can have a recipe for disaster. That's part of life, but boisterous family members can exhaust and distract you. Promise your family and yourself time to discuss everyone's agenda — a bit later. Having family discussions over dinner — not before dinner when you're only half listening — is often the best way to communicate.

However, you may be different. You may be just the opposite and love having people buzz around you as you get organized. Dinner preparation time may free you for catch-up phone chats with your friends.

But I know I function better when I have the kitchen to myself for five minutes. I can turn up the volume on some old rock 'n roll without hearing grunts from my kids and start slicing and dicing. For a list of my favorite cooking tunes, see Chapter 4. (I envy cooks who can chop, stir, and have meaningful conversations at the same time. They must have twice my powers of concentration.)

Whether you're better surrounded by people or you prefer a little solitude, choose the style that suits you best. Don't try for some image that doesn't feel comfortable to you. You and those around you won't be pleased with the outcome.

Asking for Help

Delegate, delegate, and delegate some more. Unless dinner for one is your standard scenario, you probably have a few extra hands that you can put to work. What are you waiting for? Take advantage of the situation.

Having help means that you can get a meal assembled faster. It may not seem that way at first. In fact, you're probably saying that cooking by yourself is easier than having little helpers spill rice on the floor or bang pots or otherwise add to your confusion. The chaos won't last. After a few lessons, your kitchen "staff" knows how to measure rice or gently pull a pot from the cupboard without starting an avalanche. You'll welcome the help.

You're also helping children build their skills. I know no child leaves home not knowing how to pour milk, but you want your children to feel confident doing a number of basic tasks and bringing them into the kitchen is a good way to start.

If you're cooking with a significant other, asking for assistance is a way of telling your partner that you value his contributions. Some cooks prefer having their helpmates in the kitchen from the start. I like to get organized first. After I know what I'm doing, I call everyone back to the kitchen.

I have to emphasize the importance of giving everyone meaningful tasks or letting people choose tasks for themselves. Always peeling the potatoes or taking out the garbage isn't much fun.

Letting Others Cook

Falling into the trap of thinking that you're the only person who can cook dinner becomes self-fulfilling. Even if you love nothing more than cooking dinner, letting others cook as well is important. Remember the adage: "Teach a man to cook, and he'll eat for a lifetime." Apply that to everyone in your household. You want your family to be self-sufficient in the kitchen and that happens when family members take turns doing the cooking.

Friends of ours rotate meal responsibilities. Each night someone else makes dinner. The youngest child, age 9, contributes hot dogs and chips, while the teenager serves everyone a tofu concoction. The family specialties aren't going to make the cover of *Gourmet* magazine any time soon, but every one is well fed and happy with the arrangement.

If you're cooking for one, letting others cook can mean picking up a healthful salad to go with a steak that you're grilling. Don't forget that you can turn last night's restaurant dinner into a delightful meal tonight. (Read Chapter 16 for plenty of ways to renew a doggy bag.) Or you can form a cooking club with some friends, so you can prepare meals and dine together once a month.

Having Fun

This sounds pretty obvious. Of course, you don't want to come to the dinner table with a sour disposition, and you may not even be aware that you're grouchy. But if you notice that you frequently use mealtime as an opportunity to vent, lighten up. Constantly complaining may inhibit your ability to get dinner on in 30 minutes or less, because complaining and the attitude that goes with it can diminish your energy level. Besides, it isn't good for your health. Your bad mood affects your ability to regulate how much you eat or even how well you digest food. People who are anxious, feeling blue, or irritable are less likely to eat a wholesome amount of food. And research shows that blue moods can spread through your family affecting everyone.

Dinnertime at our house provides everyone an opportunity to talk. We go around the table and everyone gets a chance to discuss something that happened during the day. We try to save the really heavy stuff for after dinner when we spend time discussing any worries. This is effective, because we're rested and ready to listen.

If you're dining alone, use the time to unwind, enjoy pleasurable music, and focus on the delicious food you're eating. Create a dinner ritual that restores you.

Getting Real

Food magazines are in the business of enticing you into trying and buying new things. Looking at the publications for inspiration or vicarious pleasure is fun, but don't worry if your menu or table doesn't resemble what you see on glossy magazine pages. You can have an enjoyable and quick dinner, even if you don't use extra-virgin olive oil extracted from the olives of 1,000-year-old trees along Italy's Amalfi Coast. Dressing up the table with candles and wine glasses is loads of fun, especially when you have a celebration with your family or friends. But eating formally every night takes time. So to keep within your 30-minute time frame, leave off the fine china, your heirloom silver, and the linen napkins. Whatever you do, keep it simple, and let everyone be part of the party.

Coping with Bumps in the Road

Power outages happen, people forget things, and soccer games run late. You can't prevent situations that limit your ability to cook dinner, but you can make light of many glitches. So what if the power is out. You can serve cereal and milk by moonlight. No one is going to mind an occasional change from the usual dinner fare.

Stocking your cupboard and refrigerator as I suggest in Chapters 3 and 4 means that you have ingredients for a meal at home in case of a snowstorm. And when the chef can't make it home on time, having a plan that your family can set in motion makes life simple. Call home and have someone else put a pot of water on to boil. Let your children or spouse prepare dinner, so you can remain calm if you happen to get caught in a traffic jam.

Sharing

This book is all about cooking meals in 30 minutes, but other factors can make or break you getting your meal on the table in 30 minutes. Getting some satisfaction from the cooking and mealtime experience can help to speed the process. In fact, sharing time together is the most valuable aspect of dinner. If time constraints mean boneless, skinless chicken breast three nights a week or sandwiches for a couple of meals, that's okay. Or if it means assembling a quick salad at a friend's place, that's okay, too. The important part is sharing the experience with people you care about.

Metric Conversion Guide

● ●

*N*ote: The recipes in this cookbook weren't developed or tested using metric measures. Quality may vary in some cases when converting to metric units.

Common Abbreviations

Abbreviation(s)	What It Stands For
C, c	cup
g	gram
kg	kilogram
L, l	liter
lb	pound
ml	milliliter
oz	ounce
pt	pint
tsp	teaspoon
Tbsp	tablespoon

Volume

U.S Units	Canadian Metric	Australian Metric
¼ teaspoon	1 mL	1 ml
½ teaspoon	2 mL	2 ml
1 teaspoon	5 mL	5 ml

(continued)

Volume (continued)

U.S Units	Canadian Metric	Australian Metric
1 tablespoon	15 mL	20 ml
¼ cup	50 mL	60 ml
⅓ cup	75 mL	80 ml
½ cup	125 mL	125 ml
⅔ cup	150 mL	170 ml
¾ cup	175 mL	190 ml
1 cup	250 mL	250 ml
1 quart	1 liter	1 liter
1½ quarts	1.5 liters	1.5 liters
2 quarts	2 liters	2 liters
2½ quarts	2.5 liters	2.5 liters
3 quarts	3 liters	3 liters
4 quarts	4 liters	4 liters

Weight

U.S. Units	Canadian Metric	Australian Metric
1 ounce	30 grams	30 grams
2 ounces	55 grams	60 grams
3 ounces	85 grams	90 grams
4 ounces (¼ pound)	115 grams	125 grams
8 ounces (½ pound)	225 grams	225 grams
16 ounces (1 pound)	455 grams	500 grams
1 pound	455 grams	½ kilogram

Measurements

Inches	Centimeters
½	1.5
1	2.5
2	5.0
3	7.5
4	10.0
5	12.5
6	15.0
7	17.5
8	20.5
9	23.0
10	25.5
11	28.0
12	30.5
13	33.0

Temperature (Degrees)

Fahrenheit	Celsius
32	0
212	100
250	120
275	140
300	150
325	160

(continued)

Temperature *(continued)*

Fahrenheit	Celsius
350	180
375	190
400	200
425	220
450	230
475	240
500	260

Index

FOR DUMMIES®

The easy way to get more done and have more fun

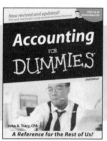
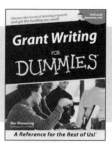

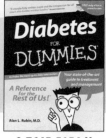

FOR DUMMIES®

A world of resources to help you grow

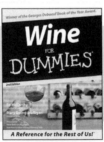

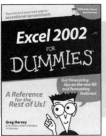 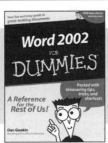 

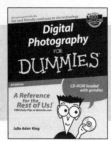

FOR DUMMIES®

The advice and explanations you need to succeed

SELF-HELP, SPIRITUALITY & RELIGION

0-7645-5302-X

0-7645-5418-2

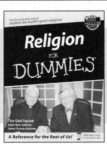
0-7645-5264-3

Also available:

The Bible For Dummies
(0-7645-5296-1)

Buddhism For Dummies
(0-7645-5359-3)

Christian Prayer For Dummies
(0-7645-5500-6)

Dating For Dummies
(0-7645-5072-1)

Judaism For Dummies
(0-7645-5299-6)

Potty Training For Dummies
(0-7645-5417-4)

Pregnancy For Dummies
(0-7645-5074-8)

Rekindling Romance For Dummies
(0-7645-5303-8)

Spirituality For Dummies
(0-7645-5298-8)

Weddings For Dummies
(0-7645-5055-1)

PETS

0-7645-5255-4

0-7645-5286-4

0-7645-5275-9

Also available:

Labrador Retrievers For Dummies
(0-7645-5281-3)

Aquariums For Dummies
(0-7645-5156-6)

Birds For Dummies
(0-7645-5139-6)

Dogs For Dummies
(0-7645-5274-0)

Ferrets For Dummies
(0-7645-5259-7)

German Shepherds For Dummies
(0-7645-5280-5)

Golden Retrievers For Dummies
(0-7645-5267-8)

Horses For Dummies
(0-7645-5138-8)

Jack Russell Terriers For Dummies
(0-7645-5268-6)

Puppies Raising & Training Diary For Dummies
(0-7645-0876-8)

EDUCATION & TEST PREPARATION

0-7645-5194-9

0-7645-5325-9

0-7645-5210-4

Also available:

Chemistry For Dummies
(0-7645-5430-1)

English Grammar For Dummies
(0-7645-5322-4)

French For Dummies
(0-7645-5193-0)

The GMAT For Dummies
(0-7645-5251-1)

Inglés Para Dummies
(0-7645-5427-1)

Italian For Dummies
(0-7645-5196-5)

Research Papers For Dummies
(0-7645-5426-3)

The SAT I For Dummies
(0-7645-5472-7)

U.S. History For Dummies
(0-7645-5249-X)

World History For Dummies
(0-7645-5242-2)

Available wherever books are sold. Go to www.dummies.com or call 1-877-762-2974 to order direct.

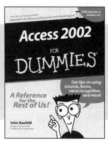